# MARRIAGE AND DEATH NOTICES FROM THE SOUTH WESTERN BAPTIST NEWSPAPER

Compiled by
*Michael Kelsey*
*Nancy Graff Floyd*
*Ginny Guinn Parsons*

HERITAGE BOOKS
2007

# HERITAGE BOOKS
*AN IMPRINT OF HERITAGE BOOKS, INC.*

### Books, CDs, and more—Worldwide

For our listing of thousands of titles see our website
at
www.HeritageBooks.com

Published 2007 by
HERITAGE BOOKS, INC.
Publishing Division
65 East Main Street
Westminster, Maryland 21157-5026

Copyright © 1995 Michael Kelsey,
Nancy Graff Floyd and Ginny Guinn Parsons

Other Heritage Books by Michael Kelsey, Nancy Graff Floyd, Ginny Guinn Parsons:
*Miscellaneous Alabama Newspaper Abstracts
Volumes 1 and 2*
*Miscellaneous Texas Newspaper Abstracts: Deaths
Volumes 1 and 2*
*Texas Masonic Deaths with Selected Biographical Sketches*

Other Heritage Books by Michael Kelsey:
*The Southern Argus: Obituaries, Death Notices and Implied Deaths,
June 1869 through June 1874*

All rights reserved. No part of this book may be reproduced or transmitted in any form or by any means, electronic or mechanical, including photocopying, recording or by any information storage and retrieval system without written permission from the author, except for the inclusion of brief quotations in a review.

International Standard Book Number: 978-0-7884-0338-5

MARRIAGE AND DEATH NOTICES FROM THE SOUTH WESTERN BAPTIST NEWSPAPER

## TABLE OF CONTENTS

NEWSPAPER ABSTRACTS ............................... 1
ALABAMA COUNTY COURTHOUSES DESTROYED BY FIRE ..... 204
NAME INDEX ......................................... 205

MARRIAGE AND DEATH NOTICES FROM THE SOUTH WESTERN BAPTIST NEWSPAPER

## INTRODUCTION

The South Western Baptist began publication in 1850 at Marion, Perry County, Alabama. The newspaper removed first to Montgomery, Montgomery County, in 1852, then to Tuskegee, Macon County, in 1854. The abstracts contained in this book are from issues published during the years 1850 through 1862.

Marriage and death notices were submitted to the South Western Baptist from throughout the south. Notices from Alabama strongly centered around the area in which the newspaper was being published.

The genealogical researcher will find information in the South Western Baptist to be extremely important due to the abundance of information contained in the death and marriage notices. Typically, the death notice included the deceased parents names; maiden name; dates and places of birth, baptism and death; former counties and states of residence; cause of death; name of church and location of church membership and baptism; and even names of grandparents. The Civil War obituaries are extremely informative in that they provided detailed accounts of military skirmishes and battlefield reports, as well as insight into family life during the turbulent time of the Civil War. Any praise or hymn included in the notice was not abstracted. Marriage notices usually contained the names of the parents and their places of residence. The earliest birth date contained in the notices was in 1758; the earliest death was in the mid-1750s.

Microfilm copies of the original newspapers may be ordered from: Alabama Department of Archives and History, Records Analysis and Appraisal Division, Micrographics and Imaging Section, Box 300100, Montgomery, AL 36130-0100. The researcher is encouraged to consult the original newspaper to verify any pertinent notice.

Michael Kelsey<br>
Nancy Graff Floyd<br>
Ginny Guinn Parsons

## Marriage and Death Notices From The South Western Baptist Newspaper

## NEWSPAPER ABSTRACTS

8-7-1850
Married in this place on the 23rd ult. by the Rev. S. R. Wright, Mr. James M. Underwood to Mrs. Ann Fife.
Died in Tallahatchie County, Mississippi on Monday the 15th of July last, Mrs. Mary Slack, wife of Major Joseph Slack.

8-21-1850
Married in this place on Thursday evening the 8th inst. by Rev. A.W. Chambliss, Mr. Thomas H. Evans of Greene County to Miss Mary Davis of Perry.
Married on the 6th inst. by the Rev. Mr. Stilman, P. B. Lawson, esq. of Marion to Miss Catharine T., daughter of Mr. & Mrs. Jannett Carrel of Eutaw, Greene County.
Died in Marion on Tuesday July 30th, Augustus R., infant son of E. A. Blunt, age five months, six days.
Died in Milledgeville, Georgia on the 24th ult. in the fifty-fifth year of his age, Judge Alfred M. Horton, formerly of Hancock County but for many years a resident of this city. (*Federal Union*).

8-28-1850
Married on the 6th by Rev. Joseph Mitchell, Mr. E.L. Cater to Miss Francis S. Green, all of Conecuh, Alabama.
Died of congestive fever in Marion on Friday morning the 16th inst., W.K. White, in the forty-third year of his age, leaving his bereaved companion and seven children to realize their unspeakable loss...... He resided in Clarendon, Sumpter District, South Carolina up to December 1846 at which time he removed to Alabama.
Died at her residence in Union Parish, Louisiana on the 24th of July at 7 o'clock p.m. of a chronic disease of the liver, Mrs. Mary P. Everett, consort of the Rev. George Everett, in her thirty-eighth year. Sister Everett was born in Bertie County, North Carolina and was married to Mr. I.S. Jordan on the 27th of August 1835. Her former husband, Mr. Jordan, died in Dallas County, Alabama on the 23rd of April 1844, and she again married to the Rev. George Everett on the 13th of February 1849.

9-11-1850
Married on the 22nd ult. by Rev. J.G. Collins, Mr. I.P. Willis to Miss Martha Ann Rolen, all of Dallas County.
Died in this place on the 2nd inst. of inflammation of the bowels, Mr. Edwin Greene, Professor of Music in the Judson Female Institute. The deepest sympathy is felt for his bereaved widow and fatherless child.....

## MARRIAGE AND DEATH NOTICES FROM THE SOUTH WESTERN BAPTIST NEWSPAPER

9-18-1850
Married in this town on the 10th inst. by Rev. M.P. Jewett, Felix Tait, esq. of Wilcox County to Miss Narcissa Goree of Marion, eldest daughter of J.R. Goree, esq.
Died on Wednesday the 4th inst. of typhoid and intermittent fever at the residence of his father, Rev. James Tubb, Mr. John Tubb, age twenty years, eleven months, nineteen days.

10-2-1850
BISHOP BASCOM: Died in this city, says the *Baptist Banner* on Sunday morning, 8th inst., after a protracted and painful illness, Rev. Henry B. Bascom...
Died at the family residence near Brooklyn, Conecuh County, on the 5th inst. after a severe illness of about six weeks, Mrs. Mary A. McCreary, consort of Elijah McCreary, in the twenty-fifth year of her age. She leaves a husband and five little children...
Nathan Parks was born in Lawrence District, South Carolina, October 25, 1788.... He removed to Benton County, Alabama in 1835. In July 1850 he left home on a visit to some of his children in Chickasaw and Yalobusha Counties Mississippi. During his stay in the latter county he was attacked with a carbuncle on his right shoulder, which disease terminated his life on the 27th of August 1850 at his son's house in Chickasaw County.

10-9-1850
Died September 14th, R.H., son of Tam?ey and R.H. Vaughan, age two years, five months, sixteen days.
Died at her residence near Carthage, Tuscaloosa County, Alabama on Sunday, September 22nd, 1850, Mrs. Olivia Norris, in the seventy-third year of her age. She was born in Edgefield District, South Carolina on March 2nd, 1778. Her parents were Evan and Olive Morgan. The maiden name of the latter was Newsom, a pious woman who died early leaving the subject of this notice an infant. Her father, Evan Morgan, was a native of Wales who from ill treatment of a step-mother at the early age of twelve years left his home and his country and came to America. He, too, became a devotedly pious man, a member with his wife of a Baptist Church on Big Stephen's Creek, Edgefield, South Carolina.

Olivia Morgan was married to David Quarles, esq., July 1795, who died March 1807 leaving four children. In December 1809 she was married to Thomas Norris, who afterward became a Baptist minister of wide notoriety and usefulness, removed with his family to Alabama in 1833, and finished his course at the family residence September 1842, age sixty-three years.... her mortal remains were consigned to the tomb on Monday afternoon, September 23rd, 1850.

# MARRIAGE AND DEATH NOTICES FROM THE SOUTH WESTERN BAPTIST NEWSPAPER

10-16-1850
Married at the residence of Mr. John Scarborough's on the 10th inst. by R. Holman, Mr. John W. Smith to Miss Mary Ann Brown.
Tribute of respect on the death of William L. Mosley.
DEAR BROTHER DYER: It becomes my mournful duty to announce to you and the many readers of the *Advocate* the decease of the aged and toil worn Mrs. McCoy. She was released by death from suffering on the morning of the 12th inst. at the residence of Mr. J.C. McCoy, near Westport, Missouri...

10-23-1850
Married in Baltimore on the 8th inst. at Christ Church by the Rev. C.W. Bolton, Lieut. McLancthon B. Woolshy, U.S. Navy, to Miss Mary L. Morrison of Wheeling, Virginia.

10-30-1850
Died at Eutaw, Greene County, October 19th Mrs. Juliet B. Coleman, age thirty-six years, wife of Mr. James C. Coleman and sister of the Rev. D.P. Boster. [Bestor]
Died at the residence of his brother, Wesley Marshall, in Pickens County, Alabama on Monday the 12th of August last, Brother Francis S. Gardner; age twenty-one years, six months, ten days.... He was buried at Bethany Church, Pickens County...

11-13-1850
Dr. Cote who has been for some time associated with the Grand Ligne Mission in Canada breathed his last at Hinesburg, Vermont, September 17th, where he was attending an Association...

11-20-1850
Died in Greene County on the 20th of September last, Mrs. Mary Windham, age forty-eight years...

11-27-1850
Married at the residence of John M. Lucas, esq. of Dallas County on the 7th inst. by the Rev. J.G. Collins, Mr. John L. Daniel to Miss Susan W. Lucas; and at the same time and place by the same, Mr. Edmund D. Rolin to Miss Mary Z. Lucas.
Departed this life on the 7th of November 1850, John D. Travis, eldest son of Elder A. Travis, age thirty years...
Died in this county on the 4th inst. seven miles north of Marion, Mrs. Jane Sanders, consort of John Sanders, and daughter of the late Wm. Cannon of Kemper County, Mississippi. Mrs. Sanders was a native of Pendleton District, South Carolina, from whence she removed to Alabama with her parents in

## Marriage and Death Notices From The South Western Baptist Newspaper

early life. She was married to Mr. S. on the 24th of September 1829, with whom she resided in Perry County...
Died on the 17th of October 1850 at the residence of her husband in Union Parish, Louisiana, Mrs. Ann, wife of the Rev. Elias George. Sister George was born in Wayne County, North Carolina on the 18th of June 1812, married to Elias George of Perry County, Alabama, January 10th, 1828, and immigrated to Louisiana in 1847...

12-4-1850
Married near Forkland, Greene County, Alabama on the 20th ult. by Rev. M.B. Clement, George W. Randolph to Cornelia Ann, daughter of Robert Flemming, esq., all of Greene County.
Died of pulmonary consumption on the 22nd inst., Mrs. M. Louisa Billingslea, wife of Dr. C. Billingslea of this place...

12-11-1850
Died at Portersville, Connecticut, October 1, 1850 in the twenty-eighth year of her age, Mrs. Abby Deslar Breaker, wife of Rev. J.H. Breaker, pastor of the Baptist Church at Key West, Florida... She has left a devoted husband and three children...
Died in this city on the 28th day of November last, John C. Herbc?t, in the thirty-fourth year of his age, after a lingering illness for several months.....He has left an aged father.......(Montgomery, 2 December 1850)

12-18-1850
Married on the 14th ult. by the Rev. N.G. Phillips, Dr. John S. Wilson of Columbus, Georgia to Miss Martha E., daughter of Mr. Ennis Loftin of Marengo County, Alabama.
Died in this place on the 11th inst. of dysentery, Miss Mary Ann Wilkerson of Tuscaloosa County, in the sixteenth year of her age.
Died in this place on 26th November last, Miss Martha T. Benson, daughter of Gabriel and Rosanna Benson, deceased.
Died of fever in Louisville, Barbour County, on the 12th of September 1850, Amanda, daughter of M.M. McLendon, aged thirteen years, six months, six days.
Died of erysipelas at the residence of her husband in Montgomery County on the 9th day of November last, Mrs. Speare, consort of Rev. P.W. Speare, after a painful illness of four days... Mrs. S. was the daughter of Hooper Calf?, esq. and a native of Guilford County, North Carolina, born June 1st, 1816...
The *Montgomery Atlas* will please copy.

# Marriage and Death Notices From The South Western Baptist Newspaper

1-1-1851
Married on the 5th ult. by the Rev. Willis Burnes, Mr. Isaac M. Crow of Perry County to Miss Louisa D. Pierson of Tuscaloosa County, Alabama.
Married on the 12th ult. by the Rev. James K. Clinton, Mr. Alonzo L. Brown of Yazoo County to Miss Agness E. Brumby of Holmes County, Mississippi.
Married in Lowndes County, Mississippi on the 13th ult. Joseph K. Murray to Miss Ann M. Dailey.
Married in Sumter County on the 18th ult. Mr. Thomas Kennedy to Miss Sarah Jane Phillips.
Died at the residence of the Rev. J.C. Perkins, his beloved consort, Hannah Perkins, in the sixty-third year of her age. This aged and pious couple were united in marriage in Wilkes County, Georgia on the 1st day of November 1810, having lived in the strong bonds of conjugal love forty years lacking but eight days, when the pure ties of earth were severed by the unsparing hand of death... She has left a tender and affectionate husband and six daughters and a large number of friends in Georgia, Alabama, and Mississippi...

1-8-1851
Died at Suggsville, Clark County, Alabama on 17 December 1850 in the fifty-first year of her age, Mrs. Francis G. Starke, wife of Mr. Turner Starke... Georgia & South Carolina papers will please copy.

1-15-1851
Died at the residence of her father near Orion, Pike County, Alabama on 16 December 1850 Miss L. [Louisiana] E. Simpson, daughter of A. Simpson, esq., age eleven years, ten months, eight days, after an illness of ten days...
Died at the residence of her son, J.D. Bullock, in the city of New Orleans on the 21st day of July 1850, Mrs. Susan Bullock, in the sixty-fifth year of her age.
Mr. Robert Hicks Vaughan died of cholera December 24th, age thirty-six years. This afflictive event occurred while on his removal with his family from Warren County, Mississippi to a new location in Arkansas, ten days after his departure...

1-22-1851
Died of typhoid fever at his residence in Montgomery County, Alabama on the 21st inst., Rev. William A. Cone, after an illness of twenty-six days.

2-12-1851
Died at his residence twelve miles north of Marion on the 16th of January of inflammation of the bowels, George B. Tubb, son of the Rev. James and Hinson H. Tubb, age twenty-one years, five months, sixteen days... he leaves a wife, one son, and a daughter...

## Marriage and Death Notices from The South Western Baptist Newspaper

Died at the residence of her husband, Mr. James Derdin, thirteen miles north of Marion, of consumption, sister Elizabeth Derdin, age twenty-nine years. Tribute of respect on the death of Condy R. Billingslea from the students of Howard College. [see below]

2-19-1851
Died on Thursday the 30th of January of typhoid fever, Condy R., son of Dr. C. Billingslea, in the seventeenth year of his age. [see above]

3-5-1851
Married on the 9th inst. by the Rev. F.C. Eager, Mr. Richard Hearison to Mrs. Frances M. Crawford, both of Warren County, Mississippi.

3-12-1851
Died at her residence in Edgefield District, South Carolina in the eightieth year of her age, Mrs. Mary Anderson, consort of Allen Anderson, deceased, after nearly a year's protracted intense affliction... member of the Big Steven's Creek Baptist Church....
Died on the evening of the 21st ult. Leonard Butler of Perry County...

3-19-1851
Died: Departed this life in Holmes County, Mississippi on Thursday morning, January 9th 1851, Mrs. Mary Elvira Denson, in the fiftieth year of her age... Mrs. Denson was a native of Sumpter District, South Carolina, and the daughter of Thomas Brumby, Sr., deceased.

3-26-1851
From the *Vicksburg Whig* of February 18: Died on the 23rd ult. at the residence of his ?? in the city of Philadelphia, William Bond...
Died at his residence in Perry County on Thursday the 29th ult., Mr. Leonard Butler of typhoid fever. The subject of this notice was born in South Carolina, June 5th, 1808, and when a youth emigrated to this state with his father Dr. E. Butler... In December 1828 he united with the Ocinulgee Baptist Church...
Died in this city on the 10th inst. Mrs. Harriet E.T. Kenney, wife of Rev. T.C. Kenney. The deceased was a native of South Carolina.
Aberdeen, Mississippi, March 14, 1851.
Died near McMa??'s, Tuscaloosa County, Alabama on the 7th of February 1851 Mrs. Ann C. Carroll, wife of Rev. W.H. Carroll, age twenty-three years. Departed this life at half past 4 o'clock on Sunday the 2nd of March 1851 at the residence of James Larkins of Macon County, Mrs. Ann Brown, consort of Samuel N. Brown, of Montgomery, Alabama. The deceased had been for many years an exemplary member of the Baptist Church, first at Eufaula and then in Montgomery, to which place she removed with her husband in 1848. She has left a bereaved husband and five children...

## Marriage and Death Notices From The South Western Baptist Newspaper

4-2-1851
Died at his residence at Elm Grove, De Soto County, Mississippi, 13 February 1851, James Alfred Wooten... He was born in Greene County, Georgia, April 20th, 1801. During a protracted meeting held at the Mountain Creek Baptist Church, Harris County, Georgia in the month of August 1838, he was hopefully converted and joined the church... he was ordained a deacon of the Bethel Church, De Soto County, September 1840...

4-9-1851
Died at his residence in Macon County, Alabama on Sunday the 9th of March 1851, Brother Frederick G. Thomas, Sen., in the eightieth year of his age. The subject of this notice was born in North Carolina April 8th, 1771. His father moved to Georgia when he was very young. After his marriage he became a member of the Baptist Church in the year 1825. In 1836 he moved to Russell County and in 1840 to Macon County, Alabama; united with the Baptist Church in Aberfoil, called Lydia.
Died on the 10th day of March 1851 Catharine W. Whitten, wife of A.F. Whitten. Sister Whitten died of bronchitis after a long protracted illness. Sister W. joined the Baptist Church at Little River, Franklin County, Georgia in the year 1828.     Wharton, March 20, 1851.

4-16-1851
Died in Dallas County on the 27th of February, Mr. E.J. Underwood, Sr. in the eighty-second year of his age. The deceased was a native of North Carolina but at an early age removed to South Carolina... For the last twelve or fourteen years he was a citizen of the county in which he died... The *Greenville Mountaineer* please copy.
Died on the 1st of March 1851 at the residence of her husband, Elijah Tabor, sister Susan Tabor...
Died March 22nd in this place in the forty-fourth year of his age, Col. Edward T. Fowlkes. He was born in Lunenburg County, Virginia. In the 1832 he married in North Carolina, Miss Mary Foster, who now with eight children mourns her sad bereavement. About a year ago he removed to this state and soon became extensively known as the landlord of the King House in Marion....

4-30-1851
Married on the 6th of April by Rev. Rufus C. Burleson, T. H. Mundine, esq. of Washington County to Miss Catharine B. Merrill of the city of Houston, Texas.
Married in Hayneville, Alabama on Wednesday the 23rd inst. by the Rev. D.P.J. Murphy, Dr. P.N. Cilley of Lowndesboro to Miss Caroline S. Safford, daughter of the late Hon. Reuben Safford of Dallas County.

## MARRIAGE AND DEATH NOTICES FROM THE SOUTH WESTERN BAPTIST NEWSPAPER

5-7-1851
Departed this life at the residence of her husband in the county of Lafayette, Missouri on the morning of the 31st inst., Mrs. Ann Baylor Starke, consort of Burwell Starke and eldest daughter of Elder Wm. Hatch??, of Hanover County, Virginia... Born in King William County, Virginia on the 5th day of October 1818...
Died in Woodford County, Kentucky on the 27th February Mrs. Amanda M., the wife of Elder John L. Waller, senior editor of the *Baptist Banner* and publisher of the *Western Baptist Review*.

5-14-1851
Died at the residence of her husband H.M. Caffey in Macon County on the 1st day of April 1851, Mrs. Mary A. Caffey, in the twenty-seventh year of her age.
Married near Marion on the 7th inst. by Rev. M.P. Jewett, Joseph T. Lumpkin, esq. of Athens, Georgia to Miss Margaret E. King, daughter of Gen. E.D. King.
Married on the morning of the 6th inst. by Rev. D.D. Sanderson, Dr. Geo. W. Browder to Miss Rebecca, daughter of John Cunningham, esq., all of this county.

5-21-1851
Died at his residence in Jefferson County, Alabama on the 13th day of March 1851, Wm. Sanders, age ninety years, nine months. He was born in Cartwright County, North Carolina, June 13th, 1760 and there spent his early life. During the struggle for Independence he enlisted as a volunteer, serving about eight months, of which six was under Gen. Lincoln. A few years after the happy termination of the war he with his wife sought the more inviting field of Tennessee. Here, about the year 1802, he made a profession of religion, united with the Baptist Church... Having moved to Christian County, Kentucky, many sad trials visited him, but on the breaking out of the war in 1812, though he was growing old he joined a scouting party under Col. Skinner and served until peace was declared... In 1816 he immigrated to Morgan County, Alabama, and thence in about two years to the place first mentioned, there remaining till death...
Died on the 2nd of May 1851, Mrs. Francinia B. Dupree, wife of Daniel Dupree, deacon of the Baptist Church at Sharon, Noxubee County, Mississippi. The deceased was a native of Georgia. She made a public profession of religion in Alabama in the year 1833...

6-11-1851
Tribute of respect on the death of John H. Elliott.

## Marriage and Death Notices From The South Western Baptist Newspaper

Married on the 24th ult. in the Baptist Church at Houston, Texas by the Rev. R.C. Burleson, Mr. Frederick C. Mahe to Miss Aurelia O. Hadley, all of that place.
CAUTION: Dear Brother Chambliss: You will please give the following preamble and resolutions two insertions in your excellent paper, and send one number to the church, Liberty, Mississippi and forward your account to the same, Viz:
Whereas Y.F. Grifling, a member of this church, holding a letter of dismission from the church in full fellowship, has been guilty of gross, immoral conduct, and whereas knowledge of the same has come to the ears of the church, well authenticated, and a letter from the clerk of the Vernon Baptist Church, Louisiana, signed officially, is in the possession of this church giving testimony to the facts and also stating (he, said Grifling) had absconded from justice and gone he knew not where: Therefore, resolved unanimously by this church, that Y.F. Grifling be and he is hereby excommunicated from the fellowship of this church... [included due to unusual content]

6-18-1851
Died in Enon, Alabama, April 27th, 1851 Archibald Seals in the seventieth year of his age.
Died in this place on the evening of the 8th inst. of measles, Abner Johnny, infant son of the Rev. A.G. and Mrs. S.S. McCraw, age sixteen months, twenty-three days.
Died in Yalobusha County, Mississippi on Monday 26th of May 1851, Mrs. Martha M. Talbert, in the fortieth year of her age. She leaves a husband and a large family of children... [see below]
Died in Yalobusha County, Mississippi on the 7th inst., Marion McRae Talbert, infant son of Hillary and Martha M. Talbert... [see above]

6-25-1851
Died of cholera in Houston, Texas on the 5th of June, Mr. Stephen House. Brother House was a native of England. He removed to Texas in 1849.

7-2-1851
Departed this life at his residence in Dale County near Daleville, on Tuesday the 10th inst. in the fifty-fourth year of his age, John Bryan, after an illness of many months, from asthma and dropsy... Brother Bryan was born and raised in what is now Taliaferro County, Georgia. He became a member of the Bethel Baptist Church about the year 1823. Two or three years after he moved to Monroe County, where he lived four years, thence to Houston, where he resided until his removal to Dale, about five years ago... Brother Bryan has left an aged wife and numerous offsprings...

## Marriage and Death Notices From The South Western Baptist Newspaper

Died in Green County, Alabama on the 10th of May Mrs. Ann May, wife of Mr. Jonathan May, in the sixty-second year of her age. The deceased was born in South Carolina, married in 1815, and moved to this county in the year 1817...

Died on the 4th of June in the vicinity of Providence Church, Sumter County, Alabama, Mrs. Eliza P. Oliver, consort of Capt. Lewellen Oliver.

Died in Marysville, Guila County, California on 17 March last Mr. Henry J. Pope, late of Forsyth, Monroe County, Georgia and more recently of Macon County, Alabama, age twenty-three years. In the early part of the year 1850, Mr. Pope in company with five other men left Alabama for California, where in common with thousands of others he was allured by the golden dreams of fortune...

7-9-1851
Died in this county on the 17th of May, Mrs. D.H. Brame, relict of the late Judge George Brame. Mrs. Brame was born in Mecklenburg, County, Virginia, 11 April 1786.

7-16-1851
Died at the residence of her husband, Thomas Ashcraft, in Randolph County, Alabama on 19 September 1850, Mrs. Catherine Ashcraft, in the sixty-fourth year of her age. She was the daughter of Rev. Ephraim Abel, and was born in Orange County, Virginia, May 28th, 1787. On the 24th December 1805 she was married to William Stigler and was baptized by her father in the summer of 1806. Her husband dying about 1813, left her with three small children. On the 15th of March 1815 she was married again to Thomas Ashcraft...

Died in Jefferson, Marengo County, Alabama on Friday evening 26 June 1851, Mrs. Bethia Cain Williams, wife of Col. Caleb Williams. The deceased was the daughter of William and Mary Cain of Sumter District, South Carolina and was thirty-eight years old in October last. She was married to Mr. Williams in December 1830, united her self with the Baptist Church in 1834, emigrated to Alabama in 1843, where she remained up to the hour of her death. Mrs. Williams was severely and distressingly afflicted about four weeks...

*Camden Journal* & *Sumter Gazette* please copy.

7-23-1851
Died in Pontotoc on the 4th inst., Talitha Cumi Davis, third daughter of Rev. James Davis, after an illness of one hundred fifty-four days... She was thirteen years, two months, twenty-four days...

Died at Grand Gulf, Mississippi on the 6th of March 1851 of erysipelas after an illness of seven days, Mrs. Vasht? Brock, wife of Rev. V.W. Brock, in the thirty-eighth year of her age. A husband and six children remain to mourn an

## Marriage and Death Notices From The South Western Baptist Newspaper

irreparable loss. Mrs. B. was a native of Louisiana. She made a profession of religion and was baptized on the second Sabbath in June 1829 in the Mississippi River, opposite Bruins Bend...

7-30-1851
Died at his residence in Yalobusha County, Mississippi, Dr. Howel N. Edmunds, in the forty-sixth year of his age, leaving a widow and three children to mourn their loss...

8-6-1851
Died in Warren County, Mississippi on the 31st of May, sister Lucinda Estes, in the forty-eighth year of her age. Sister Estes was born in Spotsylvania County, Virginia in 1803, married Brother J.W. Estes in 1817, removed to Mississippi in 1826, and the following year was baptized in Adams County by Dr. D. Cooper. Having removed to Warren County and into a region then thinly settled Brother Estes and his wife united with four others, and in 1837 were constituted into what has since been known as Flower Hill Church... Her disease was pulmonary consumption, the effects of which began to appear nearly two years before her death. But she was not confined to her room more than three months...
Died at Hernando, Mississippi, July 14th, Kate Shepherd, infant daughter of Rev. W. Carey and Catherine J. Crane, age nine months, fourteen days.

8-13-1851
Died in this place, August 7th, 1851 Mr. John Chambliss, father of the editor of this paper, age sixty-four years, ten months. The deceased was a native of Darlington District, South Carolina, where he spent the larger part of his life...
Died the 4th inst. in this town of pulmonic affection, Mr. J.J. Bradford, age about twenty-six years. Mr. Bradford had been a resident of this town for the last seven or eight years... On the morning previous to his death he rode into town from some several miles in the country, visited and conversed freely. For some days he had been making preparations to travel for the improvement of his health and had proposed to start the following morning. But about 10 o'clock at night his spirit took its journey to that land from whence no traveller returns. On the 5th a funeral discourse was preached over the remains, which were afterwards deposited by his friends and many citizens in a grave by the side of the resting place of a departed niece...
Died, July 11th at his residence in Dallas County, Mr. William Gardner, in the thirty-seventh year of his age, after a short but severe attack of fever... The deceased was a native of South Carolina... An aged father and mother mourn the loss of a dutiful son and a brother and two sisters of an affectionate brother. A wife (with whom his destines had been united only six months) to grieve for a tender and confiding husband...

## Marriage and Death Notices From The South Western Baptist Newspaper

Died on the 4th inst. at the residence of Brother J. Wood, thirty-six miles from Marion, Alabama, of an affection of the bowels, while on her way home, Miss Georgiana Borders, daughter of John and Cynthia Borders of Benton County, in the fifteenth year of her age...

Died in Dallas County, July 13th, Mr. John Hardy, Sr., in the sixty-third year of his age. The deceased was a native of Edgefield District, South Carolina. There he was united in marriage with Miss Clarissa Roebuck. In 1809 he made a profession of religion... In the fall of 1818 he removed to this state and was one of the constitution of Town Creek Church...

Died on the 17th of July last in Perry County, Alabama, Mrs. Elizabeth Ford, wife of Franklin Ford, in the twenty-ninth year of her age. The deceased was the mother of three children. The two eldest being daughters, the youngest a son...

8-27-1851
Died at his residence in Greene County, Alabama on the 17th of June 1851 after a painful illness of several days, Mr. W.L.B. Tilman, son of Daniel W. and Melissa Tilman, in the twenty-fourth year of his age. The deceased was a native of this county... A wife and baby are left to mourn his loss...

Died in Selma, Alabama on Monday morning June 9th, 1851, Laura Elouisa, infant daughter of Richard and Margaret Furman, age one year, two months, fourteen days.

9-10-1851
Died in Perry County, Alabama, August 16th, 1851, Mrs. Milly B. Morton, wife of John R. Morton, age forty-nine years and nine months... Mrs. M. was born in Oglethorpe County, Georgia, October 28th, 1801, moved to this state with her father, George Y. Farrar, December 1819; married Mr. Morton January 9, 1820. In the year 1822 she made a profession of religion and united with the Baptist Church at Concord and continued a member until about the year 1835 when she became a constituent member of the Pisgah Church... the heaviest stroke has fallen on the husband and three children...

9-17-1851
Died in Issaquena County, Mississippi on Wednesday the 31st of July, Mr. James Bland, in the thirty-fifth year of his age. The deceased made a public profession of religion in the year 1842; and united himself with the Ogden Baptist Church in Yazoo County... In the year 1847 he moved from Yazoo to Issaquena County where he remained until his death...

9-24-1851
Died in Perry County, Alabama on the 5th day of September 1851 Mrs. Milly Holmes; leaving many children, grandchildren, and great-grandchildren... Her age was not precisely known but, from the best information that can be

## MARRIAGE AND DEATH NOTICES FROM THE SOUTH WESTERN BAPTIST NEWSPAPER

gained by her surviving children she was upwards of ninety years of age. She was a woman, grown during the Revolutionary War, who used to relate many incidents of the Revolution that occurred in her immediate neighborhood. This venerable lady was born in Edgefield District in the state of South Carolina and resided there until the year 1833, at which time she immigrated to Alabama. She embraced religion and united herself to the Baptist Church at Red Bunk, Edgefield District in the year 1804...
Died on the 17th of August 1851 at the residence of her husband in Union Parish, Louisiana, sister Permela Rimer.

10-1-1851
Died at Kemper Springs, Mississippi on the 26th of August 1851, Dr. Robert W. Washington, in the fifty-sixth year of his age. The deceased was born in Brunswick County, Virginia. He grew up and received his education in the same county; having read medicine with Dr. Miller. After attending medical lectures and receiving his degree in the Medical Department of the University of Pennsylvania, in the city of Philadelphia, he located in Edgefield District, South Carolina. Here he practiced his profession for fifteen years with success and reputation. In December 1825 he was married to Hannah P., daughter of Stephen Spencer, Sr. of the same district.

During the summer of 1830 Dr. W. made a public profession of Christ, receiving baptism at the hands of that truly apostolic man, the sainted Nicholas Hodge. He emigrated with a number of relatives and acquaintances in 1832 to Sumter County, Alabama where he resided till his recent decease, having been removed to Kemper Springs as a last resort, a few days before his death...
Died on the 15th inst. at the residence of her father in Green County, Alabama of a congestive chill, Alice Manorah, second daughter of Brother R.Y. Woods, age three years, six months, fourteen days...
Died in Yalobusha County, Mississippi on Thursday morning September 11, 1851 of congestive fever, Joseph C. Talbert, in the twenty-fifth year of his age...
Died on the 31st of July 1851 at his residence in Union Parish, Louisiana, Mr. Thomas Fuller. Mr. F. emigrated to this state from Perry County, Alabama some six or seven years ago... He left a wife and six dear little children.....

10-8-1851
Died near Robinson Springs, Autauga County, Alabama, on Wednesday the 17th of September 1851, Mrs. Margaret A. Drummond, consort of Benj. J. Drummond, and daughter of Jas. B. and Eliza C. Robinson, in the twentieth year of her age. She leaves a husband and four children.
Died on the 7th of September 1851 after a few days illness, Miss R.R. Cole, daughter of Capt. S. and Mrs. R. Cole, in the twenty-third year of her age, being born in Nottoway County, Virginia, December 6, 1827. At the age of

## Marriage and Death Notices From The South Western Baptist Newspaper

thirteen she made a profession of religion and joined the M.E. Denomination of which she remained a consistent member until the removal of her father in 1844 to Madison County, Mississippi where in 18?? she united with the Baptist Church. In the early part of the present year her father moved to Benton, Mississippi...

Married on Wednesday the 1st of October by the Rev. J.S. Ford, Rev. Elias George of Union Parish, Louisiana to Mrs. Sarah E. Ross of this county.

Died at the residence of his father in Union Parish, Louisiana on 16 August 1851, Brother Wm. Edmonds, after a short illness of eight days.

10-15-1851
Tribute of respect on the death of David S. Fike.

Died on the 29 September 1851 at the residence of her brother, R.D. Marshall, in Marengo County, Alabama, Mrs. Sarah B. Mills, age about thirty years. The deceased was a native of Virginia, daughter of Captain Thomas and Elizabeth Marshall, leaves a husband and four children...

10-22-1851
Died in Pickens County, Alabama on the 5th of July 1851 Mrs. Mary Mullins, wife of Brother Uriah Mullins, age thirty-nine years. The deceased was born in Lincoln County, North Carolina, and at about three years of age removed with her parents to South Carolina where she was raised. In 1837 she removed with her mother to Alabama and in April of that year she was married. In 1842 Mrs. Mullins became a member of the Baptist Church in her neighborhood...She has left a husband and six little children...

Departed this life September 25, 1851 at his residence in Tuscaloosa County, Alabama, Mr. William Stoker, a deacon of the Bethel Baptist Church. Had the deceased lived to the day of his burial he would have been eighty-one years of age. He was born on the Nottoway River, Amelia County, Virginia. After the close of the Revolutionary War he removed with his father to Long Creek, Montgomery County, North Carolina... His next removal was to Stephen's Creek, Edgefield District, South Carolina, thence to Georgia (what is now Hall County, near the upper Shallow Ford on the Chattahoochee) afterwards to Campbell County, Georgia; finally in 1835 he emigrated to Alabama and settled in Tuscaloosa County...

Tribute of respect on the death of Theophilis Ogden, who departed this life of the 2nd day of August 1851. [see below]

OBITUARY: Died August 2nd, 1851 in the lower part of Yazoo County, Mississippi in the twenty-ninth year of his age, Theophilus Ogden, the only remaining son of George Ogden, an old and well known citizen of this county... Brother Ogden was born in Wilkinson County April 9th, 1823, and emigrated while young to the place of his death. At the age of twenty-three he was united in marriage to Miss Mary Jane Spires of the same neighborhood in which he lived... [see above]

**MARRIAGE AND DEATH NOTICES FROM THE SOUTH WESTERN BAPTIST NEWSPAPER**

10-29-1851
Married on the 22nd inst. by Rev. M.P. Jewett, Alexander J. Warford of Cahawba to Miss Catharine L. Cole of this county.
Died in Tuscaloosa, Alabama on the 25th of September 1851, in the sixty-third year of his age, Hon. Arthur Foster. He was born in Columbia County, Georgia in 1788 where at an early age he engaged in political life. His father, Col. John Foster, while a candidate for re-election to the Senate, was thrown from his horse and so injured that he died and he (Arthur Foster) yielding to the importunities of his fellow citizens, took his father's place and was elected a member of the Senate of Georgia... When thirty-five [?] or forty years old he removed to Cherokee County, Alabama, was elected in 1841 a member of the Alabama senate from Cherokee and De Kalb Counties. In 1843 he removed to Tuscaloosa, and in 1844 was elected President of the State Bank... His bereaved widow, his adopted daughter, his two surviving brothers, his sister, and a large circle of relatives and friends feel deeply sensible of their loss... united with the Baptist Church at Abilun, in Columbia County, Georgia...
Died on the 27th of August 1851 in Caldwell Parish, Louisiana, sister Elizabeth Meredith, daughter of Bagwell and Sarah Bailey and wife of Rev. John J. Meredith, in the thirty-sixth year of her age... United with the Baptist Church in 1845... Sister Meredith was attacked in June 1850 with erysipelas, the disease which terminated her mortal life... She has left a devoted husband, seven children...
Died Mrs. Mary W. Dockery. This estimable lady departed this life on Friday morning, 26th September, in this place. She was born March 9th, 1815, and was the second daughter of Benjamin Whitfied of Tuscaloosa, Alabama... She was married to Professor James C. Dockery, then of the University of Alabama, April 3rd, 1843... the survivor left with three small children...

11-5-1851
Died on the 3rd day of October 1851 at the residence of her husband in Lowndes County, Alabama, Mrs. Martha McQueen, in the thirty-ninth year of her age. The subject of this notice was born in the state of Georgia and emigrated to this state with her father in the year 1818. She was baptized by her father, Rev. James McLemore, on the 18th of February 1832 and united with the Baptist Church at Elam, Montgomery County, from which she was dismissed by letter on the 18th of June 1836 and joined the church at Lowndesboro... She has left a doting husband, eight children, a mother, brother, and sisters...
Died at his residence ten miles west of Marion on the 31st. August, Mr. Elihue Carlisle, after an illness of only five days. The deceased was born in Lincoln County, Georgia on the 18 April 1812. He married Miss. Lucretia C.M. Norton in Goshen, Connecticut, whom with one little son about five years old he has left to mourn his sudden and unexpected departure... He

## Marriage and Death Notices From The South Western Baptist Newspaper

spent the greater part of his life in this vicinity... He followed in a few short months his aged mother to the land from whence no traveller returns.

11-12-1851
Died of congestive fever on Friday, October 3, 1851 in Union County, Arkansas, Mrs. Frances M.F. Traylor, wife of Mr. Randolph B. Traylor and daughter of Mr. Ennis and Mrs. Maria H. Ford, age twenty-five years... Mrs. Traylor was born in Perry County, Alabama...
Married in Selma, Alabama on Wednesday, October 15th, by the Rev. A.G. McCraw, Dr. Clement Billingslea of Marion, Alabama to Mrs. E.D. Douglass of that place.
Married on the 7th of October 1851 near Brownsville, Hinds County, Mississippi by the Rev. J.M. Knight, Mr. Zeno P. Walker to Miss Ester I. Young, both of Texas.
Married on the 14th of October 1851 by the Rev. J.M. Knight, George B. Granberry of Madison to Miss Pamella Cockerham of Hinds County, Mississippi.

11-26-1851
Married on the 13th November by Rev. F.H. Moss, Mr. William Gilmore and Miss Martha J. Bean, daughter of Col. M.J. Bean, all of Pike County.
Married on the 26th ult. near Benton by the Rev. J.M. Knight, E.A. Moore, esq. of Yazoo County, Mississippi to Miss Ann M. Wynne of North Carolina.
Married on the 18th inst. by the Rev. J.S. Ford, Mr. D.Y. Steadman to Miss Rebecca Anderson, all of this county.

12-10-1851
Died in Warren County on the 23rd of September of congestive fever, Sarah Ann Jenkins, wife of W.M. Jenkins and daughter of John and Clarisa Slater, in the twenty-second year of her age. She left behind an afflicted husband and two little children, the youngest only twenty-five days old. At her death her husband, who had been suffering under disease for several months, was not able to go from one room to another without help.
Died at the residence of his uncle, Austin Bowlin in Macon County, Alabama on the 11th of November 1851, John H. Brooks, in the twenty-ninth year of his age. The deceased was an amiable and pious member of the Baptist Church, which he joined at Sardis, Macon County, Alabama in July 1849; with which he remained until about a year before his death when he became a member of the Union Springs Baptist Church...
Died of erysipelas on the 18th November 1851 at his residence in Green County, Alabama, Mr. George Randolph, in the twenty-eighth year of his age... mentions wife, aged mother, and sister...

## MARRIAGE AND DEATH NOTICES FROM THE SOUTH WESTERN BAPTIST NEWSPAPER

12-17-1851
Married on Thursday morning, 11th inst., at the residence of Rev. J.S. Ford, by him, Mr. S.A. Heard to Miss Sarah E. Stewart, all of this county.

12-31-1851
Married on the evening of the 11th December by the Rev. Levi Moore, H.S. Goodenough, esq. to Miss Josephine E. Kidd, daughter of Ibrey W. and Mrs. M.A. Kidd, all of Shelby County, Alabama.
Married on the 11th inst. by the Rev. J. Reeves, Mr. Caleb Williams, to Miss Mary Hudson, both of Jefferson, Marengo County, Alabama.

12-31-1851
Died, sister Catharine Madison, consort of Brother Strother Madison of Marengo County, Alabama, departed this life on the 7th inst., in the fifty-third year of her age. She was born and raised in South Carolina, Abbeville District, and moved to this state in 1818...

1-6-1852
Married on the 11th of December by Rev. J.T.S. Park, Mr. R. Sheer to Miss Sarah J., daughter of the late Col. Robert Smilie, all of Pike County, Alabama. OBITUARY: The subject of this notice Brother Phillip Shet?lesworth, a member of the Mt. Moniah Baptist Church, Bibb County, Alabama... He removed at an early age from the state of South Carolina to Tennessee and from there to this state...

1-21-1852
Died of typhoid pneumonia in Hinds County on Sunday evening, 28 December 1851, Miss Nancy Kelley, daughter of Col. Samuel D. Kelley, in the twenty-fourth year of her age. She was baptized early in the fall of 1849 into the New Salem Church near the residence of her father.

2-4-1852
Tribute of respect from Perry Lodge #34, dated Thursday morning, 29 January 1852 on the death of John R. Goree... [see below] Also tribute of respect on the death of fellow brother, Theophilus H. Lockett...
Died in the city of Mobile on the 25th inst., John R. Goree, esq. a resident of this place. Mr. Goree was born 3rd June 1811 in South Carolina, but was raised principally in this neighborhood. His disease was of the lungs and liver which protracted his illness some two months after his first attack... He was a lawyer and commission merchant of Mobile. [see above]
Departed this life on the evening of the 14th inst., Mrs. Martha T. Caldwell in Shelby County, Alabama, age about thirty-eight years, leaving her aged parents, sisters, and three orphans... Mrs. Caldwell united with the Baptist Church at Big Spring three or four years ago... Her disease was consumption.

## Marriage and Death Notices From The South Western Baptist Newspaper

Married on the 14th inst. by the Rev. A. VanHoose of Aberdeen, Mississippi, Mr. James M. Armstrong to Miss Ella S. Parke, both of Montgomery County, Alabama.

2-11-1852
Departed this life in La Grange, Georgia on the 21st ult. Mrs. Sara E. Talbird, age nearly sixty-two years... She was baptized in Beaufort, South Carolina... subsequently she united with the Baptist Church at Hilton Head. Recently she removed to La Grange and became a member of the church in this place... Three of her children survive to mourn her death, one of them extensively known as a learned, pious, able, and useful minister of the gospel, the Rev. Henry Talbird of Alabama. Mentions son-in-law the Rev. Mr. Seriven.

2-18-1852
Rev. William R. Meadows: We have received intelligence within a few days past of the death of this dear brother... He died at the residence of Mr. John C. Pharres of Sumter County on Friday morning the 6th inst...
Died in Conecuh County on the morning of the 1st of January, Mrs. Media, consort of Joel Lee, Sr. in the seventy-ninth year of her age. The maiden name of the deceased was Media Lassater. She was born in Sampson County, North Carolina, A.D., 1772; was married to Joel Lee in '95 and emigrated with their family to Alabama in 1818 and in '21 became a member of the Bethany Baptist Church... She was a mother of eleven children, eight of whom are now living; five of them, two sons and three daughters, in Conecuh, two sons in Lowndes County, and one at present in Early County, Georgia.
Died near Coffeeville, Alabama on the 6th inst. in the forty-third year of her age, Mrs. Ann C. Harris, wife of Rev. Dr. F.F. Harris. Sister Harris was a native of the city of New York. At an early age she came south and engaged in teaching in Savannah, Georgia where she resided eight years. In 1834 she became the wife of our Brother F.F. Harris, then a minister in the Lutheran Church, and moved with him to Alabama where she has been engaged in teaching for about sixteen years. Her health having failed about two years ago, she abandoned her favorite pursuit and has given much of her time to religious and devotional reading. In the Spring of 1851 her lungs became seriously affected which soon terminated in a rapid consumption. In September she became confined to her bed... Mentions a husband and son.
Died at his residence in Jefferson County, November 14th 1851, Rev. Joseph Moore, age thirty-four years, twenty-nine days. The deceased united himself with the Hebron Baptist Church in October 1836... he left a widow and four children...
Departed this life on the 20th of December 1851 in the seventeenth year of her age, Miss Cornelia E. Posey, daughter of Joseph H. and Caroline W. Posey of Harpersville, Shelby County, Alabama.

# Marriage and Death Notices From The South Western Baptist Newspaper

3-3-1852
Tribute of respect on the death of Rev. Isaac C. Perkins... which occurred on the 9th inst., sixty-three years of age.

3-10-1852
Died in Noxubee County, Mississippi on the 25th December 1851, Mrs. Susan Frazier, wife of Thomas Frazier and daughter of Featherson and Mary Walden. She was born December 14, 1813 and lived thirty-eight years nine days. She was married 17 August 1831. She left a husband and six children...

3-17-1852
Our venerable brother, the beloved father of the church at Mine Creek, Rev. Isaac C. Perkins, is no more! He closed his earthly career at his residence in this county on Friday 9 January 1852, age nearly sixty-three years. Mr. Perkins was born in North Carolina in the year 1789. Mr. P. lived in Georgia and afterwards in Alabama, and removed to Arkansas, and settled at Mine Creek in the year 1835... He was interred on the next day, at the Mine Creek burial ground with Masonic honors... Mine Creek, Arkansas 15 January 1852. Departed this life on the 13th of February, about noon, at her father's residence in the village of Gaston, Sumter County, Alabama, Mrs. Harriet, consort of Mr. J.J. Watson, age twenty-four years, twelve days. She was the second daughter of Pleasant and Frances White and was born near Greensboro, Green County, Alabama, 6 February 1827... was married 22 November 1847.
Died on the 22nd ult. at the residence of her uncle, D. McNeely, Madison County, Miss Margaret Jane McNeely, age twelve years, two months.

3-24-1852
Died: Mrs. E.G. Shuck of the Shanghai Mission, China.
Died near Carrollton, Pickens County, Alabama, Mrs. Martha Curry, wife of William Curry, Sr., age near fifty-eight years. She was first attacked by pneumonia and after six weeks typhoid fever supervened, which resulted fatally on the 25 ult. after an illness of about eleven weeks. A bereaved husband and ten children are left... The subject of this notice was a native of Fairfield District, South Carolina. She removed to Pickens County in the year 1835, and united with the Big Creek Church...
Died in Perry County on the 24th of January 1852, Dr. J.F. Jacobs, at the residence of S.B. Ford, his father-in-law. Dr. Jacobs was born the 14th of February 1818 in South Carolina, Greenville District; came to Alabama in the year '41, commenced the practice of medicine in Perryville and its vicinity in '42... Dr. Jacobs was married to Miss Nancy Ford the 12th of November 1845; in '46 volunteered his services in the war with Mexico... Dr. Jacobs died of consumption... He has left an affectionate wife, an infant daughter...

## MARRIAGE AND DEATH NOTICES FROM THE SOUTH WESTERN BAPTIST NEWSPAPER

Died in Pickens County on Thursday the 4th day of March 1852 of typhoid fever, Rev. John H. Taylor, age nearly sixty years... He leaves a wife and six children... Mr. Taylor was born in Fairfield District, South Carolina on the 20th of March 1797; was baptized in the year 1822 or 23; was married in the year 1834; was licensed to preach in the year 1828, and was ordained a Baptist minister on the 20th of August, 1831. He removed to Pickens County, Alabama in the winter of 1834...

Married on the 15th inst. by Rev. J.H. DeVotie, Mr. Wm. W. Lumpkin of Athens, Georgia to Miss L.M. King, daughter of Gen. E.D. King, Marion, Alabama.

3-31-1852
Died, January 27th of a short illness in Noxubee County, Mississippi, Mrs. Jane Hudson, wife of W.B. Hudson. She was young, had been married but little more than a year...

4-7-1852
Tribute of respect on the death of Richard Tubb, student of Howard College. Departed this life on Tuesday the 6th day of January 1852, David Atteberry, after ten days illness, of typhoid pneumonia. The subject of this obituary was born in the state of South Carolina, Chester District, and was in the thirty-fourth year of his age. For the last fifteen or sixteen years has been well known in this county (Pickens) as an excellent teacher in the various branches of the English Literature. On the 22nd January 1845 he was married to Ann Catharine, oldest daughter of Thomas and Frances Taylor.
Died near Marion, Alabama, March 22nd, 1852 Mrs. T.T. Jones, age twenty-one years, five months.

4-14-1852
Married on the 7th inst. by Rev. P.B. Lawson, Mr. William A. Corbin of this town to Miss Mary E., daughter of Rev. Jacob Creath of Palmyra, Missouri.
Married in the Baptist Church in Carlowville, Dallas County, on Wednesday (at noon) 16th inst. by Rev. Platt Stout, W.W. Waller of Montgomery, Alabama to Miss M.A. Stout, daughter of Rev. Platt Stout of Carlowville.
Deacon Henry Fox was born in Richland District, South Carolina on the 12th day of June 1768. At about the age of thirty-two years he professed religion and united with the Congaree Baptist Church, of which he was a member until the year 1814, when he removed to the state of Tennessee, Cocke County, and joined the Big Pigeon Church. In 1840 he removed to the state of Alabama, Tuscaloosa County, and united with the Big Creek Church. Subsequently he united with others in a new constitution (Bethany) near to him. In 1836 he emigrated to Mississippi, Choctaw County, and for a short time was a member of Fellowship Church; he again united in the constitution by the name of Bethany, near the place of his residence, of which church he

# Marriage and Death Notices From The South Western Baptist Newspaper

remained... until his death... he died the owner of considerable property, (more than forty slaves)... Nine years or within a few months of that time, before his own death, his wife died... On Sabbath, the 18th day of January, A.D., 1852, after an illness of some days, in the eighty-fourth year of his age, leaving a number of children...

4-21-1852
Died on the 20th of March at the Female Academy in Demopolis, Alabama of bronchitis, Henrietta Rebecca, second daughter of Levin M. Connella of Ouachita Parish, Louisiana, in the fourteenth year of her age. A.A. Connella.
Died on the 15th day of January 1852, that aged father in Israel, the Rev. Henry Hooten, at Orion, Pike County, Alabama, in the eighty-seventh year of his age. Father Hooten was born in Bertie County, North Carolina on the 2nd day of September 1765, made a profession of religion and joined the Marattock Baptist Church the first Sabbath in June 1802... In 1807 or 1808 he removed to Washington County, Georgia, and the next year settled in Jones County where he remained about sixteen years. He was one of the first settlers in that county and was instrumental in constituting and rearing up the first Baptist Churches in that part of Georgia. In 1824 he moved to Upson County... In 1841 he moved to Macon County, Alabama... About the first of January last he removed with his only surviving child, James B. Hooten, to Orion, Pike County, Alabama where he died on the 15th of the same month. A short time before the death of father Hooten, a grandson, James F. Hooten was licensed to preach...
Died in Macon Mississippi March 31st 1852, Emilly Cunningham, infant daughter of Rev. S.S. and Frances Lattimore, age ten months, twenty-six days.
Died at his residence in Macon, Noxubee County, Mississippi on the 30th ult. David Buck in the sixtieth year of his age. The deceased was born in the state of Maine on the 17th of May 1792. In the year 1818 he removed to Alabama and settled in Tuscaloosa County... Bucksville, a village still bearing his own name... In 1838 he removed to Mississippi and settled at the place of his decease...
Married on the 25th March at the residence of Col. Billups in the city of Columbus by Rev. S.S. Lattimore, Mr. D. Dupree of Noxubee County, Mississippi to Mrs. E. Moore of Columbus.

4-28-1852
Died in Tallapoosa County, Alabama on the 8th March last after an illness of little more than one day, Mrs. Rebecca Spivey, wife of Mr. Beverly Spivey and daughter of Elder Elisha Perryman. She left to mourn their painful loss a husband and eight children...

## Marriage and Death Notices From The South Western Baptist Newspaper

Married on the morning of the 28th inst. by Rev. J.H. DeVotie, Rev. Basil Manly, Jr., Pastor of the First Baptist Church, Richmond, Virginia, to Mrs. Charlotte A.E. Whitfield Smith of Marion, Alabama.

5-5-1852
Married in Montgomery on the 28th ult. by Rev. Mr. Finley, Mr. J.A. Melcher, teacher of the Preparatory Department of Howard College, to Miss Catharine E. Dewey of Wetumpka.
Died, sister S. Woodward, who departed this life in this place of a pulmonary affection, a few weeks since... She was upwards of fifty years of age... She leaves a husband and four affectionate and pious daughters... Memphis, Alabama, April 29, 1852.
Died on the 3rd inst. of pneumonia, Miss Rebecca J. Harris, age sixteen, a student of Judson Female Institute. Miss Harris was from Greene County...

5-12-1852
Died at the residence of his father in Macon County, Alabama on Tuesday night 20th of April, A.J. Robertson, son of Rev. John Robertson, in the thirty-sixth year of his age.

5-19-1852
Married on the 21st ult. by the Rev. C.C. Lee, Mr. H.S. Black to Miss Mary Odum, all of Madison County, Mississippi.
Died, April 30th at his residence near Forkland, Green County, Alabama, Deacon Robert Fleming, age fifty-four years. The deceased was a native of North Carolina. In 1831 he made a profession of christianity and united with Cedar Fork Baptist Church in Wake County... In 1833 he emigrated with his family to this state... [see below]
Died, May 13th of congestive fever, at the residence of his father near Forkland, J. Robert Fleming, M.D., age twenty-two years. [see above]

5-26-1852
Died after a short but painful illness at her residence in Montgomery County, Alabama on the 26th of April 1852, Mrs. Margaret S. McLemore. The deceased left behind a husband and three daughters.

6-2-1852
Died in Hayneville on the 9th inst. of the prevailing epidemic, Mrs. Lydia E. Stone, wife of J.B. Stone, in the twenty-ninth year of her age. [see below]
Died in Hayneville on the 11th inst. Arthur L. Stone, son of S.B. and Lydia E. Stone, in the seventh year of his age. [see above]

## MARRIAGE AND DEATH NOTICES FROM THE SOUTH WESTERN BAPTIST NEWSPAPER

Josiah Ricks, in the sixty-seventh year of his age, a native of North Carolina, and member of the Baptist Church for near twenty years, has been gathered to his Father's after a painful illness of some months... He is the father of nine children... the mother had departed sometime before him.

6-23-1852
Married at the residence of Mr. Wm. Walker, Greensboro, on the evening of the 2nd inst. by J.H. DeVoteo, Mr. O.D. Shelman of New?an, Georgia to Miss Sarah J. Walker.
Died at his residence in Washington County, Texas on the 9th of March 1852, William Jefferson, son of William and Jane Dorroh, in the twenty-fifth year of his age. The subject of this notice was born near Marion, Perry County, Alabama in the year 1827, from which place he removed in early life with his parents to Noxubee County, Mississippi. In the year 1813 he professed religion and was baptized by the Rev. Wm. Lloyd into the fellowship of the Baptist Church at Elam. In the fall of 1851 he emigrated with his family to Washington County, Texas...
Died on the 1st inst. at the residence of her husband, Dr. James A. Dillard, Crawfordsville, Lowndes County, Mississippi, after a short but severe illness, Mrs. Sarah Louisa Dillard, in the thirty-ninth year of her age. The subject of this notice was a native of Virginia... She has left a husband and six children...

6-30-1852
Married on the 22nd inst. by the Rev. W. Wilkes, Mr. James A. Lake of Dallas to Miss Ann E. Wallace of Perry County.
Died on Thursday morning the 24th inst. Felix Tarrant, only child of Rev. Russell and Lucinda M. Holman, age eighteen months, nineteen days.
Died in Sumter County June 25th, Mrs. E.J. Bestor, wife of the Rev. D.P. Bestor, in the forty-third year of her age.
Died at Dr. Woodfin's in Marengo County, Alabama on the 31st of May, Mary E., only child of Mr. Edward B. and Lucy C. Woodfin, age thirteen months, five days.

7-14-1852
Died on the 6th ult. four miles west of Port Gibson, Mississippi, Mrs. Frances N. Venable, consort of John Venaqle in the twenty-fourth year of her age.
Died at the residence of his father in Coosa County, Alabama, May 22, 1852, William Holtzclaw, in the twenty-fifth year of his age.
Died on the 5th day of June, Mrs. Mary Thomas, wife of John Thomas, deacon of the Rocky Spring Church, Claiborne Parish, Louisiana, in the sixty-ninth year of her age.

## Marriage and Death Notices From The South Western Baptist Newspaper

7-21-1852
Departed this life in Oak Grove, near Woodville, Wilkerson County, Mississippi, 7 February 1852, Martha Elizabeth, daughter of Capt. Samuel and Martha L. Thomas, formerly of Brunswick County, Virginia, age twenty-one years...

8-4-1852
Departed this life on the 17th July at his late residence in Perry County, John Cunningham, after a short and painful illness of six or eight days. The deceased was born in Lawrence District, South Carolina on the ?? September 1796, and removed to this county about fifteen years ago...
Departed this life on the evening of July 5th in the twenty-third year of her age, Mrs. M. Howlett, daughter of John and Susan Hogue and wife of John B. Howlett.
Departed this life at her residence in Auburn, Macon County, Alabama, July 23rd, 1852, the day that made her just thirty-nine years old, Mrs. Artemissa Turner, wife of Mathew Turner, after a protracted illness of several months.
Died in Bienville Parish, Louisiana, June 18, 1852, John M. Cooper, in the thirty-seventh year of his age, having accidentally shot himself, the whole load, twelve buck shot entering his right breast just below the collar bone, six shots passing through the shoulder and causing almost instant death. He only lived about five hours after he was shot... The subject of the present obituary was born in Warren County, Georgia. His father removed to Putnam County when he was quite young. His mother had previously died... He came to Morgan County from Putnam where he lived some years, thence to Walton County where he married the daughter of Wm. Denson in 1839. He removed from Georgia to Louisiana in 1846, and in 1850 was one of nine who were constituted into a church in this place (Sparta). He leaves a wife and six children...
Dear Brother Chambliss. It becomes my painful duty to record the death of one of the deacons of our church in this place Brother _____ Morrow departed this life on the 19th of this month... Brother Morrow was born in Wilkes County, Georgia, and died at his residence in Minden, Louisiana, in the fifty-second year of his age. He left an affectionate wife and seven children.

8-11-1852
Died near Cameron, Milam County, Texas on the 22nd ult., Mary Clay???, daughter of Alsey and Mary C. All????, of Lowndes County, Alabama, age two years, ? months, eighteen days.
Died at her residence in ? County on the 24th ult., Mrs. Martha ?, wife of deacon Dent Lamar.

## Marriage and Death Notices From The South Western Baptist Newspaper

8-18-1852
Died at Tampa Bay, Florida, July 5th 1852, Mrs. Mary W. John, wife of Dr. S.W. John of Marion and daughter of Dr. Clement Billingsly of Selma... age twenty-two years, two months...

8-25-1852
Departed this life August 5, 1852 of congestive fever at his residence in Caddo Parish, Louisiana, Noah B. Cole, age fifty-seven years, six months, twenty-five days. The deceased was a native of South Carolina. He emigrated with his parents in early life to the state of Georgia, in which he grew up to manhood. He thence removed to Alabama where he raised a large family of children, most of them are now married. In January 1848 Mr. Cole emigrated to this parish...
Tilman R. Brassfield departed this life at 7 o'clock on the evening of the 8th inst. after a painful illness... He was buried with Christ in baptism in the Neuse River near Raleigh, North Carolina during the summer of 1831... He officiated as clerk of Friendship Baptist Church, near Forkland, Green County, Alabama for the last ten years. He left a wife and two small children, several brothers and sisters... He was born in Wake County, North Carolina, 20th April 1814...
Died in Pickens County, Alabama on the evening of the 11th August 1852 after an illness of about nine days at the residence of her father, Nancy M., daughter of Nathaniel and Margaret West, age eleven years, ten months, one day.

9-1-1852
Died at the residence of Mr. John Mayo in Tuscaloosa County, Alabama of bloody dysentery on August 16th 1852, Rev. Henry R. Morgan. Brother Morgan was born in Montgomery County, North Carolina about the year 1817. In the year 1821 his father removed with his family and settled in Greene County, Alabama. About the time he arrived at the age of manhood Brother M. entered a store as a clerk in Pickens County and in this occupation remained one year...
Departed this life July 17, 1852 at Homer in Pope County, Arkansas, Mary D., wife of Rev. James Veazey, in the forty-third year of her age...

9-8-1852
Died of typhoid fever at the residence of her father near Wetumpka on the 25th ult., Miss Victoria Baker, daughter of A.C. Baker, in the fifteenth year of her age.
Departed this life on the 30th July at the residence of her father in Camden, Arkansas, Miss Elizabeth Brodie Hartwell, age twenty-one years. While a pupil of the Judson Institute she embraced religion and joined the Siloam Baptist Church at Marion, Alabama...

## Marriage and Death Notices From The South Western Baptist Newspaper

Died on the 12th of July 1852, Mrs. Mary E.B. Dossey of Laurel Hill, Marengo County, Alabama. She was the daughter of George Outlaw of Bertie County, North Carolina, and became the wife of Wm. Dossey and his solace for more than forty years.

Died in Dale County, Alabama on the 16th inst., sister Clarisa A., consort of Brother A.N. Thompson, in the twenty-seventh year of her age. Sister Thompson was born and raised in Seriven [Screven] County, Georgia and removed to Alabama with her family in 1849... Mentions husband, infant daughter, mother.

9-15-1852
Died at the residence of his son in Montgomery County, Alabama on the 27th of July last, Deacon Green B. Pinkston, in the eighty-first year of his age, having been a member of the Antioch Church thirty years and a deacon twenty-eight.

9-22-1852
Departed this life on Sunday morning, 29th of August 1852, Miss Susan Smith, only daughter of J.S. and V. Amanda Smith, of Wilkerson County, Mississippi... being only twelve years, five months, seven days old...
Died on Saturday the 31st of July, Mrs. Nancy A. Gooch, age fifty-eight years, one month. Born in South Carolina and emigrated from there to Shelby County, Alabama, where she resided until the day of her death...

9-29-1852
Tribute of respect upon the death of James Cadenhead who departed this life 15 August 1852...
Departed this life September 6th, Mrs. Amanda C. Edwards, wife of John Edwards, and daughter of Samuel T. and Ann Harrison, in the twentieth year of her age. She had about eleven or twelve months ago entered into holy wedlock with Mr. Edwards and left an infant daughter but a few days old.
Died of typhoid fever at ??? Monroe County, Alabama, William Henry Longmire, son of Rev. Garret Longmire... in the nineteenth year of his age...

10-6-1852
Married on the 28th September by the Rev. Sam'l Henderson, Dr. William A. Hooten of Orion, Pike County, to Miss Parisade Jett of Macon County, Alabama.
Mrs. L. Ella O'Bryan, wife of S.G. O'Bryan, died of consumption, 27 August 1852, at the residence of Mr. John Echols in Burleson County, Texas... Sister O'Bryan was born in Mathuen, Massachusetts in 1827 but raised in New Hampshire. Her father, Jonathan Swan, was familiarly known as a deacon of the Baptist Church in Denmark, Iowa...

## Marriage and Death Notices From The South Western Baptist Newspaper

Died on the 25th September, Marcella Henrietta, infant daughter of Dr. Olfa L. Shivers, age eight months, eighteen days.

Died on the 23rd inst. at the residence of W.H. Griffin, Dallas County, Alabama after the brief existence of five hours, infant son of Rev. P.E. and Eliza C. Collins.

Died near Demopolis, September 16th, Letitia, second daughter of Dr. Jasper and Mrs. Ann Palmer, age seven years, seven months, eleven days.

10-21-1852
Tribute of respect on the death of John A. Holmes from the students of Howard College. [see 10-28-1852]

Died at Sumterville... Eliza, child of Col. I. Chapman and Mary Brown, age thirteen months.

Married on the ?? inst., by Rev. P.H. Lunds, Stephen H. Pearce of Autauga County to Miss Sarah Virginia Tatum of Lowndes County.

10-28-1852
Married by the Rev. John S. Ford, October 5th, 1852 Mr. Bryant Boroughs of Perry County to Miss Jane Spratt of Lowndes County, Alabama.

Died of typhoid fever at the residence of his father in Perry County on the 15th of September, John A. Holmes, in the twentieth year of his age. He was the youngest son of Anderson and Louisa Holmes. This amiable young man had been a student at the Howard College for the last two or three years and had returned home to spend the vacation with the family... had attached himself to the Concord Baptist Church in Dallas County... [see 10-21-1852]

Died near Carlowville, Dallas County, on the 8th inst., William Edward, infant son of Jas. A. and Mary E. Fountain, age one year, five months, twenty-three days.

Died at her residence three miles southwest of Moulton, Lawrence County, Alabama on the 30th of July last, Mrs. Elizabeth N. Walker, wife of John N. Walker. Sister Walker was the daughter of Samuel and Catherine Young; born May 9, 1827, died in the prime of life, being in her twenty-sixth year.

Died in Marion on Wednesday morning the 27th inst., Frank William, only child of Dr. Wm. W. and Lucy M. Sanger, age twenty-three months, ten days.

11-3-1852
Tribute of respect from the Adelphi Society on the death of J.A. Holmes.

Rev. John S. Maginnis, D.D., Professor of Systematic Theology in the Rochester Theological Seminary, died on the 15th ult.

Departed this life at his residence in this county on the 5th ult., Brother Young Goodwin, age forty-seven years, one month. Brother G. was born in Hancock County, Georgia; moved to Alabama in 1818, and was married in Dallas County; moved to Talladega, and was baptized into the fellowship of Mt. Zion

## Marriage and Death Notices From The South Western Baptist Newspaper

Church in 1845. In 1846 he moved to this county with his family and united with the Rehoboth Church...

11-10-1852
Died in Pike County on the 7th of August 1852, sister Sarah McCall, age seventy-five years. Born North Carolina, 19 August 1777, and was raised in South Carolina...

2-4-1853
Married by Rev. C.D. Oliver on the 2nd inst., B.P. Reese of Virginia to Miss Laura I. Grigg of Montgomery.

2-11-1853
Married by Rev. G.R. Foster on the evening of the 27th ult. Mr. James Montgomery of Benton to Miss Martha D. Goode of this city.
Married on the 31st ult. Rev R.C. Burleson, President of Baylor University, to Miss Georgiana Jenkins, both of Independence, Texas.
Married on the 13th ult. Mr. Cameron of Texas to Miss Emma A. Dailey of Mississippi.
Married on the 12th ult. Albert G. Prewett, esq. to Miss Elizabeth Holliday, both of Aberdeen, Mississippi.
Married on the 18th ult. Mr. Haughton to Miss Margaret E. Askew, both of Maury County, Tennessee.
Married in Galveston, Texas, _____Jones to Miss Mary Sydnor.
Died in the city of New Orleans on the evening of the 1st inst. Mr. George Emmet Chisolm, in the forty-second year of his age. The deceased had been for many years a citizen of this place and had but recently taken up his residence in New Orleans. [mentions a mother, daughter, brother and sisters]
Tribute of respect from the Philomathic Society, University of Alabama, on the death of A. Judson Foster.
Tribute of respect from the Philomathic Society of the University of Alabama on the death of Horace Southworth Pratt, age eighteen years... He was born in St. Mary's, Georgia on the 4th September 1835... parents were the late Prof. H.S. Pratt and Mrs. Isabel A. Pratt; brought him to his city on their removal in 1838...

2-18-1853
Died of consumption on the 5th inst. at her residence in Gainesville, Alabama, Mrs. Maria E. Robertson, wife of Mr. James G. Robertson, in the twenty-ninth year of her age. The deceased was born in Lancaster County, Virginia, but while young moved with her father, Mr. Wm. H. Dandridge, to Alabama. In June 1841 she was married... A widowed husband, two little girls, and aged father...mourn her loss...

## MARRIAGE AND DEATH NOTICES FROM THE SOUTH WESTERN BAPTIST NEWSPAPER

2-25-1853
Tribute of respect on the death of Dr. W.F. McMath...

3-4-1853
Married on the 1st inst. by Rev. I.T. Tichenor, Dr. W. H. Rives and Mrs. Sarah H. Wray, all of this city.
Married on the 24th inst. by the Rev. Prof. H.H. Tucker at the residence of President Henry H. Bacon in Tuskegee, the Rev. J.H. Foster, pastor of the Baptist Church in Tuscaloosa, and Miss Frances Cornelia Bacon, formerly of Liberty County, Georgia.
Tribute of respect from Hermathenian Hall, Green Springs, 21 February 1853 on the death of Lewis M. Stevens of Greensborough, Alabama...

3-11-1853
Married on the 10th day of February by the Rev. Leonidas T. Eubanks, Mr. Edward Denkins and Miss Lucy Perry, all of Russell County, Alabama.

3-25-1853
Tribute of respect on the deaths of Mrs. Minerva Pylant, Mary Butler, and Serena Griffin, all of last year. Dated Coosa County, Alabama, February 1st, 1853.
Tribute of respect from Mt. Zion Baptist Church, Talladega County on the death of Alexander Oden, who died 1 March 1853, in the sixty-fifth year of his age.
Died on Sunday morning the 20th inst. at the residence of her mother in Tuskegee, Miss Mary Elizabeth Bailey, in the sixteenth year of her age.
Died in this city on the 22nd inst., Mr. A.B. Vickers, son of Martha A. Vickers, age two years, two months.
Tribute of respect from Auburn Lodge #76 on the death of Sandford Thornton, who died on Thursday night 3rd inst...

4-1-1853
Died at Loachapoka, Macon County, Alabama, March 24th of consumption, Miss Catharine Ann, daughter of Isaac and Mary Ann Winter, in the nineteenth year of her age, formerly of Baltimore, Maryland.

4-8-1853
Married on Tuesday the 13th March by the Rev. James F. Hooten, Col. W.W. Battle and Miss Elizabeth Sharp, daughter of the late Dr. Sharp, all of Macon County.

4-15-1853
Married on the 7th inst. by Rev. D. Culberson, Rev. J. C. Burruss and Miss Francis A.T. , daughter of Rev. Charles Burks of Macon County, Alabama.

## Marriage and Death Notices From The South Western Baptist Newspaper

4-22-1853
Married in the city of Houston on the 15th March by the Rev. Thos. Chilton, George Erving to Miss Sarah E. Perkinson.
On the 17th by the same, Mr. George W. Broderick to Mrs. Eliza Conger.

4-29-1853
Married on the 21st inst. by the Rev. Dr. A.A. Lipscomb, Col. L.C. Jurey of New Orleans to Miss Mary E. Holt, daughter of Dr. Samuel D. Holt of this city.

5-6-1853
Rev. Alfred Wright, a missionary among the Choctaw Indians, died recently at the missionary station at Wheelock, Choctaw Nation, Arkansas...
SUICIDE: An individual, a stranger, whose name has since been ascertained to be J.F. Arnot of Texas, walked into the courthouse on Monday evening and deliberately blew out his brains with a pistol charge... (*Journal*)

5-20-1853
Died at his residence in the city of Montgomery on the 9th inst. of consumption, Dr. Andrew McBryde, age thirty-nine years, six months. He was a native of Charlotte, North Carolina. His parents moved to Montgomery in the year 1822... He has left a wife and three children, a mother and a brother...

6-3-1853
Died at his residence in Tuskegee on the 9th ult., Green B. Marshall, in the sixty-first year of his age. He was born in South Carolina, lived in Columbia for a number of years, then removed to Augusta, Georgia. In 1839 he transferred his residence to Montgomery County, Alabama where he continued to reside until about the last of January of the present year...
Tribute of respect on the death of Dr. W.F. McMath. Dr. W.F. McMath was born 1 December 1815 in Tuscaloosa County, Alabama. In 1835 he married Miss Amanda L. Edmonson... The fruits of this union are five living children. In 1843 he with his family emigrated to Texas... At the battle of Mier he was taken prisoner... In 1845 he returned to Alabama and located in Tuscaloosa County...

6-10-1853
We have just received the painful intelligence of the death of Brother Green Rives of Lowndes County... He had just returned from his plantation in Louisiana...
Married in Montgomery, Alabama on the 5th inst. by the Rev. Mr. Oliver, Mr. Ezra B. Mershon of Columbus, Georgia to Miss Rebecca Eady, daughter of Absolom Eady of Auburn.

## Marriage and Death Notices From The South Western Baptist Newspaper

Married on Monday the 2nd of May by the Rev. Lewis Johnston, Rev. J. Veazey of Pope County to Mrs. Rebecca Nours of Johnston, all of Arkansas.
Died in Marion on the 30th ult. of dysentery, C. Perry Jones, Professor of Natural Science and of Modern Languages in the Judson Female Institute, age twenty-eight... Buried on Tuesday at set of sun...
Died on the 28th May 1853 at the residence of Mr. Robert Rives in Lowndes County, Alabama, Mrs. Elizabeth A. Traylor, consort of George H. Traylor. Sister Traylor was the daughter of Brother Jonathan and Sister Nancy Mealing. She was born in Edgefield District, South Carolina on 26th March 1810; was married to Brother Traylor on 15th August 1827. She joined the Baptist Church at Mt. Gilead in July 1833... She has left a husband, three orphans, an aged father, a step-mother... four sisters and brother...
Died at his residence, Grove Hill, Clarke County, Alabama, May 26th, George D. Megginson, age fifty-three years, four months, two days. The object of this brief notice was the son of Thomas and Elizabeth Megginson; was born in Montgomery County, North Carolina, 24 January 1800. Soon afterward, his father removed to Smith County, Tennessee. In this state his relatives now dwell. In 1812 he removed to Alabama and settled in Clarke County; was married in early life to Sarah N. Hill... Removing to Macon (now Grove Hill) he united by letter with Horeb Baptist Church... He has left a widow, six sons and a daughter...

6-17-1853
Married in this county on the 26th May by the Rev. A.T.M. Handey, Mr. James S. Seaman of Wetumpka to Miss Frances A. Hagerty of Montgomery.
Married at the residence of Mr. B. Gibson, near Tallassee, on the 7th inst. by the same, Mr. J.F. Ashust to Miss Frances E. Johnson.
Married in this county on the 8th inst. by the same, Mr. Edward S. Ready of Wetumpka to Miss W. Amanda Sledge of Montgomery County.
Died in Talladega County, Alabama at the residence of Rev. E. Martin on the 21st of May 1853, Elijah Chalmon, age eight years, ? months, twenty-two days.
He fell asleep at half past 9 o'clock in the morning; and on the same day at 6 o'clock, thirty-five minutes in the evening, Garrett Grose departed this life, age ten months, twenty-three days; on the 26th of May, Champ Marable died with the same disease (the flux), age eleven years, ? months, twenty-five days... Also, on the 31st of May, George A?? Judson departed this life, age thirteen years, five months, two days...
Departed this life in Lowndes County, Georgia on the 19th of May in the sixty-fifth year of her age, Mrs. Rhoda Gaulden, wife of the Rev. Jonathan Gaulden, after an illness of only one week. She has left a husband, four sons and one daughter... Her children had been assembled to witness the marriage of her youngest and only surviving daughter, and the next day she was taken sick...

## MARRIAGE AND DEATH NOTICES FROM THE SOUTH WESTERN BAPTIST NEWSPAPER

7-1-1853
Died in Jefferson, Marengo County, on the 4th inst., Mrs. Elizabeth L. Ringgold, wife of Benjamin Ringgold of Linden... was in her thirty-eighth year... She had been the subject of disease (consumption) for two or three years...

7-8-1853
A gentleman by the name of J.B. Kerlin fell from a window in the fourth story of the Madison House on Friday night the 1st and was instantly killed... We learn that Mr. K. was an overseer and resided in the neighborhood of Line Creek... (*Advertiser*)
Extract from a letter dated Carlowville, Dallas County, Alabama, Monday, June 30, 1853:... We went to the neighborhood of Canton Church (of which Elder Hare is pastor) where on Tuesday we were joined by Elders Jones and Samuel Wright, (Elder Hawthorn being prevented by the illness of his brother's wife which proved fatal the latter part of this week.)...

7-22-1853
Died at the residence of her husband in Foster's Settlement, Tuscaloosa County, Alabama, June 18th, 1853 at 8 o'clock, p.m., Mrs. Julia F. Morgan. She was the daughter of Isaiah and Elizabeth Jones, was born in Abbeville District, South Carolina, April 12, 1812. She was married to Robert C. Morgan, esq., 27 January 1830...
Died on the 7th inst. at the residence of her father, D.A. Outlaw, esq. in Oktibbeha County, Mississippi, Miss Ann R. Outlaw, age sixteen years.
Married by Rev. John S. Ford on the evening of the 13th inst., Mr. Benjamin R. Coleman of Louisiana to Miss Fidelia N. Melton of Perry County, Alabama.
Died in Wilcox County, Alabama in the seventeenth year of her age, Miss Martha Scott, daughter of John B. and Susan Scott.

7-29-1853
The Rev. William Dossey died at Laurel, the place of his abode, in Marengo County, Alabama, 3 July 1853. It is known that he was born 26 January 1779, consequently he was in his seventy-fifth year at the period of his decease. He was married to Mary E. Outlaw, of Bertie County, North Carolina, 31 October 1809; and this admirable lady, the light of his house and the help-meet of his ministry, had preceded him to the rest of the saints a little less than a year, having died 12 July 1852, in her sixty-first year... About 1814, upon the withdrawment of that venerable man of God, the Rev. Daniel White, from the pastorship of the Welch-Neck Baptist Church, Brother Dossey removed to Society Hill, Darlington District, South Carolina, and became its pastor...
Married at Tampa, Florida on the 10th July 1853, by Rev. J.M. Hayman, Rev. J.H. Breaker of Key West to Miss Eliza J. Spencer of Tampa, Florida.

## Marriage and Death Notices From The South Western Baptist Newspaper

8-5-1853
Married at Athens, Pennsylvania on the 27th ult. by the Rev. Mr. Elmer, Mr. E.A. McWhorter of Montgomery County, Alabama to Miss Anna G. Shepard of the former place.

8-12-1853
Died at his residence in Trinity County, Texas on 5th inst. after a painful illness of three months, Dr. Langston Goree, age fifty-nine years, ten months. The disease which terminated his existence was abscess of the hip joint, terminating in mortification... mentions relations in South Carolina and Marion, Alabama...
Died at his residence in Eufaula on the 14th inst., Gen. Reuben Clark Shorter, in the sixty-seventh year of his age. He was a native of Culpeper County, Virginia. Left at a tender age an orphan... studied medicine, and in 1809 settled in Monticello, Georgia where he devoted himself to the successful practice of his profession until about 1818 when he embarked in mercantile life and about 1826 abandoned that for the life of a planter. In 1836 he removed to Eufaula where he resided to the time of his death...

8-19-1853
Died at his residence in Autauga County on Sunday 24th ult., Elder Enoch Hays, an old and faithful Minister of the Gospel in the Baptist Church; leaving an aged wife and many children...

8-26-1853
Died at Springfield, South Carolina, Brother Luke Smith on the 2nd day of July, 1853, which was his birthday, making his age fifty-six years. Brother S. on the 20th of May last left his home in company with his wife and a brother-in-law to visit his relatives and acquaintances in Newberry District, South Carolina. He had the pleasure of reaching his place of destination and of spending some three weeks among his friends with great satisfaction, when he was attacked with the bloody flux, a disease then prevailing in that county...

SPRING GROVE, PICKENS COUNTY, Alabama, August 15th 1853. Dear Brethren, Allow, if you please, to an affectionate community, space enough to record the death of our dearly beloved and greatly lamented brother, Elder Montgomery H. Curry. He departed this life at his residence near Starksville, Mississippi on Saturday evening the 6th of August 1853. Brother Curry was a native of Fairfield District, South Carolina, and was born on the 19th of March 1815. He was baptized on the 2nd of December 1832 at Beaver Creek Church by our esteemed Brother Elder D. Duncan, now of this county; and in 1836 with his family and many connections removed to Tuscaloosa and thence to Pickens County... [see 9-9-1853]

## Marriage and Death Notices From The South Western Baptist Newspaper

9-2-1853
Departed this life August 9th 1853 of malignant congestive fever at his residence in Coffee County, Alabama, Abram Burk, in the forty-sixth year of his age. Mr. Burk was a native of Screven County, Georgia; was married to Miss Jane J. Scarbor in 1828... Mr. B. left home on the 19th of June on an exploring trip to the West and came home on the 3rd of August, well pleased with his new scenes... He emigrated to Alabama in 1840 where he has raised a portion of a large family of children... Mr. B. has left an affectionate wife and ten children...
Died at Oakland, his residence near Columbus, Mississippi, August 19, 1853, James Brownlee, in the forty-ninth year of his age, after three months confinement of consumption. The subject of this notice was the son of James and Mary Brownlee who formerly resided in Abbeville District, South Carolina. He moved to this state in early life and was married to Miss Prudence Taggart... He has left a widow, three sons and two daughters...

9-9-1853
Tribute of respect from the Baptist Church at Starkville, Mississippi, 22 August 1853 on the death of Rev. Montgomery C. Curry. [see 8-26-1853]

9-16-1853
Died in Montgomery on Monday the 5th inst. John B. Harvell [Harwell?] in the sixth year of his age. He was the son of Samuel B. and Martha Ann Harvell of Columbus, Georgia.

9-23-1853
Departed this life on the 27th August 1853 in Tallapoosa County, Alabama, Lucinda A. Maxwell, consort of Frances M. Maxwell, and daughter of Jacob and Nancy Carraker of Talbot County, Georgia. The deceased died of typhoid fever. Her attacks were violent and she lived only eight days after she was confined to her bed...
Mrs. Ariana A. Hudson was the daughter of Rev. James J. and Mrs. W.E. Harris of Glennville, Alabama. She was born on the 27th February 1833, was married to Dr. N.L. Hudson April 3rd 1853, and died in Hancock County, Georgia on the 23rd of August last.
Died at the residence of Jackson C. and Jane A. Curry, Marengo County, their second son Jabez, August 22nd; age five years...
Died at the residence of her husband August 4,1853 after a short illness, Sister Margaret W. Smyly, consort of Brother W. Smyly, age fifty years.

## Marriage and Death Notices From The South Western Baptist Newspaper

9-30-1853
Died at the residence of her husband, Mr. C.B. Bacon, on Sabine River, Texas, Mrs. Maria Jane Bacon, in the twenty-sixth year of her age. She was and had been for the last thirteen years a member of the Missionary Baptist Church... Mentions relatives in Alabama & Mississippi.
Departed this life Wednesday, September 14th 1853, Sister Mary Francis Bussey, consort of Brother Nathan A.T. Bussey, age twenty-five years, five days. She was married to her now disconsolate husband on the 26th day of March 1848...
The numerous friends will regret to hear of the death of James B. Elston. He died at his father's residence in Talladega County on the 1? inst., in the thirty-seventh year of his age. Mr. Elston was a resident of Mobile for a number of years... He suffered for near two years with consumption... left parents, brothers and sisters...

10-7-1853
Died at Bickley's Landing, Marengo County, Alabama, September 11, 1853, Mrs. Sarah, consort of S.S. Taylor, age thirty-two years. She was the daughter of Strother and Elizabeth Madison.
Col. Thomas Williams died on Friday, 16th September, inst. at the residence of Col. Lewis M. Stone in this county after an illness of twelve days. Col. Williams was born in North Carolina on the 9th of July 1787; his age was when he died sixty-six years, two months, seven days. He was removed while an infant to Georgia, settled in Tuscaloosa County, Alabama in 1818 and removed to Pickens in 1831 where he has ever since resided.
Died in Auburn, Macon County, Alabama on the 16th of September of consumption, William H. Swanson, son of John and Elizabeth C. Swanson in the twenty-second year of his age... In the year 1849 he graduated at Mercer University...

10-14-1853
Departed this life on the 1st of September last, Lucinda Gibson, a native of Georgia, age twenty-six years, leaving a husband and three children...
Died on the 4th September last, Charles Wintworth. He was baptized in the sixteenth year of his age and ordained to the office of deacon at Apalachicola, Florida in 1845...
Died at the residence of her father, Isaac Oakes, in Claiborne Parish, Louisiana, Miss Susan F. Oakes, age sixteen years, five months, one day. The subject of these lines made a profession of religion and joined the Shiloh Church, Perry County, Alabama...

10-21-1853
Died on the 10th inst., Mr. John Henley, in the forty-fourth year of his age, at the residence of his mother-in-law, Mrs. Thomas Molton, in this county.

## Marriage and Death Notices From The South Western Baptist Newspaper

Died in this city on Sunday morning the 16th inst., Mrs. Abagail Mulder, in the sixty-second year of her age. The deceased was born in the state of South Carolina, near the "Old Nation Ford" in York District, and removed to this city in the month of October 1837. Mrs. Mulder made a profession of religion and was baptized into the fellowship of the Baptist Church, in Columbia, South Carolina in the year 1832; and upon her removal to this city attached herself to the Baptist Church in this place... She was attacked with a chill on Thursday morning the 13 inst. from which she never recovered... Montgomery, 18th October '53.

Houston, October 8, 1853: Died of yellow fever in the city of Houston, Texas on the 3rd inst., Mrs. A.R. Garrett, consort of Mr. W.R. Garrett, in the thirty-ninth year of her age... in the year 1851, in the month of November, together with her husband and only daughter, she emigrated to this state, settling in this city.

Died on the 5th October at the residence of his relative, Capt. Lewellen Oliver, near Warsaw, Sumter County, Alabama of fever and a complication of chronic disorders, Thomas W. Oliver of Panola County, Mississippi; age twenty-five years.

Tribute of respect from Liberty Lodge #65, held at Athens, July 9th on the death of Wm. C.P. Holmes...

10-28-1853

Died at his father's residence three miles from Claiborne, Monroe County, Alabama on the evening of the 12th October, Richard Alexander, only son of Francis P. and Apphia W. Clingham; age fourteen years lacking six days.

Died at his residence near the town of Talladega, Alabama on the --- of September last, Mr. William Shaffer, Sr. in the seventy-fourth year of his age. He was by birth a native of Virginia. In his thirteenth year his parents moved and located in Fairfield District, South Carolina. Early in life he became a member of the Baptist Church... In 1831 he came to this state and was at the time of his death a member of the Baptist Church in the town of Talladega...

Died at Sylacauga, Talladega County, Alabama on the 10th inst. Mrs. Malinda T., consort of John T. Gibson, in the twenty-fifth year of her age. She was by birth a native of Franklin County, North Carolina and came to this state in 1833; was married in 1844 and professed the religion of our lord Jesus Christ, was baptized by Brother O. Welch at Tallassahacha Church in 1845. She not long after became a member of Mt. Zion Church where with her husband she remained till her death...

Mrs. Lucinda Lee, the subject of the following memoir, was born in Edgefield District, South Carolina, August 9th, 1815. In the Autumn of 1817 her parents, John and Clarissa Hardy, moved to Dallas County, Alabama. In the month of July 1833 at the age of eighteen... was baptized into the fellowship of the Baptist Church at Town Creek, Dallas County. The August following, she was married to Brother Jesse Lee, since a distinguished minister of the Gospel...

## Marriage and Death Notices From The South Western Baptist Newspaper

She was a member of the church sixteen years in Alabama when she transferred her membership to Summer Grove Church, Caddo Parish, Louisiana, where she remained a member until her death on the 5th day of June 1853... Her disease was one of almost unexampled severity, and continued for near two years with no hope of recovery. Indeed, her sufferings were so intense that it was necessary for her to consume about fifty bottles of morphine during her illness... leaves husband, two boys and two girls.

Departed this life on the 4th of October 1853 at the residence of her husband, Jno. B. Scott, Susan Scott, after an illness of ten days... She has left a husband and ten children...

11-4-1853
Died on the morning of the 19th of October 1853 at the residence of her? parents in Lowndes County, Alabama, Lebanon [Zebulon?] Rudulph, Jr., in the fifty-fifth year of his age. He was a native of South Carolina, born near Camden, and had resided successively at Columbia in Edgefield District and in Lowndes County, Alabama... about the year 1826 he joined the Baptist Church at Red Bank in Edgefield District, South Carolina; and he ever adorned that profession by a well ordered life... He had been twice married. First to Miss Mims of Edgefield. Next to Miss Watson of Abbeville. But each of his wives was taken from him a few months after marriage. The latter left an infant son now approaching manhood...

Died in the town of LaFayette, Chambers County, Alabama on the night of October 1?th, 1853, Brother William I. Stamps, son of Brother Britton Stamps, age twenty-four years, eleven months, six days... He left a wife and two children, a father and step-mother and several brothers and sisters...

Died at Perryville, Perry County, Alabama on Friday, October 21st, 1853, Mrs. Melissa W. Gary, wife of Dr. ____Gary. The deceased, a daughter of the Rev. A.G. McCraw, was born on the 31st October 1822 so that her age at death was about thirty-one...

Married near Sumterville, Alabama on the 19th inst. by Rev. E.B. Teague, Rev. William Howard, pastor of the Baptist Church at Gainesville, to Miss Caroline L. May.

11-11-1853
Died on the night of the 3rd inst. after an illness of three days, Elizabeth Ellen Whatley, daughter of B.J. and Sarah J. Whatley, of this city, age one year, eight months, eleven days.

Departed this life on the 8th October 1853 after a brief illness at the residence of her husband, James H. Draughon, esq. in Claiborne, Alabama, Mrs. Jane Smith Draughon, in the sixty-first year of her age. Mrs. D. was the daughter of Isaac and Rachel Williams and was born in Cumberland County, North Carolina; was for several years subsequent to her marriage with

## Marriage and Death Notices From The South Western Baptist Newspaper

Mr. Draughon, then a merchant of Wilmington, North Carolina, a resident of the latter place; and for the last thirty-four years of Claiborne, Alabama. Married on the evening of the 2nd inst. by Rev. W. Wilkes of Selma, Mr. Joseph Barron to Miss Eliza B. Nelms, both of Perry County, Alabama.

11-18-1853
Departed this life at her residence in Prattville on the 28th of October of consumption, Mrs. M.A. Anderson. She was born in Orangeburg District, South Carolina, August 11th, 1806.
Married on Sunday morning, October 30th by Rev. J.T.S. Park at his residence in Helicon, Alabama, Mr. Geo. M. Dews and Miss Laura S. Walker, both teachers during the last session in Helicon Academy.

11-25-1853
Died, June 17th, M.S., daughter of Levi Shackelford, age ten months, seventeen days...
Died of yellow fever at his father's residence, 28th September, A.J. Shackelford. He was born in the city of Montgomery, Alabama, 21 January 1840...
At the same place and of the same disease, 10 October, L.D. Shackelford. He was born in Casey County, Kentucky, 28 August 1828...
At the same place and of the same disease, 14 October, Mariah S., consort of Levi Shackelford...
On the 15th inst. of the same disease, Texana Shackelford. She was born in Nacogdoches County, Texas, 28 July 1840.
Died in Selma on the 7th inst. of yellow fever, J. Travis McGraw [McCraw ?], age twenty-one years. The deceased was the eldest son of Rev. A.G. McGraw...

12-2-1853
Married on Tuesday the 15th November in the vicinity of Tuskegee by the Rev. Samuel Henderson, Mr. Samuel L. Harris of Chambers to Miss Eugenia S. Pinkard of Macon County, Alabama.
Died in Tuskegee on Tuesday the 22nd of November 1853, Mr. William Calvin Porter, after an illness of ten days, in the twenty-eighth year of his age.
Died in Noxubee County, Mississippi on the 19th of October, Miss Mary Ann Sanders, in the twenty-fifth year of her age.

12-9-1853
Died in Rockford, Coosa County, Alabama on the 15th November 1853, Sister Elenor Manning, consort of Brother Benjamin W. Manning, age twenty-five years, one month, seventeen days. Sister Manning was born in Monroe County, Alabama and lived there until she was married... has left an affectionate husband and five small children...

## Marriage and Death Notices From The South Western Baptist Newspaper

Married by Rev. J.S. Abbott at the residence of Mrs. Gewin, November 17th, Mr. Francis M. Moore of Perry County to Miss Elizabeth J. Gewin of Greene County, Alabama.

12-16-1853
Married on Thursday the 1st day of December by Rev. J.H. DeVotie, Mr. David S. Hogue to Miss Martha S. Tubb, all of Perry County, Alabama.
Extract from a letter, dated Henry County, Alabama, December 1st, 1853:... it became my duty to announce through your columns the death of our dear Brother, Elder B.M. Roberts... He died on the 12th September at his residence in Abbeville, in the forty-eighth year of his age, of a long and complicated disease, which however finally terminated in chronic diarrhea... Brother Roberts was a native of Georgia... He married Miss Harriet Hardivick, who still survives together with several children and grand children. He was baptized by his father, Elder Joseph Roberts into the church at Long Creek, Warren County, Georgia... In 1839 he moved with his family to Lee County in the same state... In 1846 he removed from Baker to Abbeville in this State...
James D., son of Asa and Nancy Whitlock, was born in Greene County, Mississippi, 29th of November 1827, and departed this life, October 24th, 1853, age twenty-five years, ten months, twenty-seven days...

12-23-1853
Died at his residence near Fredonia in Chambers County, Alabama on the 11th day of November 1853, Jesse Gunn, Sr., in the seventy-fourth year of his age. He was born in what was formerly Caswell, now Person County, in the state of North Carolina on the 22nd of November 1779. He united with the Baptist Church of Christ at Sargon Creek in Morgan County, Georgia on the 18th of October 1831. He died of a disease of the heart after a protracted illness of eighteen months...
Married on the 14th day of December by Rev. Wm. T. Rogers, Mr. Jeremiah Haney to Miss Frances S. Burks, all of Coosa County, Alabama.

1-12-1854
Married in Charleston on the 5th inst. by Rev. J.R. Kendrick, the Rev. J. Lewis Shuck, Missionary to the Chinese in Calito??ia, and Annie L., second daughter of the late Gen. G.J. Trotti of Barnwell C.H., South Carolina.
Married in Marion on the 3rd inst. by Rev. M.P. Jewell, A.J. Brazelton, esq. to Miss Rebecca Pierson, late Governess in the Judson Female Institute. *New York Recorder* & *Baptist Register* please copy.
Married on the 21st ult. by the Rev. J.S. Ford, Mr. John W. Melton to Miss Clarinda J. Mahan, all of Perry County, Alabama.
Married in Tuskegee on the 12th inst. by Rev. A.J. Battle (?), Rev. Wm. H. McIntosh of Eufaula to Mrs. K.A. Billingslea of Tuscaloosa.

## Marriage and Death Notices From The South Western Baptist Newspaper

Died in Tuskegee on Friday morning the 30th ult. Mrs. Amelia Womack, in the fifty-fourth year of her age... Sister Womack was a native of Hancock County, Georgia; born on the 29th of March 1800... In June 1842 she removed to Tuskegee...

Died at his residence near Fredonia, Chambers County, Alabama on the 26th November 1853, Leroy McCoy, in the sixty-sixth year of his age. He was born in Hancock County, Georgia in the year 1788...

Died of typhoid near Summerfield, Alabama on the 2nd ult., Benjamin F. Culbreth, son of Joel & Mary Culbreth, age twenty-two years, nine months... born in Walton County, Georgia on 2 March 1831.

Died at the residence of her husband, Mr. Joseph Ratcliff, on the 18th October 1853, Mrs. Rebecca Ratcliff, in the thirty-first year of her age. Sister R. was the daughter of Rev. David Elkins of Russell County, Alabama. She was married in 1846... leaves a husband and three children and stepchildren...

1-19-1854

Married on the 25th day of December 1853 by Rev. Thomas M. Lynch, Mr. James G. Haynes to Miss Eliza A. Shores, all of Coosa County, Alabama.

Died at his residence near Notasulga, in this county, on the 6th day of January 1854, Mr. David Lanier, age sixty-three years. He had an attack of something like St. Anthony's fire...

2-2-1854

Married on the 25th inst. by Rev. A. VanHoose, Mr. A.W. Herst to Miss N.R. Armstrong, all of Montgomery County, Alabama.

Married in Auburn on Thursday evening the 19th inst. by Rev. William Williams, Mr. Geo. C. Dillard and Miss Mary Frances Williams, all of Auburn.

Paul Tillman, youngest child of George W. and Mary Ann Gunn of Tuskegee, was born July 13, 1852 and died of teething January 20, 1854...

Died in La Grange, Georgia after a brief illness on the morning of the 10th of January, George W. Calloway, in the twentieth year of his age. The subject of this notice became a member of the Baptist Church...

2-9-1854

Died in Tuskegee on Friday the 3rd day of February inst. Mrs. Elizabeth J. Gwinn, consort of Mr. Thomas Gwinn, age thirty-eight years, leaving five children, the youngest an infant of only five weeks old...

Died at his residence on Blue Creek in Lowndes County, Alabama on the 2nd day of January last, Thomas Jordan in the forty-second year of his age, a native of Virginia... His disease was bloody flux...

Died of puerperal convulsions resulting in paralysis at the residence of her husband, T.U. Wilkes, in Eatonton, Putnam County, Georgia, Mrs. Maria Louisa Wilkes, in the thirty-fourth year of her age...

## Marriage and Death Notices From The South Western Baptist Newspaper

Died at his father's residence in Macon County, Alabama on the 29th day of January, William M. Richardson, son of George D. Richardson, in the fifteenth year of his age. Disease oppression of the brain.

2-?-1854
Died, January 20th, 1854 in the city of Montgomery in the forty-eighth year of his age, R.P. Rogers... He was laid in his grave the Sabbath after, near his residence in Coosa County... [see below]
Died at her residence in Coosa County, Alabama, February 6th, sister E. Rogers, in the seventy-first year of her age. Thus shortly after the son was the mother taken from the family...[see above]

3-2-1854
Died at the residence of ???, of Talbot County, Georgia, 31st December 1853, Jas. A. Stringer of Lowndes County, Alabama.
Died in Putnam County, Georgia on the 30th of November 1853 at the residence of her husband, P.G. Dawson, Mrs. Sarah Dawson, in the eightieth year of her age... She was brought from North Carolina, her native state, to South Carolina during the Revolutionary War. She was married in 1796 and united with the church in 1808 being baptized by Rev. Samuel Marsh. In 1810 she moved to Putnam County where she remained some twenty years, and after an absence of twenty years returned...

3-9-1854
Married in the vicinity of Helena, Arkansas on the evening of the 6th inst. by Rev. Reuben Jones, Dr. Wm. F. Newsom, to Miss Ella S., daughter of Rev. T.S.N. King.
Died at her residence near Allenton, Wilcox County, Mrs. Mary E. McConico, half past 3 o'clock, a.m., January 1st, 1854, in the sixty-second year of her age, after a long and painful illness. Mrs. McConico was the daughter of Charles and Mary Span and was born on the 4th of March 1792 in the state of South Carolina, Sumter District... On March 24th 1711 [1811?] at the interesting age of nineteen she was married to Mr. William W. McConico of the same state and district. They moved to Alabama in 1817 and settled in Monroe County near the town of Claiborne where they lived... In the Fall of 1827 Mr. and Mrs. McConico made a public profession of religion and were at the same time baptized into the fellowship of the Claiborne Baptist Church... They remained active and influential members until the death of Mr. McConico which occurred December 1830. After the death of her husband, Mrs. McConico remained at Claiborne until the year 1833 at which time she moved to Allenton where she remained until the time of her death... Her funeral took place on Tuesday, January 3rd. The funeral services were ???? in the parlor of her late residence after which her body was conveyed to the Allenton Graveyard...

## MARRIAGE AND DEATH NOTICES FROM THE SOUTH WESTERN BAPTIST NEWSPAPER

Died of pulmonary consumption at her residence in Carroll County, Mississippi, Mrs. Mary Ann Lancaster, in the sixty-fifth year of her age. Sister Lancaster was born, reared, and married in Alabama. She was married to Aaron Lancaster in the fifteenth year of her age and moved with him to this state. Her husband has been dead about three years...

3-16-1854
Married at Union Cross Roads, Louisiana on the 16th of February by the Rev. S.J. Larkins, Mr. G.W. Everett, son of Rev. George Everett to Miss Ellen R. Jordan, all of Union Parish, Louisiana.
Died at Union Springs on Tuesday morning, March 7th, Corbin Hunter, son of Henry R. and Sarah J. Rugeley, age three years, one month.

3-30-1854
Mr. Andrew J. Bodell departed this life on last Tuesday morning at 8 o'clock. Died on the night of the 12th inst. at the residence of her husband, Mrs. Lucenda Gilmore, wife of George Gilmore, age about 3? years...
Died at her residence in Taylor County, Georgia on the 23rd December last, Mrs. Martha Sears, former companion of Dr. Wm. Lockhart of Knoxville and later of Wm. Sears, who was one of the first settlers of Talbot County and who died at Daviston in 1848... She has left behind four sons, three by the former husband and one by the latter...

4-13-1854
Died on the night of Sunday the 2nd inst. at the residence of Rev. A.T.M. Bandy in Macon County, Alabama, Mrs. M.R. VanHoose, in the twenty-fourth year of her age. The deceased was a native Alabamian and professed religion in Greenville, Butler County in September 1848... On the 21st of December 1849 she was married to the Rev. A. VanHoose. In 1850 and '51 they resided in the city of Tuscaloosa where Brother V. held the pastorate of the Baptist Church and the two years following they spent in Aberdeen, Mississippi. At the beginning of the present year they moved to Tuskegee where they resided at the time of her death...

4-27-1854
Tribute of respect on the death of W.S. Lloyd.
Married on the evening of the 19th inst. by the Rev. J.P.W. Brown, Mr. Leonidas S. Thompson to Miss Catharine L. Long, all of Russell County, Alabama.

5-4-1854
Married by the Rev. C.B. Sanders at the house of Mr. I.B. Gladney on the evening of the 11th inst., Mr.T.B. Gardner to Mrs. Mary Jane Gardner, all of Pickens County, Alabama.

## Marriage and Death Notices From The South Western Baptist Newspaper

5-18-1854
Married on the 9th inst. by Rev. R.M. Saunders, Mr. Demosthenes R. Hayley of Auburn, Alabama to Miss Sarah A.F. Bass, daughter of Lewis Bass of Troup County, Georgia.

5-25-1854
Married in Selma on the 5th inst. by Rev. A.G. McCraw, Mr. Lewis A. Tidwell of Mobile and Miss Virginia Dillard of Greensboro.
Married in Selma on the 10th inst. by Rev. A.G. McCraw, Mr. William B. Fraser of Camden, South Carolina to Miss Anna E. Burr of Selma.
Married at the house of John Miles near Tuskegee on the 18th inst. by M.S. Kelton, esq., Mr. David Reeves to Miss Sarah A. Miles, daughter of John Miles.
Died at his residence in ??? County, Alabama on the 16th April 1854, Deacon B. Gardner at about ?5 years old... He was born in Maryland, moved to Edgefield, South Carolina, thence to Alabama... He has left an aged widow and some two or three children... He was a member of the Town Creek Church.
Died on Sunday evening the 30th April 1854 at her residence in Pickens County, Alabama, Mrs. Elizabeth Locke, wife of Deacon Thomas Locke, in the fifty-fifth year of her age. Sister Locke was the daughter of Philip and Nancy Noland and was born in Chester District, South Carolina in August 1799. She removed with her parents to Alabama in the year 1820 and was married to Mr. Locke in March 1821.
Mrs. Edna Malone was born in Newberry District, South Carolina, May 18th, 1778, and departed this life at Warrior Stand, Macon County, Alabama, April 25th inst. in the seventy-sixth year of her age...

6-8-1854
Died at her residence near Coffeeville, Clarke County, Alabama on Tuesday the 16th inst., Mrs. Martha E. Pendleton, in the fifty-fifth year of her age. She was a daughter of the late Rev. Joseph Williams, who with his family emigrated from Sumter District, South Carolina as early as the year 1810...

6-22-1854
Died Rev. Joshua S. Callaway... at his residence near Jonesborough on the 23rd of May last... Born Wilkes County, Georgia, 30 May 1789, baptized at Sardis, Wilkes County, 23 September 1809.

6-29-1854
Married on the 4th inst. by Rev. Saml. Henderson, Mr. Richard Conine and Miss Martha E. Gwin, daughter of Thomas Gwin of Tuskegee.
Died on the 30th day of May at his residence in Pike County, Alabama, Brother Elias Devore, in the forty-ninth year of his age...

MARRIAGE AND DEATH NOTICES FROM THE SOUTH WESTERN BAPTIST NEWSPAPER

Also on the 1st day of June at the same house, Brother John W. Devore, eldest son of Elias and Elizabeth Devore, in his twenty-fourth year...
Also on the 7th day of June at the same place, sister Elizabeth Devore, wife of Elias Devore, in the fifty-fourth year of her age...
Also on the 7th day of June at the same place, sister Elizabeth Adams, a sister of E. Devore, about fifty-five years old...

Died near Gaston, Sumter County, on the 11th inst., Mrs. Emma White, wife of John W. White, in the twenty-eighth year of her age...

7-6-1854
Married on Thursday evening the 22nd of June by the Rev. James H. DeVotie, Mr. J.L. Deyampert to Miss Ann Judson King, daughter of Gen. Edwin D. King of Marion, Alabama.
Died at his residence near Tuskegee on Wednesday June 18th of bilious typhoid fever after an illness of ten days, William Veasy, age about forty years. Leaving a wife and four children...

7-13-1854
Married on the 5th inst. by Rev. A.T.M. Handy, Mr. Wm. C. Scott of South Carolina to Miss M.A. Cook of Macon County.
Died on Tuesday the 4th of July 1854 after a short and painful illness of two days, of cholera morbus, at the residence of his son, Rev. J.M. Jackson, Chambers County, Alabama, Rev. Wyche Jackson, in the seventy-fifth year of his age. The subject of this notice was a member of the Baptist Church at Rehoboth, Wilkes County, Georgia, for more than thirty years... He left a wife, three sons...

7-20-1854
Married on the 22nd June by Rev. E.B. Teague, Mr. Berrien Cromwell to Miss Nannie K. Washington, daughter of the late Dr. Robert Washington of Sumter County.
Married on the 5th of July by the same, Mr. Solomon Sessems of Oktibbeha County, Mississippi to Miss Hannah Eliza Hibbler, daughter of Maj. Wm. H. Hibbler of the same county.
Departed this life June 13th, 1854 in the eighteenth year of her age, Mrs. Mary F. Jones, consort of Mr. Tignal W. Jones of Talladega. The deceased was born November 5, 1836... She was married December 20th, 1853...
Died at his residence in Germany, Monroe County, Alabama, Samuel H. Nettles, Deacon of Concord Baptist Church, June 12th, 1854, after a painful illness of eight days, of bloody flux. Brother Nettles was a native of South Carolina, and was born December 7th, 1800; being at the time of his death fifty-three years, seven months, five days old... Brother Nettles professed religion, and with his excellent wife, Martha M. Nettles, was baptized into the

## MARRIAGE AND DEATH NOTICES FROM THE SOUTH WESTERN BAPTIST NEWSPAPER

fellowship of the Gravel Creek Church, Wilcox County, in the Fall of 1835... In the course of a year or two he removed from the neighborhood of Gravel Creek to Allenton, in the same county (Wilcox)... He subsequently moved to Dallas County, and was a member of the County Line Church. About nine years ago he settled at the place of his late residence...

7-27-1854
On the 3rd day of July, William, infant son of Benjamin F. and Amanda C. Dupree of Notasulga died, age about eight months; and on the 14th, Mrs. Dupree died after an illness of but a few days in the nineteenth year of her age. Mrs. Dupree was a daughter of the late Dr. Phillips of Notasulga, so long and favorably known as one of the first citizens of that town. She was married, I believe, sometime in December 1852...
A painful visitation has befallen us at this place in the removal by death of our beloved Brother Eli H. Lide, a deacon of Centre Ridge Church. Brother Lide had sold his premises, and having taken letters of dismission for those of his household who were members of the church to the number (I think) of nineteen, including himself and companion, children and servants, was removing to Texas with family of nearly one hundred persons. Somewhere in the vicinity of Woodville, perhaps, in Jasper County, Texas, that fearful scourge, the cholera, arrested their course and himself with several of his servants were cut down as we understand in a few days...

8-3-1854
It becomes my painful duty to inform you and the public of the death of sister Matilda B. Coats, consort of W.W. Coats, who departed this life at her residence near Gaston, Sumter County on the morning of the 7th inst. in the thirty-fifth year of her age. Sister Coats was confined to her sick chamber eight days. In her illness she was surrounded by a devoted husband, six children and numerous relatives and friends...
Died at the residence of her father in Warren County, Georgia on Saturday the 24th of June, of cold taken after a severe attack of measles, in the sixteenth year of her age, Mary Susan Ann McCrary, daughter of Mr. Jasper and Mrs. Drucilla McCrary, formerly Miss Drucilla Wood of Jefferson County. Tribute of respect from Providence, Chambers County, Alabama upon the death of Rev. Wyche Jackson, who died the 4th inst. in the seventy-fifth year of his age.

8-10-1854
Died on the 14th of July, Taylor L., infant son of William and Jahaza J. Todd of Union Springs, age six months, twenty-nine days.

## Marriage and Death Notices From The South Western Baptist Newspaper

8-17-1854
FROM THE *WESTERN RECORDER*: Died in Chenango County, New York on the 8th of July, Mrs. Eliza E.P. Gibbs, wife of Rev. B.B. Gibbs, who has for the last four years been pastor of the Baptist Church at Vicksburg, Mississippi...
Our esteemed fellow citizen Judge Thomas died at the residence of Rev. Charles Stewart in this county, at 8 minutes past 11 o'clock on Monday night the 17th inst. in the fifty-fourth year of his age. Judge Thomas was born in Kentucky in the year 1800. He came to Tuscaloosa about the year 1818 and to this county in 1835...

8-24-1854
Married on the 1st inst. by Rev. ? H. Foster, Mr. John S. Caldwell and Miss Sarah L. Terrell at the residence of her father, Wm. H. Terrell, in Tuscaloosa County.
Died on the 15th of July 1854 in Pope County, Arkansas William Walter, infant son of James M. and Susan E. Veasy, age seven months, twenty-five days.
Died at his late residence in Greene County on the 26th July 1853 ?, John Richardson. The deceased was born in Lunenburg County, Virginia, September 29th, 1798; married to Sally N. Coleman, 1824, by whom he had eight children who survive to mourn the loss of both parents; about 1830, having previously removed to Georgia, he professed conversion; ...removed to Alabama in 1836... In 1850 Mr. Richardson was married a second time, to Jane J. Ward, which pious and excellently lady survives him...

8-31-1854
REV. THOMAS CHILTON IS NO MORE: It is with a sad heart that we announce to our readers the demise of this eminent servant ... he died on the 15th of August...
Died at her residence at Cross Keys, Macon County, Alabama, August 6th, 1854, Mrs. Lucy M. Miller, wife of Mr. George Miller. Mrs. M. was born in Middletown, Connecticut June 15th, 1820... She was married August 5th, 1845 and removed with her husband to Macon County, Alabama in the Fall of 1848... After appropriate religious services her remains were committed to the tomb where they quietly repose beside those of her first-born, Maria Elizabeth, who died May 31st, 1849, age two years, three months... She has left behind a bereaved husband and three small children...
Mrs. Louisa L. Park was born in Fairfield District, South Carolina, May 31st, 1807, and departed this life at her residence in this county August 8th, 1854. She had just returned from a visit to her daughter when she was attacked with the disease, which despite the skill of her physicians and the care and solicitude of friends and relatives, in a few days bore her to the grave.

## Marriage and Death Notices From The South Western Baptist Newspaper

Departed this life at the house of George B. Nuckolls in Tuskegee, Alabama on Sunday August 27th after a lingering illness of several months, of liver disease and chronic dysentery, Mr. Edmund Bullock, formerly of Louisa County, Virginia, in the sixty-fifth year of his age...

Died in Columbia County, Arkansas on the 2nd August 1854 of the flux after a short illness of four days, excruciating pain and agony, Rachel Agnes, daughter of Thomas J. and Elizabeth E. Watts, age four years, nine months, eighteen days.

9-7-1854
Died in the city of Galveston on the 11th inst. of consumption at the house of S. Cole, in the thirty-sixth year of his age, the Rev. T.T. Hopkins, recently from Lafayette, Chambers County, Alabama.
Married on Thursday evening the 31st August last at the residence of Mrs. Sarah Pinckard by Rev. J.R. Hand, Dr. Joseph Hand and Miss Lucia Pinckard, all of Macon County, Alabama.

9-14-1854
Died in Columbia County, Arkansas on the 17th August inst. of the flux, Mary, daughter of Thomas J. and Elizabeth E. Watts, age two years, five months, twenty days.
Died at the residence of her father, John Jarrell, in Tallapoosa County on the 24th of August Miss Bethena Jarrell, age nineteen years and nearly ten months, as she was born October 30th, 1834...
Died at the residence of her husband, Mr. Wm. S. Means, Greene County, Alabama on the 16th August, Mrs. Amanda A. Means, daughter of Col. Simeon Maxwell. The deceased was born 8th December 1822, married 11th August 1844 to Wm. C. Williams of Louisiana, by whom she leaves two children; married a second time 10th January 1854 to her late husband....
James Waldren, the subject of the following brief memorial, was born in Edgefield District, South Carolina on the 18th March 1795. He moved to Clark County, Alabama in 1816.
Died, Elisha Henderson, age fifty-eight years. He died on the 23rd of August of typhoid fever at his residence in Walton County, Georgia after an illness of twenty-three days...

9-21-1854
Mrs. Elizabeth Frances Danforth, consort of James Danforth, died at the residence of her brother, John W. Simmons, in Henry County, Alabama on the 2nd of August last, age nearly twenty-one years... Mrs. Danforth was the daughter of John T. and Mary Simmons, and was born and principally reared in Hancock County, Georgia... While yet an infant her mother died...

## MARRIAGE AND DEATH NOTICES FROM THE SOUTH WESTERN BAPTIST NEWSPAPER

9-28-1854
Married at LaGrange on the 14th inst. by the Rev. Otis Smith, Mr. Benj. B. Davis of Montgomery, Alabama to Miss Mary E., daughter of Rev. Wm. A. Callaway of the former place.
Died in Auburn, Macon County, Alabama on the 8th inst. of inflammation of the stomach, Eliza M. Perryman, infant [consort?] of Edmund D. Perryman, in the forty-eighth [?] year of her age.

10-5-1854
Judge Nimrod E. Benson died in Montgomery on the 27th inst., it is supposed of yellow fever.

10-19-1854
Thomas Obadiah Echols, son of Col. J.W. Echols of Auburn, died on Sunday the 15th inst. in the seventeenth year of his age. He had been confined for several weeks with typhoid fever, and it was supposed that he was recovering, when quite suddenly, about 10 o'clock on last Lord's day, he was attacked with hemorrhage and in four hours he was a corpse.
Died September 2, 1854 in Tampa, Florida, Mrs. Eliza Jane, wife of Rev. J.H. Breaker, age eighteen years, nine months.
Died of consumption on the 18th September at the residence of her husband, Mrs. Francis B. Harrell, consort of Solomon Harrell of Kinchafoonee County, Georgia. Mrs. H. was the second daughter of William and Elizabeth Murphy, and was born in Wilkes County, October 20, 1805, where in early life she attached herself to the Baptist Church at Fishing Creek, then under the care of the Rev. Jas. Armstrong by whom she was baptized. On the 6th of January 1831 she was married to Churchill Blakey with whom she moved to Harris County and lived in the full discharge of all the duties incumbent upon her as a wife, mistress and christian, until the 29th of September 1844 when he was taken from her by that fell destroyer death. She then moved to Sumter County and on the 22nd day of April 1847 was married to Solomon Harrell of Stewart, (now Kinchafoonee) County with whom she lived to the time of her death...
Departed this life, September 27th 1854, Allen K. Curry of Talladega County, Alabama. He was born in Lincoln County, Georgia May 25th, 1805, consequently was at the time of his death in his fiftieth year. He remained in the county of his birth until removal to Alabama in 1842. In 1843 he moved to Talladega County the place where he died... his sickness which was that of bilious fever of about ten days continuance...

10-26-1854
Departed this life in Chambers County, Alabama on the 13th inst. of teething, an infant, the daughter of Charles T. and Nancy Callaway, age about fourteen months...

## Marriage and Death Notices From The South Western Baptist Newspaper

11-2-1854
Married on the evening of the 12th inst. by Rev. A.G. McGraw, Rev. W. Wilkes of Selma to Miss Mary E. Lamar of Autauga County.

11-9-1854
It becomes my painful duty to announce the demise of Elder John Calfee which occurred at his residence near Syllacauga, Talladega County, Alabama September 23rd, 1854, age about forty-eight years. The deceased was born in Adair County, Kentucky in 1806 removed from there to Franklin County, Tennessee in 1812, thence to Bibb County, Alabama in 1818, and in 1835, shortly after his marriage, to his last residence near Syllacauga.
Departed this life on Thursday morning the 19th inst. Mrs. Anne Elston, wife of Allon Elston, esq., in the sixty-third year of her age. The deceased was born in Pendleton District, South Carolina on the 15th March 1792. She was the daughter of the late Col. Blair of Georgia... Three promising sons in quick succession were hurried to untimely graves, the two last victims of pulmonary consumption...
Tribute of Respect: Whereas an all-wise providence has seen fit to remove from our midst our much esteemed Brother B.H. Tarver, who departed this life July 28th, 1854, in his sixty-fourth year. The deceased was born in Robeson County, North Carolina and removed with his father, the Rev. Jacob Tarver, to the state of Georgia...

11-16-1854
Departed this life in Shelby County, Alabama on the 24th inst. after a short but severe illness Mrs. Mary F. Kidd, daughter of William and Amy O'Neal, now Mrs. Wadsworth. She was born in Lincoln County, Georgia, March 15th, 1829, and was married to Col. John M. Kidd, her surviving companion, November 24, 1852. She professed religion in the fall of 1848 and shortly after joined the Baptist Church at Spring Creek, Alabama in which she continued a useful and pious member till death severed the tie.
Married on Wednesday evening, October 8th at the residence of Mr. Daniel Rast of Lowndes County by the Rev. P.H. Lundy, Mr. Andrew J. McLemore of Montgomery County to Miss Sarah C. Smith of the former county.
Departed this life on the 19th of October, James William Slaughter, in the seventeenth year of his age, at his father's residence in Chambers County, six miles from West Point...

11-23-1854
Married on the 16th inst. by the Rev. Dow Perry, Mr. Milton A. Campbell of Tuskegee to Miss Mary J. Hamilton of Macon County.
Died in Marion, Perry County, Alabama, November 8, 1854, Mr. Anderson H. Talbert, son of Ansel and Rachel L. Talbert, in the twenty-second year of his age. Mr. Talbert was born in Edgefield District, South Carolina, but was

## MARRIAGE AND DEATH NOTICES FROM THE SOUTH WESTERN BAPTIST NEWSPAPER

brought by his parents to Alabama August 1838... In the burning of the edifice of Howard College on the night of October 16th he sustained the injury which terminated his youthful career...

Pike County, Alabama, November 15, 1854: Departed this life on Thursday morning, 7 minutes before 9 o'clock, Mr. Samuel Moore, age about forty-five years. The deceased was a member of the Baptist Church some twelve years before the grim monster death marked him for his victim.

11-30-1854
Died in Tuskegee, Alabama on Friday the 24th inst. at 7 o'clock a.m., Mrs. K.A. McIntosh, wife of Rev. Wm. H. McIntosh of Eufaula. [see 12-7-1854]
Died at his father's residence in Barbour County on the 23rd November, Samuel Stratford Starke, age fourteen months, twenty days.

12-7-1854
Died in Tuskegee, Alabama on Friday the 24th ult. Mrs. K.A. McIntosh, in the thirty-third year of her age. Mrs. M. was a daughter of Dr. James Guild of Tuscaloosa, where she was born April 2nd, 1822... She was a member of the celebrated school of Dr. Dagg where in 1840 she graduated with the highest honors of the first class sent out by that institution. In April of the succeeding year she married William B. Billingslea, a young lawyer of unusual promise, with whom she was permitted to pass but two and a half years when the happy connexion dissevered by the death of the husband... she formed the acquaintance of Rev. W.H. McIntosh, pastor of the Baptist Church in Eufaula, to whom she gave her hand in marriage on the 12th of January 1854... [see 11-30-1854]

12-14-1854
Died in Talladega County on Saturday November 11th, 1854, Isaac Adams, in the thirty-eighth year of his age. Mr. Adams was born in Chester District, South Carolina, and moved to Alabama about 1839 with his godly father. In the Fall of 1846 he was baptized into the fellowship of Lebanon Church...
Married on the night of the 14th by the Rev. John Motley, Mr. F. Stevens to Miss Frances Moon, all of Macon County, Alabama.

1-11-1855
Married on the 31st December 1854 by Rev. W.S. Barton, Rev. W.H. Carroll of Marion to Mrs. V.D. ?ay of Greensboro, Alabama.
Married at the house of David Gordon in Lowndes County, Alabama on the 3rd day of January 1855 by Rev. I. Lyon, Mr. Eldred W. Hardy of Dallas County to Miss Sarah A. Sherror.
In the *Tennessee Baptist* of Dec. 16th, 1854 we find an obituary of Elder Green B. Waldrop of Panola County who bade adieu to all earthly things at the residence of C. B. Young in October last, age six-? years, five months,

## Marriage and Death Notices From The South Western Baptist Newspaper

twenty-four days. He was born in Lawrence District, South Carolina, April 6, 1791, made a public profession of religion in 1821, and was baptized by Elder Joseph ??? into the fellowship of the church called "Five Miles" Green County, Alabama in 1829...

Died in the city of Montgomery, Alabama on the 18th of June 1854 at the residence of her daughter, Mrs. Elizabeth Winter, Mrs. Sarah L. Gindeat, wife of the late deacon John Gindeat, deceased. She was born in Augusta, Georgia July 9th, 1794. She was married in early life and removed with her husband and settled in Montgomery in 1823...

Departed this life on the 14th of December 1854, Brother William Jenkins, Sr. in the eighty-seventh year of his age. The deceased was born in Chester District, South Carolina... He moved to Alabama in the Fall of 1835 and joined the Talladega Church... He was married three times... His last wife is living... His children were all buried before him... Only one grandchild survives him...

1-18-1855

Married at Hickory Grove on the 11th inst. by Rev. A. VanHoose, Mr. G.R. Williams to Miss Nannie Coleman, all of Lowndes County, Alabama.

Married at the residence of William M. Stakely, esq. in Madisonville, Tennessee on the 10th inst. by the Rev. Mr. Wilson, Mr. H.C. Hooten of Orion, Alabama to Miss Nannie J. Stakely.

Died at Hickory Grove, Lowndes County, Alabama on the 10th inst. William Moncrief, deacon of Hickory Grove Church.

1-25-1855

Departed this life Dec. 5th, 1854, Mr. William H. Kellam, son of Robert and Elizabeth Kellum, in the twenty-fourth year of his age. The deceased was on a visit to the home of his childhood (Monticello, Georgia) where he was seized with that terrible scourge typhoid pneumonia. Being at the house of his uncle, Judge F.M. Swanson, every attention that affection and professional skill could render was bestowed...

Died at the residence of his mother in Chambers County, Alabama on the 12th day of December 1854 of consumption, Mr. James T. Eberhart, age twenty-two years, two months, twenty days. The deceased was the son of Mr. James Eberhart and Elizabeth Eberhart.

2-1-1855

Married on the 25th January by the Rev. Mr. Dalzell, Maj. James Philips of Russell County, Alabama and Mrs. Martha H. Sherwood of Columbus, Georgia.

Departed this life at his residence near Carlowville, Dallas County on Thursday December 21st, 1854, Deacon Come B. Watts of Centre Ridge Baptist Church. Brother Watts was born in Hancock, Putnam County, Georgia, September 20th, 1801, being the eldest of a large family of sons

## MARRIAGE AND DEATH NOTICES FROM THE SOUTH WESTERN BAPTIST NEWSPAPER

and daughters. He was married to Mary Patton, his present bereaved and disconsolate widow in Butler County, Alabama, January 27,1825...
Henry J. Herrick, son of Smith and Eliza Herrick, was born March 9th, 1825 in Duchess County, New York but chiefly reared in Vermont. He came south in 1845 and devoted his time in the useful and honorable avocation of teaching until attacked with his last illness which was in October 1854 and he departed this life December 20th, 1854. He joined the Baptist Church in September 1853 of which he continued an acceptable member till his death... He has left a wife and two children...    D. Perry.

2-15-1855
It becomes my painful duty to chronicle the death of our faithful and much esteemed Brother Wm. Moncrief, who departed this life at his residence (Hickory Grove) on the 10th of January last. Brother Moncrief was born February the 8th, 1807 in the state of Georgia. At the age of fourteen his parents moved and settled with their son in Montgomery County, Alabama. On the 18th of December 1828 he was married to Elizabeth Armstrong with whom he lived a peaceable and happy life for twenty-eight years. Our Brother had been suffering and on the decline for some eighteen months. During the summer he traveled to some of the watering places in the state of Tennessee but received no special benefit... He has left a wife and eight children to mourn their loss.
Died on the 30th of January last (from the effects of a burn which she got by her clothes taking fire) Ann Elizabeth, daughter of Joseph and Elizabeth Prather of Chambers County, Alabama, age five years, one month, nineteen days.

2-22-1855
Died in Chambers County, December 11th, 1854, Elijah H. Parker, age seventeen years, three months, nine days, leaving a fond father, four sisters, and a large circle of friends and relatives to mourn his loss... He was an only son...
Died at his residence near Boston, Bowie County, Texas on the 14th day of January 1855 after a short but severe case of dropsy, Doctor Martin Read, age about fifty-two years. The doctor was a native of Halifax County, North Carolina. He married in May 1826 and resided in the town of Halifax until the year 1834 when he emigrated to Wilcox County, Alabama where he remained until December 1854 when he again removed to Texas and where he died. He has left a devoted companion and six children...

3-15-1855
Married at La Place on the 14th of February by Rev. A.T.M. Handy, Mr. Amos G. Tuttle to Miss Margaret Cloud, all of this county.

## Marriage and Death Notices From The South Western Baptist Newspaper

Married on the 28th February at Cubihatchee by the same, Mr. Ernest K. Wilkerson to Miss Sarah A. Griffin, all of Macon County.

Died in the Mountains about the 16th of November last, John B. Hodgens, in the eighty-eighth year of his age. Brother Hodgens was born in England, and at the age of seven years he went to sea and lived a sea-faring life until he was nineteen years old. Then he came to America and settled in South Carolina. Then he married and raised a family and after he lost his wife emigrated with his son to Alabama and settled in Bibb County and professed religion, and was baptized into the fellowship of the Cahawba Valley Church in the eighty-fourth year of his age, four years before his death. The circumstances of his death were about as follows: He lived in a very thinly settled part of the county, but few were living nearer than from five to seven miles. He being very old and childless would frequently start a morning along some cow trail or trail made by hunters, and always come home at night, until the 16th of last November he walked his last. The night came on and he did not return. The family became alarmed and spent the night in diligent search for him. The people of the neighborhood being notified of it, were the next day and for two or three weeks perhaps, from twenty-five to fifty men in search of him, but without success. At length after all hopes were gone, he was found by a company that was out on a camp hunt after he had been gone three weeks to the day, and what is a little singular is that some twelve or fifteen years ago there was another man about the same age that got lost and died on the same creek.

Died in Macon County, Georgia on the 31st of January at the residence of Henry L. Corbin, his wife Adaline, in the thirty-seventh year of her age. Mrs. Corbin was a native of Columbia County which is still of some of her relatives and the place where her parents, Lemuel and Elizabeth Steed are buried. This lady was in the year 1836 married to Henry L. Corbin of South Carolina with whom she shortly after moved to Crawford County in this state and after seven years residence there moved to Macon County where she closed her life... she rests under her green walnut tree, near the ???? she adorned so much...

3-22-1855
Married near Philadelphia, Montgomery County, Alabama on the 6th February by Rev. J.A. Fonville, Mr. Mitchell Wisham to Miss Susan Dillard.
Married in Russell County, Alabama, March 1st. by Rev. L.T. Eubank, Mr. David Walker to Miss Ann J. Perry.
Married at the residence of Mr. John Odom in Muscogee County, Georgia on the 8th inst. by Rev. Thos B. Slade, Mr. Charles P. Watt and Miss Sarah F. Eley.
Married on the 11th February by Elder P. Love, Mr. Robert L. Williams to Miss Martha Ann Goss, daughter of J.D. and Ann Goss, all of Autauga County, Alabama.

## MARRIAGE AND DEATH NOTICES FROM THE SOUTH WESTERN BAPTIST NEWSPAPER

Departed this life at his residence in Dallas County, Alabama on Friday February 2nd, 1855 William C. Jones, Sr., deacon of County Line Church, age sixty-eight years.

Died at his residence in Perry County, December 12th, 1854, Jesse Cole, a deacon of Hopewell Baptist Church and one of the most estimable and worthy members of society. He was born in Newberry District, South Carolina, January 19th, 1799. In November 1819 he removed to Alabama and settled at the place where he died...

Departed this life on Wednesday morning the 28th ult. at his family residence in Conecuh County, Alabama, Hin?hey Warren, esq., in the sixty-eighth year of his age. Mr. Warren was one of the first settlers in the county...

3-29-1855

THE LATE ZEBULON RUDULPH: This worthy gentleman was of German extraction on his father's side and Welch on his mother's. His paternal grandfather, Michael Johannes, was born on the Prussian part of the Rhine and served seven years in the army of Frederick the Great. Removing to America with his wife Anna he settled at Elkton, Maryland, where his son Jacob was born, September 8th, 1726. Jacob Rudulph, by a second marriage with a lady of Welsh origin (whose maiden name was Jacob), was the father of Zebulon Rudulph, the subject of this notice, born at Elkton, Maryland, Jan 30th, 1770. From Michael Johannes down, the family were all tenacious of the spelling and pronunciation of the name, with the letter "u" in the second syllable, not "o". Michael Rudulph, so distinguished in the American Revolution, as a Captain in Lee's Legion, was a son of Jacob, by his first marriage, half brother to Zebulon, and a little more than twelve years older than he.

Zebulon Rudulph commenced business on his own account as a merchant and miller at Elkton in 1794. In 1797 he was married to Abby Murray of Philadelphia, a lady most honorably connected there and in 1798 they removed to Camden, South Carolina. From that place they removed to Columbia, South Carolina in 1811, to Edgefield District in 1821, and to Lowndes County, Alabama in November 1839.

The greater part of his early life was spent in the profession of a merchant. He settled a plantation, however, on the Congaree in 1813 and from that time till the close of his long life he continued to interest himself personally in the business of farming. His first profession of religion was in 1806 under the ministry of the Rev. Dr. Andrew Flynn...

Died at her residence near Pine Hill, Wilcox County, Alabama, March 2nd 1855, Mrs. Eleanor Thomas, in her sixty-second year.

Departed this life in Marion, Alabama, March 15th, 1855, Miss Emma M.L. Latimer, daughter of S.S. and Christiana A. Latimer, age eighteen years, ten months, twelve days... She was the eldest daughter...

## Marriage and Death Notices From The South Western Baptist Newspaper

4-26-1855
Married in Macon County, Alabama on the 22nd April at the residence of Abram Williams by Rev. M.N. Eley, Mr. Thomas Ramsey of Warren County, Tennessee to Miss Mary Jane Williams, daughter of Abram and Sarah Williams formerly of Hancock County, Georgia.
Died in Tuskegee on the 19th inst. of scarlet fever, Miss Mary Ann Thompson, daughter of Mrs. L.P. Allen.
Elder Jacob Rogers of Hardin County, Kentucky died at his residence on the 21st March.

5-3-1855
Died at the residence of Barnea Ivy in Barbour County, Alabama on the morning of the 27th of November last, Mrs. Sarah L., consort of Malachi Ivy, at the age of twenty-five years, two months, twenty-one days, and the only daughter of William and Jane A. Curry formerly of Edgefield District, South Carolina. The deceased was a member of the Baptist Church. She joined at Gilgal, Edgefield District in August, A.D. 1841 and was baptized by the Rev. James M. Childs... She formed an acquaintance with Mr. Ivy in Russell County, Alabama and they were married on the 27th of August 1850. She leaves behind two little sons of tender age and hearts (the oldest a stepson)...

5-10-1855
Died at his residence in Bibb County, Alabama on the 23rd inst. after a week's illness with pneumonia, Elder Henry Kirbo, in the thirty-fifth year of his age. He was for many years a Methodist... He united with the Cahaba Valley Baptist Church of which he continued a member until his death... He left to mourn his lost, four churches, an afflicted companion and eight small children... He left his family in indigent circumstances and on the day of his burial the Cahaba Valley Church raised some ninety or one hundred dollars for their relief.
Died at the residence of his son Elder John R. Humphries in Chambers County, Alabama on the 26th of April Uriah Humphries, in the seventy-eighth year of his age. The deceased was born in North Carolina, and raised in Franklin County, Georgia. In early life he became the subject of christian hope and united with the Baptist Church at Cabin Creek, Jackson County, Georgia... His aged companion had preceded him several years...
Died at the residence of her father Dr. P. Philips in Russell County on Thursday 26th April, Mrs. Mary S. Shelton, wife of Geo. W. Shelton of Auburn, Alabama. She leaves a husband and two small children...
Married on the 10th inst. in Montgomery County by Rev. A.T.M. Handy, Mr. J.T. Green and Miss Eugenia Zimmerman.
Married in Macon County on the 25th April by the same Mr. James M. Bonds and Miss Hester E. Lloyd.

## MARRIAGE AND DEATH NOTICES FROM THE SOUTH WESTERN BAPTIST NEWSPAPER

5-17-1855
Died in Campbell County, Georgia of scarlet fever at the residence of his father on the 12th May 1855, John William, age four years, nine months, twelve days, youngest son of Wm. E. Russell, formerly of Chambers County, Alabama.

5-24-1855
Tribute of Respect upon the death of William Curry, Talladega County, Alabama, May 1855.

5-31-1855
Died in Tuskegee on the 19th of April Miss Mary Ann Thompson, daughter of Mrs. L.P. Allen, in the eighteenth year of her age.

6-14-1855
Died after a short but severe illness in Opelika, Russell County, Alabama on the 27th of May 1855, Mrs. Elizabeth Watson, wife of David Watson, and eldest daughter of William Trother, in the forty-second year of her age, leaving a husband, one single son, two married daughters, and three grandchildren... She united with the Missionary Baptist Church at Bethlehem, Chambers County, Alabama about the year 1839.
Died at the residence of his father in Coosa County on Sunday the 27th of May, James Henry Bozeman, eldest son of Col. D.W. Bozeman, in the nineteenth year of his age...
Mary Elizabeth Miller, daughter of Col. Wm. M. Miller and Louisa Elizabeth Miller (now Mrs. D.R. Lide) was born in Sumterville, South Carolina, January 7th, 1841, and died at the East Alabama Female College, Tuskegee, Alabama, May 29th, 1855.
Died in Perry County, Alabama on the 16th of May 1855, Mrs. Rosanna S. Trammer, wife of Elias E. Trammel, age thirty-four years, nine months, twelve days. The deceased was a native of the state and county in which she died. She was married to Mr. Trammel on the 14th day of March 1837... Mrs. T. died of typhoid pneumonia just four weeks from the time she was taken, about sunrise on Wednesday morning her dissolution took place.

6-28-1855
Married on the 12th of June 1855 by the Rev. Wm. D. Harrington, Mr. Wm. J. Dodson of Russell County, Alabama to Miss Samantha J. Hodge of Chambers County, Alabama.
GEORGE HARRISON COBB: Wm. S. Meek, writing to the *Tennessee Baptist*, gives an outline of the life and death of the above named Brother... He was a native of Lincoln County, Tennessee but removed with his parents to Tuscaloosa County, Alabama. He united with the Baptist Church in December 1832. In 1840 he removed to Saline County, Arkansas. In the

## Marriage and Death Notices From The South Western Baptist Newspaper

Spring of 1841 he was ordained a deacon of Philadelphia Baptist Church. On the 20th October 1842 he was married to Jane McDaniel. In 1844 he removed to Union County, Arkansas. After living an exemplary and useful life he died triumphantly on the 9th of April 1855, age thirty-nine years, four months, eleven days, leaving to mourn his loss a wife and five children. The disease which carried him off thus in the prime of life was consumption.

Died at her residence near Spring Hill, Marengo County, Alabama on Tuesday the 8th ult., Mary Melvina, daughter of Brother John Danghdrill, in the twenty-first year of her age...

Died of consumption May 21st, 1855 in Baldwin County at the residence of her mother, Mrs. Elizabeth Holmes, Miss Sarah Margaret Holmes, thirty-five years of age, after an illness of nineteen months. The lamented subject of this obituary notice was the eldest daughter of the late Dr. Thomas G. Holmes. She was baptized into the fellowship of Montgomery Hill Baptist 1840, being in her twentieth year... On Sabbath morning, May the 27th [date of death is given as the 21st at start of notice] at 8 o'clock she breathed her last...

7-5-1855
Married on the 28th ult. in Tuskegee by the Rev. Samuel Henderson, Mr. Malachi Ivey to Miss Matilda Gunn, eldest daughter of Gen. Geo. W. Gunn. At the same time and by the same Mr. David P. Nuckolls to Miss Sarah E. Gunn, second daughter of Gen. Gunn.
Married on the 14th ult. by Rev. M.N. Eley, Mr. Memory ? E. Thornton to Miss Amanda Johston [Johnston?], all of Macon County, Alabama.
The subject of this notice Wm. G. Eberhart, son of James and Elizabeth Eberhart, was born August 8th, 1830 in Madison County, Georgia... this young, devoted Christian, the pride and hope of a widowed mother... on the 14th of June 1855 calmly fell asleep...

7-19-1855
Married on the 12th inst. by the Rev. Mr. Brown, Russell County Mr. John H. Smith of Pike County to Miss Marcella F. Harris, daughter of Rev. J.J. & W.E. Harris of Econ, Macon County.
Died on Sunday last at the residence of ??? father in this place after a protracted illness, William Douglas Varner, age twenty years one and a half months. The deceased was educated at the University of Georgia. He afterwards went to the Law School at Cambridge, Massachusettes, where he graduated but a few months previous to his death.

7-26-1855
Died of pulmonary consumption at the residence of his father near LaFayette, Alabama on the 29th of June 1855, Edwin R. Stamps, son of Brittain and Polly Stamps. The deceased was born in Oglethorpe County, Georgia, September 6th, 1839...

## Marriage and Death Notices From The South Western Baptist Newspaper

Died in Leon County, Texas on the 24th inst. Mrs. Eliza Bannerman, wife of George W. Bannerman, and daughter of William and Martha Blackshear. Mrs. Bannerman was born in Georgia and removed with her parents to Alabama at an early day...

Departed this life on Monday the 23rd of June at the residence of his father in this county, Mr. John R. Simmons, in the twenty-fourth year of his age. His disease was scarlet fever.

8-2-1855

Married on the 12th ult. by the Rev. J.P.W. Brown, Rev. John R. Smith of Pike County to Miss M.F. Harris, daughter of Rev. J.J. Harris of Enon, Alabama.

Elder John Sansing is no more. After a short and painful illness he breathed his last at his residence in Oktibbeha County, Mississippi on the 9th inst. He removed from Alabama to this county during the last year; and was employed the present year by the Columbus Association to travel within her bounds as a domestic Missionary...

Miss Mary Armstrong, daughter of Franklin and Charlotte Armstrong, died on the 27th June 1855 at the residence of her parents in Lowndes County, Alabama.

Departed this life at his residence in Perry County, Alabama on Sabbath evening June 10th, Mr. Davis McGee, in the sixty-second year of his age...

8-23-1855

Died on the 6th August (inst.) in Carroll County, Mississippi, Mrs. Elizabeth Echols, wife of Rev. Obediah Echols, well known as a Minister of the Gospel in Alabama for many years... She was in her sixty-sixth year...

Died in Choctaw County, Mississippi on the 11th of July after an illness of thirty-three days, Mrs. Missouri M. Gooch, consort of Henry J. Gooch, and daughter of Leroy and Nancy R. Hammond, in the twenty-eighth year of her age. The deceased left a devoted husband...

Died near Enon, Alabama, May 10th, sister Winefred Carter in the ninety-first year of her age. She professed religion and joined the Baptist Church more than sixty years ago at old Fishing Creek...

Died in Macon County, Alabama on the 12th inst. Mrs. Hannah McDonald, wife of Lovett McDonald, and daughter of Hugh and Nancy Thomas. Mrs. McDonald was born in Laurens County, Georgia, March 3rd, 1814. Deceased moved to Talbot County, Georgia in 1834... She moved to this state in 1853...

8-30-1855

Married on the 22nd August by the Rev. S. Henderson, Mr. Wm. E. Pinckard to Miss Mary Jane Swanson, eldest daughter of Mr. John Swanson, all of Tuskegee.

## Marriage and Death Notices From The South Western Baptist Newspaper

Married on the 22nd of August 1855 by the Rev. Matt Bishop, Mr. C.J.L. Cunningham to Miss H.E. Hamilton, all of Troy, Pike County, Alabama.
Died near Burnsville after a lingering and painful illness Mrs. Ohpha Andrews, consort of Rev. A. Andrews...

9-6-1855
Departed this life on the 6th of August in the sixty-fifth year of her age after lingering several months, of the liver complaint, (but particularly confined to her bed about four weeks), Mrs. Elizabeth Echols, wife of Rev. Obadiah Echols of Carroll County, Mississippi.
Died on the 26th of August 1855 in the city of Selma, "Willie", infant son of Rev. A.G. and Mrs. Sarah S. McCraw, age thirteen months, eleven days.
Died at his residence in Benton County, Alabama, G.C.P. Hughes, in the thirty-sixth year of his age...
Departed this life on the 27th day of August at his residence near Burnsville, Dallas County, Alabama, Mr. Uriah West, in the seventy-first year of his age...

9-20-1855
Died at the residence of her sister, Mrs. Elizabeth K. Taylor, on the 27th of August 1855, Mrs. Amanda M.F. Shell, daughter of Joseph R. and the late Sarah A. Moorefield.
The deceased was born in Chesterfield District, South Carolina, April 21st, 183?, and joined the M.P. Church in Macon County, Alabama in the year 1845...
Mrs. L.P. Lovell was born in Williamson County, Tennessee January the 12th, 1800, and was the daughter of Nicholas and Elizabeth Seales; was married in 1821 and moved to Greensboro, Alabama where she made a decided profession of faith, after some years, removed to her native state, from thence, at the early settlement of East Alabama, she and family settled in the town of Talladega... As late as 1848 in company with her daughter, Mrs. Lake, removed to the present village of Cape Springs, Georgia, where she rejoined the church of her choice and till death remained one of its brightest ornaments... that most insidious foe, consumption, had made upon her its mark and was slowly yet certainly doing the work of death, just previous to which event she visited her friends in Talladega, with whom she might again mingle in life, as here resided the only surviving member (save one) of a large and affectionate family, with whom she lingered a few weeks... on the morning of the 20th of June 1855, at the house of her brother-in-law, Maj. Plowman, she breathed her last...

9-27-1855
Died at his residence near Cusseta, Chambers County, Alabama on the 6th of September 1855, Deryl Hart, who was born in Edgefield District, South Carolina on the 9th of March 1789. He was married to Miss Jane Pitts in

## Marriage and Death Notices From The South Western Baptist Newspaper

1815, with whom he lived in great harmony and raised one daughter and eight sons. He was baptized at Little Stephen's Church by Elder Samuel Worthington in August 1832... In 1855 soon after moving to this state he joined in the constitution of Bethesda Baptist Church of which he remained a member in full fellowship up to the time of his death... His last illness was of several weeks duration...

Died September the 17th Mrs. Frances Harriet, wife of W. Levere B. Lane, Jun., age eighteen years, eight months. Having been married only seven months and eleven days, leaving behind an affectionate and deeply afflicted husband... Aberdeen and Pontotoc papers please copy.

Married on the evening of the 11th inst. by the Rev. Wm. Williams, Mr. George W. Cherry and Miss Frances E. Parsons, daughter of Mr. David J. Persons, all of Opelika.

10-4-1855

Died at her residence near Lafayette, Chambers County, Alabama on the 11th of September 1855, Mrs. Nancy Christian, relict of Thomas Christian. The deceased was born in Edgefield District, South Carolina in the year 1798, and became a resident of Chambers County in 1835...

Died on the 10th September '55 of bilious remittent fever, Mr. John P. Williams, in the fifty-seventh year of his age. Brother Williams was born in Buckingham County, Virginia, July 20th, 1779 [Note: This date does not correspond with his age given above], was married to Courtney Tucker Williams of Buckingham, Virginia, December 26th, 1821; was baptized near Enon Church, Buckingham, Virginia by Elder Wm. Moore, September 29th, 1840... He moved to Alabama in the Fall of 1846; lived in Dallas County, holding membership with the Carlowville Church up to the commencement of the present year when moving to Allenton he united with the Allenton Church...

Died in this city on the evening of the 23rd inst. in the twenty-first year of her age after a short illness, Miss Mary Catharine McCraw, daughter of Rev. A.G. McCraw.

10-11-1855

Married at Union Springs on the 9th inst. by Rev. T. Root, Mr. Noel S. Nelson and Miss Emma Moragne, all of this county.

Married on the 2nd inst. by the Rev. W.S. Barker at the residence of her father Jacob Murph(y?) Perry County, Alabama, Mrs. Sarah Crawford to Sidney M. Stein of Tuscaloosa.

Departed this life on the 17th of September '55, Brother E. Matthis, in the forty-fifth year of his age... Brother Matthis was long a member and served as deacon in a church which I served (Tallassahatcha)...

## Marriage and Death Notices From The South Western Baptist Newspaper

Died in Barbour County, Alabama of congestive chill on Thursday, 20th September, Mrs. Matilda Clappe, eldest daughter of James Thomas in the thirty-eighth year of her age. Mrs. C. was baptized by Rev. J. Culpepper at Cedar Creek Church, Anson County, North Carolina in the year 1835... She left no children, but a husband...

10-25-1855
Died in Tuskegee on the 8th of October, Mrs. Mary Kerr Howard, consort of Alexis Howard, in the forty-sixth year of her age. Mrs. H. was a native of North Carolina and with her husband removed to Alabama some six years ago...
Died at Athens in Montgomery County, Alabama on the 25th day of September last, the Rev. John B. Warnock, age fifty-five years. Mr. Warnock was a native of the county of Antrim in Ireland, a graduate of the University of Glasgow and a minister of the Presbyterian Church for twenty-five years.
Died on the 6th inst. Robert Simpson, son of Arthur and Martha Simpson of Pike County, Alabama. This young man was born on the 17th of February 1835, making his age at the time of his death twenty years, seven months, nineteen days.

11-1-1855
Married by the Rev. O. Welch on the 17th inst., Dr. R. Wallace of Shelby to Miss G. Mallory of Talladega, daughter of Col. William Mallory, late of Orange County, Virginia.
By the same, Mr. Wm. Griffin to Miss N. Murry, all of Talladega County, on the 9th inst.
Mrs. Emily Parish died at her residence near Marion on the 3rd day of September 1855, in the seventieth year of her age. She was a native of North Carolina, born May 1st, 1785. She was married to the late Joel Parish, deceased, December 18th, 1804. In 1820 she became a believer in the Lord Jesus and made a public profession of her faith in him uniting with the Sandy Field Baptist Church, Orange County, North Carolina. She emigrated to Alabama in the year 1833...
Departed this life at Franklin in Macon County, Alabama, Miss Cornelia Gillispie, the eldest daughter of J. and R. Gillispie, on Wednesday evening the 17th of October 1855, in the fourteenth year of her age.

11-15-1855
Departed this life on the 16th of October 1855, Martha Wood... She was the only sister of my wife... Sister Wood joined that society at Allen's meeting house in Franklin County, Georgia, and for seven years was a citizen of Carnesville. From there she moved to De Kalb County, Georgia, and lived there a few years and then moved to Floyd County. After staying there a few years she came to Alabama, Chambers County...    F. Callaway

## Marriage and Death Notices From The South Western Baptist Newspaper

Died on Sunday, 11th inst., about 12 o'clock, at his residence, John McKay, Sr., in seventieth year of his age.

Died on the 17th day of October last in the vicinity of Union Springs, Mrs. Ann T. Eley, consort of the Rev. M.N. Eley, in the thirty-fifth year of her age. Sister Eley was afflicted for several weeks before her death. Her husband was also confined a large portion of the time with the same disease, typhoid fever... She left an afflicted husband, seven children, the youngest of whom was a dear and only little daughter...

Died at the residence of her father in Macon County, Alabama on the 19th day of October 1855, Miss Mary Elizabeth Wimberly, daughter of Mack and Rocela Wimberly.

She was born in Talbot County, Georgia on the 29th day of August 1842, and lived to the age of thirteen years, one month and ?? days.

Died at his residence near Wedowee, Alabama, October the 9th, 1855 in the thirty-eighth year of his age, James H. Hand. He has left a bereaved widow and a large family...

11-22-1855
Tribute of respect on the death of Rev. Wm. Lacy, who departed this life 5 October 1855, age sixty-four years... Born Virginia in the year 1791... (County Line Church, Randolph County, Alabama)

Married on Tuesday the 13th inst. by Rev. Sam'l Henderson, Thomas S. Howard to Miss Henrietta Stratford, all of Macon County.

11-29-1855
Married at Brewer's Hotel in Tuskegee on Wednesday morning the 21st inst. by Rev. Dow Perry, Mr. Henry Key to Miss Augusta A.F. Brewer, youngest daughter of Wm. Brewer.

On the 22nd inst. by Rev. W.T. Brantley, Mr. O.P. Caldwell, formerly of this place, to Miss A. Whitman of Athens, Georgia.

On the 14th inst. by Rev. John Powell, Rev. J.R. Haggard of South Alabama to Miss Parmeliv S. Randolph.

In Enon, Alabama on the 22nd inst. by Rev. Samuel Henderson, Col. William Ivey of Clayton to Miss Amanda DuBose.

On the 18th inst. at the Magnolia Institute, Alabama by Elder A. VanHoose, Mr. S.S. Stakely of Madisonville, Tennessee to Miss S.F. Fonville, daughter of Elder J.A. Fonville.

12-13-1855
Died at the residence of his father (Overton Stephens) on the 2nd inst. after a few days illness, Henry Stephens, in the fourteenth year of his age... J.M.P. Milner, Randolph County, Alabama, 30 November 1855.

## Marriage and Death Notices From The South Western Baptist Newspaper

Departed this life at his father's residence on the 6th of November, Benjamin F. Hadin, in the thirtieth year of his age, having a bereaved widow and three little orphans, besides a father, mother, brothers and sisters to mourn their loss.

### 12-20-1855

Married on Tuesday, December 4th by Rev. Thos. W. Lynch at the house of Mr. W.C. Barnes in Coosa County, Miss Sallie Barnes to Mr. J.F. Allen of Russell County, Alabama.

Married at the residence of Ruffin Gregory in Hellicon, Lowndes County, Alabama by John Henderson, esq., John A. Peetry to Miss Margaret Ann Gregory, on the 29th inst.

Departed this life at Carlowville, Dallas County, Alabama on Thursday November 9th, 1855, in the eighty-sixth year of his age, James Lide, the Senior Deacon of the Centre Ridge Baptist Church. This aged and honored servant of God was born in Mulberry District, South Carolina, May 19th, 1770... He was first called to the Deacon's office and ordained at Mechanicsville Church, Darlington District, South Carolina about the year 1823. He, with a few others who had emigrated to Alabama and settled at Carlowville, united in their efforts to settle Dr. Hartwell at that place about the year 1837 and thus laid the foundation of Centre Ridge Church... He leaves his aged companion with whom he had walked the pilgrimage of life more than sixty years, now in her seventy-seventh year...

### 1-10-1856

Married by Rev. T. Root, Mr. Edmund Walker of Madison, Georgia to Mrs. Mary E. Carley of Marianna, Florida.

By Rev. W.B. Jones, December 6th, 1856, Rev. Joseph H. Norton to Susan B. Hagin, all of Macon County.

Died on the 5th of January 1856 of scarlet fever, Sarah Blakey, daughter of A.G. Simpson, near Notasulga, in the sixth year of her age. Her illness lasted one month.

Died on the 5th of December ult. at the residence of his brother near Flat Rock, South Carolina, of paralysis, Mr. James Drakeford, in the fifty-fourth year of his age. Mr. Drakeford had left his residence in Tuskegee but a few days before his death in his usual health to visit his relations in his native state. He had not reached his destination more than half an hour before he was attacked and he lingered but three days... A wife and two sons mourn his departure...

Died in Autaugaville, 10th of September 1855, Mary Ann Murrah, daughter of Sister V. Murrah, age six years, seven months, ten days...

Died of typhoid fever at Tallassee, Tallapoosa County, Alabama, December 27th, 1855, Miss Sarah Anne Buse, in the sixteenth year of her age...

## Marriage and Death Notices From The South Western Baptist Newspaper

1-17-1856
Married on the 20th December ult. in Tuskegee by Rev. Samuel Henderson, Mr. David Watson of Russell County to Mrs. Malinda Garrot.
Died in Auburn, Alabama on the 15th of November last Catharine B. Graham, second daughter of Mr. and Mrs. Jas. A. Graham, of Lowndes County, in her thirteenth year... Buoyant with hope and burning with ambition to take a high position in her classes she left home in summer and entered the Female College at Auburn to complete her education, but being attacked with scarlet fever, death chose her for a victim. Mr. Graham who had repaired to Auburn during the illness of his daughter contracted the disease and after his return home spread it to some extent in his family. Not satisfied with a "Delila, the King of Terrors" smites down a Benjamin. On the 3rd of December, James A., youngest son of this stricken household fell a victim to the dire scourge.
Died in Newbern, Green County, Alabama, December 27th 1855 at the residence of her brother Rev. R. Holman, Miss Phebe F. Holman, after a long and painful illness.

1-24-1856
Married in Montgomery on the 17th inst. by the Rev. J. T. Tichnor, Mr. Richard Stratford, Jr. of Macon County to Miss Frannie A. Ware, daughter of Maj. R.J. Ware of Montgomery.
Tribute of respect on the death of John Beverly.

1-31-1856
Died on the 29th December 1855 at his residence in Chattahoochee, Florida Mr. John Wooten, age fifty-two years, eight months.

2-7-1856
Married at the Mongolia Institute, Alabama on the 17th of January by Elder J.A. Fonville, Mr. E.D.F. McRie, A.B., to Miss R. Westmoreland.

2-14-1856
Married on the 17th January, Capt. E.Y. Hill of La Grange, Georgia to Miss M.L. Baptist, daughter of the Rev. Edward Baptist of Marengo County, Alabama.
By the Rev. P.R. Bland on the 14th January, Mr. Americus Hatchett of Shreveport, Louisiana to Miss Sallie C. Collier of Hayward County, Tennessee.
Died at Marion on Saturday morning, February 26th (from the croup), Willie, second son of President S.S. Sherman, in the seventh year of his age...

2-21-1856
Died at the residence of her mother in Tuscaloosa County, Alabama on Sunday, 7 o'clock p.m., January 27th, 1856 in the fifteenth year of her age,

## Marriage and Death Notices From The South Western Baptist Newspaper

Miss Sarah Ann Shuttlesworth, daughter of Phillip and Nancy Shuttlesworth. Her illness was of one month's duration (typhoid fever)...

2-28-1856
Married on the 21st inst. by Rev. R. Dickerson, Mr. W.R. Chapman of Macon County to Miss Susannah Letcher of Coosa County.
On the 17th inst. by Rev. Mr. Bentley, Mr. John DeLoach to Miss Dorathy S. Blunt, all of Macon County.
It becomes our painful duty to record the death of our highly esteemed and much beloved Brother Benjamin F. Hardy, who departed this life on the 17th November 1855, at the early age of thirty-six years...
Died in the vicinity of Union Springs at the residence of her son, Rev. M.N. Eley, on the 1st day of February, '56, Mrs. Martha Eley, in the eighty-fourth year of her age. She was born in Wake County, North Carolina, removed to Hancock County, Georgia in 1813, and to Macon County, Alabama in 1838, where after a few years her husband died.
Departed this life on the 9th inst. at the house of Col. Geo. Hill, Mrs. Adelia A. Hill, consort of the late W.C. Hill, esq., deceased, and daughter of Col. D.P. Armstrong of Knoxville, Tennessee. Early in life she became a member of the Presbyterian Church of Talladega...(mentions two children)
Died at his residence in Russell County, Alabama on the 16th of February, Abner H. Vann (formerly of Edgefield District, South Carolina) age thirty-nine years... left a wife and children...
Tribute of respect upon the death of Rev. George Granberry.
Died at her father's near Union Springs in Macon County, Alabama, on the 6th inst. after an illness of three weeks, occasioned by typhoid fever, Miss Nancy M., daughter of Mr. H.P. and Prudence Slaughter, in the fourteenth year of her age...
Married at 10 o'clock on the morning of the 14th inst. by the Rev. Cornelius McLeod, Mr. R.J. Swear?ngen to Miss C.F. Roberts, all of this county.
Married in Macon County on the 20th inst. by Rev. A.T.M. Handy, Dr. Frederick Williams to Miss Mary H. Greenwood.

3-6-1856
Died in Tallassee, Tallapoosa County, Alabama, Mrs. Elvira, consort of C.B. Garward, in the thirtieth year of her age...
Mary Ann Kinnebrew, wife of E.H. Kinnebrew, departed this life on the 7th February 1856, after an illness of ten weeks...

3-27-1856
Died in Brunswick, January 29th, James Herbert Fuller, son of James P. and Hannah Fuller, age seven years, nine months.

MARRIAGE AND DEATH NOTICES FROM THE SOUTH WESTERN BAPTIST NEWSPAPER

4-10-1856
Married on Thursday, December 6th at the residence of Benjamin Baker by Rev. C.A. Stanton, Mr. Francis M. Gilmer of Russell County and Miss Lauretta Ann Baker, of Macon County.
On the evening of the 17th inst. by the Rev. P.F. Collins at the St. Francis Street Baptist Church, Mr. Thomas J. Harris of Wilcox County, Alabama to Miss Elizabeth A. Collins.
Tribute of respect on the death of Deacon John Beverly, who died at his residence near Enon, Alabama on the 21st of December last, in the sixty-seventh year of his age.

4-17-1856
Died at his residence near Evergreen, Conecuh County, Alabama on the 12th ult. of disease of the liver, Mason L. Mosely, in the forty-ninth year of his age. The deceased was born in South Carolina and at a very early age was deprived of the cares of a father. His mother married again to John Scogin who removed to this county in the earliest settlement of it... Early in life he married Martha M., daughter of David Jay of this county, whom he now leaves a widowed mother and eleven children...
Died on the 8th of February 1856 at the residence of her father Brother Isaac N. Hall in Orion, Pike County, Alabama, Mrs. Eleanor K. Jones, wife of Brother Hansford S. Jones. Sister Jones was born September 3rd, 1827... She has left an affectionate husband and three children...
Also at the same place on the 16th March 1856, Mrs. Louisa J. Sebastian, age thirty-two years, one month, three days. In early life she was married to A. Spalding with whom she removed to Louisiana where in a short time she was a left a widow by the death of her husband, among strangers, with three children. She afterwards married Mr. Wm. Sebastian. She had been separated from her parents twelve years and had during the last two or three years set several periods to visit them, but had been providentially hindered until a few weeks since. She arrived just in time to follow her sister to the grave... From exposure during their travels, her children were taken down one after another, and during her watching and anxiety for them she herself marked by the arch destroyer as his victim. Sister S. joined the Baptist Church about two years since... Brother and Sister Hall (Hali) are left nearly childless in their old age, having buried five out of their six children...
Died in Coffman (Kaufman) County, Texas on the 22nd day of February 1856, John J. Shuttlesworth, in the twenty-second year of his age. The deceased was a son of Philip and Nancy Shuttlesworth, and was born and raised in Tuscaloosa County, Alabama; and in connection with his brother James Shuttlesworth and family removed to Texas in November 1855. On his journey Westward he was much exposed to the inclemency of the weather in consequence of which he took a violent cold, settling upon his lungs, resulted in his death.

# Marriage and Death Notices From The South Western Baptist Newspaper

Died of pneumonia at his residence in Dallas County, Alabama on the 21st of February last, Deacon Stephen Fr(e)drick, in the seventy-first year of his age...

4-24-1856
Married by the Rev. Robert Oldham on the 13th inst., Dr. William Vance of Bibb County to Mrs. Nancy Shuttlesworth of Tuscaloosa County, Alabama.
ELDER H.D. ACHER: This servant of God died in Talladega County, Alabama in January or February 1856 after a brief illness of a few days. He was cut down in the prime of live, in his forty-sixth year.
Died in Marion, Alabama on the 6th of April, Susan V. Lawson, daughter of W.B. and Jane Lawson, age eighteen years...

5-1-1856
Married by Elder H.E. Taliaferro at the residence of Maj. White of Macon County on the 27th of April 1856, Mr. Isaac Smith of Tallapoosa County to Miss Lucy Futell of Macon County.

5-8-1856
Married in Coosa County on the 15th ult. at the residence of Col. Wm. Garrett by Rev. J.J. Bullington, Col. George Hill of this county to Miss Caroline M. Henry of Coosa County.
By Rev. John H. Smith on the 24th of April 1856, George Y. Malone to Miss Tabitha E. Wallace, all of Pike County, Alabama.
Departed this life on Friday the 4th of April 1856, Laura Eugenia, daughter of T.J. and Emily M. Russell, age five years, ten months.
Also on Sunday April 6th, 1856 Gertrude Ella, daughter of T.J. and Emily Russell, age two years, three months, three days.
Also on Wednesday, April 9th, James Henry, son of T.J. and Emily M. Russell, age nine years, one month, six days. The disease... scarlet fever.
Died in the 32nd year of her age Mrs. Susan Marson, wife of Dr. W.S. Mabson, at Union Springs, Alabama, April 25th, 1856. She was the daughter of Mr. J.C. Farley, and was married to Dr. Mabson in 1844 by whom she had four
children...

5-15-1856
Married on the 6th of May at Mrs. Amanda McMath's (late widow of Dr. W.F. McMath) by Rev. Robert Oldham, Rev. Bill??? Gayle of Perry County to Miss Josephine McMath of Tuscaloosa County, Alabama.
Died at his residence in Macon County, Alabama, April 3rd, William M. Dick, in the thirty-ninth year of his age. In the fall of 1852 he joined the Baptist Church at Ebinezer...

## Marriage and Death Notices From The South Western Baptist Newspaper

Died in Macon County, Alabama on the 10th day of April, Mrs. E.J. Dick, in the twenty-ninth year of her age...

Died of consumption on the 5th of May 1856 after an illness of eleven weeks Mrs. M.A., consort of R.M. Burt of Macon County, Alabama, and daughter of Rev. William Henderson, who died in Monroe County, Georgia in 1832. She was in the twenty-ninth year of her age... She has left a fond and affectionate husband and three little daughters...

Died at the residence of her father in Pike County, Alabama on Monday morning the 21st ult. Susan Ann, daughter of Loveless and Susan Kotten, age twelve years, four months, six days...

The *Constitutionalist* of yesterday contains an obituary notice of Milner Echols, one of the purest and most honored citizens of Georgia, who died at his residence on Monday last of derangement of the liver. Mr. Echols at the time of his death was upwards of eighty-four years of age, seventy-one years of which time he has been a citizen of Georgia. He is survived by his wife...

5-22-1856

We, the subscribers, having been appointed a committee to prepare an obituary notice of the late James Tubb... He departed this life on the 20th of April 1856. His disease was thought to be an affection of the heart... He was born in South Carolina (Greenville District), July 10th, 1799 making his age at death fifty-six years, nine months, ten days. His parents moved to Tennessee (Dixon County) while he was a child. Our Brother Tubb moved from Tennessee in the fall season and took up his residence in Perry County, Alabama, November 25th, 1826, and was received into the fellowship of Union Church by Baptism in December 1828... November 1845 he called for a letter of dismission and moved to the place at which he died... He has left a wife and a large family of children...

Whereas, it has pleased Almighty God in his wisdom and providence to call from earth our worthy brother and pastor, Elder Charles Stewart, who died at his late residence near Carrollton, Alabama on the 29th of March last in the sixty-second year of his age...

Died at the residence of Felix G. Christmas near Coffeeville, Alabama on the morning of the 10th ult. after a brief illness, Mrs. Julia A., consort of Thos. A.J. Cox, age twenty years, four months, eleven days. She had been a member of the Baptist Church for two years living up to its strictest requirements. She joined at Marion, Perry County, Alabama in the summer of 1853 while going to school at the Judson Institute...

5-29-1856

Married on the 20th inst. at 8 o'clock in the morning by Rev. M.N. Eley at the residence of Mrs. Kezia Underwood, Mr. Joseph P. Eley of Green County, Georgia to Miss Carrie M. Barn?t [Barnet?] of Macon County, Alabama.

## Marriage and Death Notices From The South Western Baptist Newspaper

Died of croup after a short illness of three days at the residence of his grandfather, James H. Camron, near the town of Henderson, Rusk County, Texas, April 24th. J. Frank Camron, son of Ewing L. and Emma A. Camron, age two years, six months, twenty days...

Tribute of respect from Shiloh Church, Pike County, Alabama on the death of Mary Ann K. Owens, wife of Charles A. Owens.

6-6-1856

Died in Tuskegee, May 26th, 1856, James Daniel, infant son of John and Georgian Ann Campbell, age sixteen months, one week.

Departed this life at his residence in Russell County, Alabama on the 8th of May 1856 in the thirty-seventh year of his age, George L. Granberry, son of Rev. Thomas Granberry... Brother G.'s last illness, which was caused by the measles and lasted thirteen days, was peculiarly severe... He has left a wife and six children, and aged father and mother...

Died at his residence near La Place, Macon County, Alabama at 8 o'clock on Saturday morning the 17th inst., Mr. John Cloud, Sr., in the sixty-eighth year of his age. The subject of this notice was born in Elbert County, Georgia, February 13th in the year 1789. When quite a boy his father settled in Edgefield District, South Carolina. He was there raised, married and resided until 1846 when he emigrated to Macon County, Alabama and settled the place of his residence...

6-12-1856

Married on the 27th ult. at the residence of Mrs. A.L. McMath by Elder A.C. Thomason, Capt. John Salmons to Mrs. Amanda L. McMath, all of Tuscaloosa County, Alabama.

Died in LaFayette, Alabama on the 26th of May 1856, Sister Martha Hill, wife of Brother Wade Hill, and daughter of Rev. Wm. D. Lane, deceased, formerly of Putnam County, Georgia, in the sixty-fourth year of her age. She was a native of South Carolina, had been a member of the Baptist Church forty-five years and was baptized by Rev. Elijah Mosely, into Island Creek Church, Hancock County, Georgia...

Died of derangement of the liver in Jefferson County, Alabama on the evening of the 1st of May 1856, Mrs. Mary, consort of E. Wood and daughter of Wm. Allen, in the fifty-sixth year of her age. The subject of this notice was born in Spartanburg District, South Carolina on the 25th of December 1801... When she was about twenty years of age her father died and on his death bed requested her to remain single and take care of her aged mother and some younger children. Sometime after the death of her father she with her mother removed to Alabama and settled in Shelby County. Here she soon had to suffer the loss of her mother, leaving her to provide for the rest of the family. Sometime after this she was united by marriage to a Mr. Jordan, assuming the responsible station of a step-mother. Mr. Jordan did not live

## MARRIAGE AND DEATH NOTICES FROM THE SOUTH WESTERN BAPTIST NEWSPAPER

long and after his death she got her brother, J.P. Allen, to live with her and see to her business until the 8th of June 1845 when she was married to E. Wood of Jefferson County. Here she was again installed as a step-mother over a large family...

6-19-1856
Died in this county on Sunday the 8th of June, Mrs. Sarah Robertson, consort of the Rev. Jno. Robertson, in the seventy-first year of her age...
Departed this life at her father's residence in Russell County, Alabama on the 3rd of June 1856 in the nineteenth year of her age, Martha A. Granberry, daughter of Rev. Tho. Granberry.

6-26-1856
Married at Wetumpka on the 19th inst. by Rev. L.T. Tichenor, Mr. William Thompkins of Montgomery to Miss Mattie A., daughter of Rev. J.D. Williams of Wetumpka.
Died in Tuskegee on Thursday morning, June 5th after a painful illness of nineteen days at the residence of Dr. Fowler, Joshua Soule Sedberry, age twenty-six years. He was a native of Fayetteville, North Carolina. At the early age of fourteen years he obtained a hope in Christ and united with the Methodist Church in his native town... In April 1853 he came to Tuskegee...
Died at Creek Stand, Macon County, Alabama May 28th, 1856 Sarah Amanda Burt, infant daughter of Richard M. and Martha A. Burt, recently deceased.
Died at his residence in Dallas County, Alabama on the 12th of April last, Zachariah Rolen, in the sixty-sixth year of his age. He was born and raised in Edgefield District, South Carolina, and emigrated among the first settlers of Alabama. He joined the Baptist Church at Sister Springs, August the 27th, 1843, and ordained a Deacon of the same church, April the 26th, 1846.
Departed this life at Collirene, Alabama on the 24th day of April last, Mrs. Jerusha Rives, in the ?5th year of her age. She was born in Orangeburg District, South Carolina, and removed to Lowndes County, Alabama in the winter of 1832-1833 where she resided until her decease.

7-3-1856
Departed this life at Allenton, Wilcox County, Alabama on Wednesday, June 11th, 1856, Miss Pocahontas R. Williams, youngest daughter of the late Deacon John P. Williams of Centre Ridge Baptist Church. The deceased was born in Buckingham County, Virginia, August 6th, 1831, and moved with her parents and family to Alabama in 1846. She with a sister and three brothers were received into the fellowship of Centre Ridge Baptist Church and all Baptized...
Died in the city of Montgomery, Alabama on the 28th of May 1856, Capt. John Cook, age fifty-seven years, eleven months, twenty-four days. The

## Marriage and Death Notices From The South Western Baptist Newspaper

deceased was a native of South Carolina and was among the early emigrants to this country, and settled in Lowndes County, Alabama... Brother Cook made a profession of religion some ten or twelve years since and was united with the Cubihatchie Baptist Church, Macon County, Alabama... So far from desiring to live, he preferred to die; only wishing that his life might be prolonged so long as that he might see and embrace an only and much loved daughter, who resided in the state of South Carolina and who had, by telegraph, been advised of his illness...

7-17-1856
Married in Clinton, Hinds County, Mississippi on the 11th June 1856 R.W. Priest, Missionary of S.B. Foreign Missions to Central Africa, to Miss Clara E. Warner, a member of Clinton Baptist Church.
It becomes our painful duty to record the death of Mary F. Goodwin, wife of Thelston A. Goodwin, and daughter of Benjamin and Sarah M. Averitt, who departed this life the 16th day of June 1856, in the twenty-eighth year of her age. Mrs. Goodwin was born on the 8th of February 1828, and was married on the 24th of December 1844. At her decease left five children, three sons (one an infant) and two daughters... Her funeral is to be preached at the Mount Zion Baptist Church on the 1st Sabbath in August next by Elder David Lloyd of Bibb County, Alabama...
Died on the second day of December 1855, Mary, youngest daughter of Col. Wm. B. and Susan Haralson, of congestion of the brain, in the second year of her age...
Died of consumption on the 2nd day of March, Mrs. Susan C. Haralson, in the thirty-fourth year of her age... She was born in the county of Maury, Tennessee, November 11th, 1822, and was united in marriage to Col. W.B. Haralson in August 1840... The daughter and mother lie near each other in the burying ground at Ashe Creek Church...
Died in Lowndes County, May 19th Mrs. Atkinson, age about sixty-four. The deceased was a native of Virginia but for a number of years she resided in Monroe County, Alabama, for the last four years a resident of Lowndes County. For many years has she suffered, her disease being pulmonary consumption... The mother of twelve children, she survived them all save one. An affectionate daughter, three grandchildren, a devoted husband and many relatives and friends to mourn her loss...

7-24-1856
Married on the 16th inst. by Rev. Wm. Howard, Rev. Wm. L. Foster to Miss Sarah M. Maxwell, daughter of Col. Maxwell of Greene County.
Mrs. Sarah Elizabeth Nuckolls, wife of David P. Nuckolls, and second daughter of Hon. George W. and Mary Ann Gun(?), died at the residence of her parents in Tuskegee, July ?, 1856, in the twentieth year of her age... married in June 1855.

## Marriage and Death Notices From The South Western Baptist Newspaper

Departed this life in Clinton, Greene County, Alabama on the 28th ult. John P. Freeman, age thirty-four years. The deceased was born in Franklin County, North Carolina in the year 1822; removed to this state in 1848; was baptized into the fellowship of the Clinton Baptist Church in 1851. He leaves behind him a wife and five little orphan children...

Died in Polk County, Texas on the 3rd of June 1856 Sister Jane, daughter of Brother John and Sister Sarah Lee, in the twenty-fifth year of her age. The subject of this notice was born near Town Creek Church, Dallas County, Alabama in the year 1831... In December last Brother J. Lee (formerly Deacon of Town Creek Church) with his family removed from this to the state of Texas...

7-31-1856
Married at the Independent Presbyterian Church, Savannah, Georgia on the 12th inst. by the Rev. David H. Porter, S.M. Bartlett, M.D. of Tuskegee, Alabama to Miss Sue A. Hendree of Richmond, Virginia.

8-7-1856
Died in Autauga County, April 16th, 1856 after a short illness, Mrs. Sarah Law, in the fifty-fourth year of her age. The deceased was a native of Sumpter District, South Carolina; moved with her husband, Isaiah H. Law, to Alabama in January 1833; was left a widow with seven children in 1846, all of whom survive her...

8-14-1856
Departed this life at the residence of his father, Reubin H. Hall, in Henry County, Alabama on the 28th ult. at 9:30 o'clock a.m. John A. Hall, in the twenty-second year of his age.

8-21-1856
Died in Tuscaloosa on Tuesday the 12th inst. at 20 minutes past 12 o'clock Kate McIntosh, the infant daughter of Rev. Archibald J. and Mary E. Battle, after a painful and lingering illness of two months, age fifteen months, twenty-five days.

Died on the 2nd day of August in Marion, Perry County, Sally Strong Billingsley, daughter of Isaac and Ann Jane Billlingsley, age two years, one month, twenty days.

Died on the 13th of July at the residence of her husband, Dr. H.K. Stanford, near Waverly Hall in Harris County, Georgia, Mrs. Louisa J. Stanford, age thirty-three years. The subject of this notice was the youngest daughter of David and Frances Weaver, deceased...,united with the Baptist Church at Harmony, Putnam County. For several years she was a member of Mount Vernon Church, Talbot County... She left a kind husband and four children...

## MARRIAGE AND DEATH NOTICES FROM THE SOUTH WESTERN BAPTIST NEWSPAPER

8-28-1856
Married in Roxberry, Massachusetts this morning (August 13) by Rev. T.D. Anderson, Prop. G.W. Thomas of Tuskegee, Alabama to Lizzie L., daughter of Nathaniel Adams of R.
Died in Dallas County on the 14th inst. at the residence of her son, Maj. E. Wilson, Mrs. Sarah Wilson in the eighty-fifth year of her age. The subject of this notice was at the time of her death a member of the Selma Baptist Church...
Died at Montevallo, Alabama on the 17th inst. after a lingering illness J. Bradford, only son of Rev. F.M. and Mrs. Kate Law of Selma, age two years, nine months.

9-4-1856
Died Charles E. Treutlin on the 1st of May 1856, age fifty-eight years... Tribute of respect from the Baptist Church at Enon, Alabama.

9-11-1856
CENTRAL INSTITUTE, WILLIAMSTON, AUG 29, 1856. The melancholy intelligence of the death of Julius S. Morton, a member of this institution...
Died in Uniontown, Perry County, Alabama on the morning of the 12th ult. at the age of seven years and a few months, Clara P., the only daughter of brother James G. and M.C. Hudson.
Died at Lowndesboro, Lowndes County, Alabama on the 17th June 1856, Mrs. Caroline S. Cilley, wife of Dr. P.N. Cilley. Mrs. Cilley was a daughter of the late Hon. Reuben Saffold, and born on the 28th of January 1830 in Dallas County. She leaves two young children having lost the eldest on the 27th of April 1855. Mrs. Cilley was an intelligent lady. Educated at the Judson Female Institute...

9-18-1856
Died at her residence in Tallapoosa County, Alabama on the 16th of August 1856 of congestive fever after an illness of eleven days, Mrs. Mary Jane, consort of John R. Pearson, and daughter of John H. and Elizabeth Veazey, in the twenty-second year of her age.
Departed this life at Franklin in Macon County, Alabama on the 27th of August 1856, Miss Mary Segrest, daughter of George and Jane Segrest, in the twenty-second year of her age...

9-25-1856
Married at Jersey City in the Baptist Church by Rev. W.H. Parmly, Rev. William H. McIntosh, pastor of the Baptist Church in Marion, Alabama to Miss Helen M. Colby, daughter of Rev. Lewis Colby of New York.

## Marriage and Death Notices From The South Western Baptist Newspaper

Died in Tuskegee on the 16th inst. Mrs. H.B. Lipscomb, wife of the Rev. Dr. A.A. Lipscomb.

Died near Union Springs, Macon County, Alabama on the 4th inst. at the age of seven years one month two days, James S., son of brother G.J. and sister S.E. Pihrce. (Pierce?)

10-2-1856
Killed suddenly in Lafayette, Alabama, September 16th, 1856 by a fall from a carriage in the forty-sixth year of her age, Mrs. May Ann Hill, wife of Gibson F. Hill of Fredonia. On leaving the residence of her father-in-law, Maj. Waid Hill, the horses took fright, ran a few rods, upset the carriage against a tree and killed her instantly in sight of the house and many of her relatives. She was born in Washington City, came south soon after her marriage and lived a consistent member of the Baptist Church for more than twenty years. An affectionate husband and eight children are left to mourn her loss.

Died at the residence of Elder R.H. Taliaferro in Jackson County, Alabama on the 17th September, Francisco Eustace, only child of Ezekiel and Ann H. Williams, age three months, five days.

Tribute of respect from Uchee Lodge #77 upon the death of Laban S. Johnson...

Died on the 11th of September in Pike County, Laura Smith daughter of Alexander and Ann Smith, age one year, eleven months, sixteen days.

10-9-1856
Died at Clinton, Greene County on Friday morning the 26th inst. Augusta Josephine, infant daughter of Dr. W. Wills, age eleven months, twenty days.

10-16-1856
Married at the residence of H.P. Slaughter in this county on the 13th inst. by the Rev. M.N. Eley, Mr. Erastus L. Black of Tallapoosa County to Miss Sarah Slaughter.

Died at his residence in Russell County, Alabama on Friday the 26th September, Dr. Merrick H. Ford, in the fifty-fourth year of his age... The nature of his disease was such as to deprive him of the power of speech for several days before his death...

Tribute of respect from Gilgal Church on the death of Elder R.S. Adams...

TRIBUTE OF RESPECT: Whereas, it has pleased the Supreme Architect of the Universe to suddenly remove from our midst on the 23rd of September our worthy and much esteemed brother John C. Henderson, (treasurer of this lodge at the time of his death)... Warrior Stand Lodge, September 26, 1856

## MARRIAGE AND DEATH NOTICES FROM THE SOUTH WESTERN BAPTIST NEWSPAPER

10-23-1856
Died at her residence in Benton County, Alabama on the 26th day of September 1856 of bloody flux after an illness of over forty days, Mrs. Mahala Hodges, consort of Thompson Hodges, and daughter of Samuel and Mary Hill, in the sixty-fourth year of her age... She was born in Lancaster District, South Carolina in 1792. Her father moved to Edgefield, thence to Old Pendleton, thence to Abbeville while in her childhood. She grew up to womanhood and married Thompson Hodges by whom she had fifteen children, nine of them now living; all married... She had seventy odd children and grand children and three great grand children... was baptized by the Rev. N.W. Hodges, her brother-in-law, and received into the Church at Walnut Grove, Abbeville District, South Carolina where she lived a consistent member until 1837 when she with her husband and family moved to Benton County, Alabama...

10-30-1856
Married on the 2?rd inst. by Rev. A.T.M. Handy, Mr. Marshall H. Moulton of Montgomery County to Miss Julia T. DuBose of Enon, Alabama.
Married at the house of Mrs. Nancy Fitzpatrick on the 19th inst. by the Rev. Thomas Granberry, Mr. John H. Shank of Macon County, Alabama to Miss Elizabeth Fitzpatrick of Chambers County, Alabama.
Died in Russell County, Alabama on the 29th of last June Rev. James Salmon, in the fifty-second year of his age. Brother Salmon was a native of Spartanburg District, South Carolina... In 1835 he removed to Franklin County, Georgia and was ordained in that county to the Gospel ministry in 1837. He spent most of his time as minister in the counties of Hancock and Washington... He has left a wife and four children.
Died at the residence of John S. Barnes in Russell County, Alabama on the 10th of October, 1856, Mrs. Francis Smith, in about the eightieth year of her age...
Died in Tuskegee on the 20th, Lenora Francis, daughter of John B. and Georgia Ann Campbell, age four years, four months, five days.
Died on Wednesday night last the 16th inst. in Russell County, Mr. David Mealing at the residence of Reuben Cooper's. The deceased had been unwell for some days before his death but on the night he died he sat up and ate supper; next morning he was found dead in his bed. *Edgefield Advertiser* and *Columbus Enquirer* please copy.
Tribute of respect from the Big Creek Baptist Church of Tuscaloosa Association held the 11th day of October 1856 upon the death of Robert S. Adams...

## Marriage and Death Notices From The South Western Baptist Newspaper

11-6-1856

Married on the 28th ult. at the residence of Mr. T.A. Thornton of Macon County by the Rev. F.H. Moss, Mr. Franklin Hendrick of Pike County, Alabama to Miss Sarah Ann Thorton.

Married on the 30th ult. at the residence of Mr. Johnathan Orum by the Rev. F.H. Moss, Mr. John F. Meekin to Miss Rebecca J. Orum, all of Montgomery County, Alabama.

Married at the residence of Mrs. Sarah Eubank of Russell County on the 28th ult. by the Rev. Wm. Ross, the Rev. James N. Owens to Miss Lavinia Eubank.

Died in Selma, August 25th, 1856, Miss Fannie N., youngest daughter of John and Mary Apperson, in the eighteenth year of her age.

Died in Choctaw County, Alabama near Bladen Springs on the 11th inst. after a lingering illness Sharlotty Ryan, in the 5?th year of her age.

Tribute of respect from the Baptist Church of Christ at Tywakana, Freestone County, Texas on the death of William A. Kurvin whose death occurred on the steamship *Nautilus* between Galveston and New Orleans...

Thomas S. Howard, second son of Alexis Howard, died at the residence of his father in Tuskegee, October the 17th, 1856. Mr. Howard was born in North Carolina, July 9th, 1832. In 1850 he entered Howard College where he graduated with the highest honors of his class...

Tribute of respect from the Northport Baptist Church upon the death of Robt. S. Adams, at about the age of seventeen or eighteen years.

Died at Jackson County, Florida, October 27th, Lourena Emeline, youngest daughter of Bennett S. and Emeline M. Battle, age one year, ten months, eleven days.

11-20-1856

Died at McKinley, Marengo County, Alabama on the 30th August 1856, Mrs. Martha Morris, consort of William Morris, in the fortieth year of her age...

Died at Uchee, Alabama on the 18th of September last, Laban S. Johnson, Jr., in the twenty-eighth year of his age... leaving a wife and two children...

11-27-1856

Married on the 11th inst. by Rev. E.Y. VanHoose, Mr. Thacker V. Walker of Pike County to Miss Virginia A. Cox of Enon, Alabama.

Married on the 19th inst. by the Rev. T. Root, George Bryan to Miss Nancy E., daughter of Col. C.B. Harrison, all of Tuskegee.

Married on the 9th inst. by the Rev. S. Henderson, Mr. Wm. D. Scott to Miss Emily Brown, all of Macon County, Alabama

Died in Lowndes County, Alabama on the 15th of November after a painful illness John Elbert, eldest son of Thomas L. and Lucinda A. Traylor, age two years, five months, twenty-six days.

## MARRIAGE AND DEATH NOTICES FROM THE SOUTH WESTERN BAPTIST NEWSPAPER

12-4-1856
Married at the residence of Mrs. Julia McKinney on the morning of 2nd inst. by Rev. Samuel Henderson, Mr. Lovett McDonald of Cotton Valley to Mrs. Anna Smith of Tuskegee.
Married on the 25th ult. at the residence of Mr. William Brewer of Dale County by the Rev. Caswell Smith, Mr. Joseph Pellum to Miss Mary Ann Brewer.
Died at his residence in Selma, Dallas County, Alabama, September 17th, 1856 of congestive chill, John W. Adair, son of Farmer and Nancy Adair, age twenty-six years, four months, nineteen days. The subject of this notice was baptized into the fellowship of the Harmony Church, Autauga County, Alabama in November 1846. In May 1856 he removed his membership to the Selma Baptist Church...
Died at the residence of his mother, Mrs. Hannah Bledsoe, Chambers County, Alabama on the 10th ult. Mr. William H. Bledsoe, in the twenty-third year of his age...
BARBOUR COUNTY, ALABAMA, November 15th, 1856: Tribute of respect on the death of Capt. G.W. Cariker who departed this life on the 23rd of October 1856, in the forty-sixth year of his age. He was born in Mecklenburg County, North Carolina on the 8th of May 1811. He moved to the state of Georgia where at the age of twenty he made a profession of the religion of our Lord and was baptized.
Died on the morning of Sunday October 26th, 1856, Mr. John Himes at his residence in Russell County, Alabama, in the forty-sixth year of his age. The subject of this memoir was born in Lancaster County, Pennsylvania on the 29th day of June 1811. His parents were of the industrious German stock that settled so large a portion of that state. At an early age, Mr. Himes removed to the Eastern part of Tennessee and located in Washington County... After he was grown he left home and spent several years in wandering over various parts of the United States. In 1840 he was united in marriage to Miss Catherine Fraser of Russell County, Alabama. He immediately abandoned those dissipated habits which had been contracted during years of vicious association and entered upon the quiet, steady pursuits of a farmer's life. His early training had been religious no doubt, for his parents were attached to the primitive and peculiar sect of Dunkards, scattered throughout Western Virginia and Eastern Tennessee... In the spring of 1852 his health became impaired... In the Summer of 1854 he visited his aged parents for the last time, after an absence of nearly twenty years... His children of whom there were but two... During the past summer his health again declined. Being called to attend the session of the Circuit Court for Macon County he left home for Tuskegee about the middle of October. While there a sudden change of weather added to the fatigue of travel brought on an attack resembling asthma. He returned to his home on the 17th and was

## Marriage and Death Notices From The South Western Baptist Newspaper

immediately compelled to take his bed... The disease developed itself into dropsy of the chest, and he died after ten days of suffering... His remains were buried on his own premises...

12-11-1856
Married at the residence of A.W. Bowie, esq. on Wednesday the 26th ult. by the Rev. John Wilmer, Mr. Columbus Cunningham of Montevallo, Shelby County to Miss Sallie Bowdon of this place. (*Talladega Reporter*)
Sarah M. Oden departed this life in Talladega County, Alabama on the 17th of November 1856 in the eighteenth year of her age. She was the daughter of Benjamin Averett and Sarah M. Averett, and wife of Dempsey B. Oden... She lived but little over three years with her husband and left an infant daughter of twelve days old... We deeply sympathize with brother and sister Averett who have lost two daughters within less than a year.

12-18-1856
Died on Friday the 5th of December 1856 in the 28th year of her age, Mrs. Nancy R. McWhorter, wife of Dr. A.B. McWhorter, Jr., of Lowndes County in this state... She leaves a husband and two small children...
Died in Tuskegee, Alabama on Tuesday 25th ult. of that truly terrible disease of infancy, the croup, following a recent attack of an epidemic sore throat which had been prevalent a short time in the community, James William Goodall, youngest child of Dr. W.F. and Mrs. Caroline E. Hodnett, age four years, four months, twenty days... W.F. Hodnett
Died at his residence in Macon County, Alabama on the morning of the 21st of November, Barna Ivey, age sixty-one years, one month, twenty-nine days. He has left an affectionate wife and family... He united with the Baptist Church at LaGrange, Georgia about 22 years ago... LaGrange, Georgia and Milledgeville papers please copy.
Died in Pickensville, Alabama on Saturday night the 29th of November 1856 at the residence of Dr. A.M. Wilkins, James A.R. Hanks, fifth son of Elder A.M. Hanks, age nine years, eleven months, twenty-five days...

12-25-1856
Married at the residence of John W. Eley on the morning of the 18th inst. by Rev. M.N. Eley, Mr. Samuel A. Howell of Taliaferro County, Georgia to Miss Georgia A. Eley of Macon County, Alabama.
Mrs. Nancy Thorton, wife of deacon Dozier Thornton, died on the 18th day of October 1856. Our deceased sister was born on the 12th June 1788; and she was therefore in her sixty-ninth year when she died. She was married to her surviving husband in 1804...

## Marriage and Death Notices From The South Western Baptist Newspaper

Died in Macon County, Alabama on the 4th November 1856 after a short illness, Mrs. Caroline Henderson, wife of John H. Henderson, and daughter of Mrs. Louisa Kilkrist, in the twenty-sixth year of her age... Connected herself with the Ebinezer Baptist Church... She leaves behind an affectionate husband and two children...

Died at her residence in Conecuh County, Alabama on the 7th of September 1856, Mrs. Lavinia Straughn, consort of Fielding Straughn, age seventy-one years.

1-8-1857
Died at his residence in Shelby County, Alabama of inflammatory rheumatism, T.W. Teague, in the fifty-eighth year of his age... Born in Newberry District, South Carolina, December 14th, 1798. At twelve years old he professed religion and was baptized at Old Bush River Church by Rev. Silas Crow. In 1816 he was married to Mary Davis of the same district. In 1822 he moved to Alabama, Greene County where he resided for a short time. In the Fall he removed into Shelby County, where he remained until the day of his death. He was taken unwell on Wednesday but was not confined to his room until Saturday following, when he commenced complaining of pain in his knee which continued to increase until Tuesday morning when it attacked his head and heart, and soon dethroned his reason so that he could get nothing intelligible from him in his last hours... frequently, during the last ten or twelve years of his life he has been heard to remark: "If it were not for Martha (his idiot daughter) he would feel ready to die." [see below]

Died of bilious fever at her father's in Shelby County, Alabama, Martha A. Teague, idiot daughter of T.W. and Mary Teague, in the thirtieth year of her age. She was taken ill at the hour of her father's death with vomiting and continued of a very sick stomach until Monday night following when her spirit took its flight... [see above]

1-15-1857
Died in Montgomery, December 9th, 1856, Mary Ellen Blunt, only daughter of J.J. and E.A. Stewart. Mrs. Blunt was born in this city January 8th, 1837, graduated at the Judson Institute in 1854, was married to her affectionate and bereaved husband Wm. Blunt in May 1855.

Martha Ann Metcalf departed this life in Dale County, Alabama on the 14th of December 1856, in the twenty-sixth year of her age. She was the wife of James H. Metcalf...

Mrs. Elizabeth Keel is dead!... Mrs. Keel was born in Marlborough District, South Carolina, but for many years previous to her death was a resident of Clarke County, Alabama...

## Marriage and Death Notices From The South Western Baptist Newspaper

1-22-1857
Departed this life at her residence in West Point, Georgia on the 25th of November 1856 Mrs. Mariah, consort of W.R. Heirston, formerly Miss Langford, age twenty years, five months, seventeen days... She was married to W.R. Heirston, November 18th, 1854... She has left a babe only six weeks old... a kind husband, mother, brothers and sisters...
Died in Montgomery, Alabama on the morning of the 19th instant Mrs. E.E.S. Garrett, wife of John B. Garrett. Mrs. G. was born in Kent County, Virginia, November 28th, 1817; was married November 29th, 1835 and united with the Baptist Church in Montgomery, Alabama in 1837.

1-29-1857
Mrs. Louisiana Wallis, wife of Daniel Wallis, of Fayetteville, Alabama died of pneumonia on the 12th of January 1857, in the thirty-third year of her age. She was married to Brother Wallis in 1844; lived with him happily for thirteen years and has left five children... She attached herself to Fort Williams Church in 1842...

2-5-1857
Married on Tuesday evening January 27th at the residence of A.A. Hughes, esq. by Rev. C.A. Stanton, Mr. Thomas A. Culbreth of Russell County and Miss Sarah A. Hughes of Macon County.
Married in Milledgeville, Georgia on the 20th ult. by Rev. C.W. Lane, Col. B.B. DeGraffenreid and Miss Sarah Walker.
Married on the 15th of January last by Rev. William Boroum, Franklin Cobb, esq. of Chattahoochee County, Georgia to Miss Mary J. Collier of Jackson County, Florida.
Departed this life November 9th, 1856, James Sanford, infant son of I.K. and A.K. Lamb of Florida, age fifteen months, twenty-five days.

2-12-1857
Resolutions of respect from Loachapoka Lodge upon the death of Brother John A. Stanton.
MESSRS. EDITORS: By special request I send you a short obituary of father Samuel Ray of Autauga County who died December 9th, 1856, age eighty years, seven months, twenty-nine days. He was born April 10th, 1775 in the state of Virginia. Removed to the state of North Carolina when quite young; from thence to Georgia, Clark County... He united with the Baptist Church of Christ at Trail Creek in 1807; was baptized by Elder Isah Hale; was ordained to the Gospel ministry in 1812... He removed to Montgomery County, Alabama... He then removed to this county where he resided up to his death...

## Marriage and Death Notices From The South Western Baptist Newspaper

Died at his residence in Coosa County, Alabama on the 4th of January 1857, Brother Hiram Bentley, age fifty years, two months, twenty days. The deceased died a member and deacon of Bethesda Baptist Church in Coosa County, Alabama...

Died at his residence in Rockford, Coosa County, Alabama on the 26th day of January 1857 of measles, Brother Josiah Butts, in the forty-seventh year of his age. Brother Butts was a member of the Rockford Baptist Church, Coosa County, Alabama when he died. Brother Butts has left a wife and one daughter... The Tyler, Texas paper is requested to copy.

2-19-1857

Died near Tuskegee on Saturday night the 7th February 1857 of pneumonia, Mr. Richard Fallaw, in the forty-ninth year of his age.

Died at his residence in Shelby County, Alabama, William T. Williamson, in the twenty-fifth year of his age. This devoted young man was born in Shelby County, Alabama March 20th, 1832... baptized at Spring Creek Church, 17 August 1849 and from that time he lived an exemplary christian life to the day of his death, which was December 30th, 1856...

Died on the 31st of January in the twenty-ninth year of her age at her residence in Chambers County, Alabama Margaret A. Ratchford, daughter of Abner and Nancy Webb, formerly of Elbert County, Georgia. The deceased left to lament their bereavement a husband, four small children, a father and mother, three brothers and a sister...

Eli J. Walker of Macon County, Alabama died on the 26th of January 1857 in the city of Philadelphia. Mr. Walker was an amiable young man of promising talents; had studied medicine in this place under Dr. Johnston; went to medical College in Philadelphia, to graduate, and fell a victim by death in the twenty-sixth year of his age...

Married in Columbus, Georgia on the evening of the 11th inst. by the Rev. Thos. B. Slade, Mr. Edmund S. Roberts to Miss Mary A. Whiteside.

2-26-1857

Died in Perry County, Alabama on the 12th inst. Robert B., son of Samuel and Mary A. Richardson, age fourteen years, one month, twelve days. The deceased was taken with typhoid fever in September which brought on dropsy.

3-5-1857

Married on the 26th February by the Rev. Sam'l Henderson, Mr. James A. Wright to Miss Nancy M. Gibson, daughter of C. Gibson, all of Macon County, Alabama.

## Marriage and Death Notices From The South Western Baptist Newspaper

Departed this life on the 23rd of January 1857, Mr. Willis H. Wood, son of Matthew and Mourning Wood, late of Talladega County, Alabama, in the seventeenth year of his age. On the 24th of December he ate a quantity of ice and was on the 25th attacked with typhus fever so violently that all medical aid which could be obtained proved of no avail... During his protracted illness, which reduced him to a mere emaciated form, he bore all his suffering without complaint until the 23rd of January, a few minutes after 7 o'clock in the afternoon, when he calmly fell asleep. Mr. Wood was born on the 11th of March 1842 in Talladege County, Alabama; moved with his father to this (Smith County, Texas) during the fall of 1855...

TRIBUTE OF RESPECT from Providence Church, Chambers County, Alabama, dated 2-21-1857, upon the death of Mrs. Nancy Jackson, widow of Rev. Wyche Jackson, which occurred in the 17th February, 1857, formerly of Wilkes County, Georgia. She was in her sixty-seventh year, and had been a consistent member of the Baptist Church for nearly thirty-five years. She joined at Rehoboth, Wilkes County, Georgia, in 1822, where she lived until the winter of 1833, at which time she moved with the family to this state.

Died in Barbour County, Alabama on the 2? February 1857 of dropsy at the heart, Alexander Moton, son of William J. and Eliza Ann Bush, age six years, four months, three days. The *Charleston Christian Advocate* will please copy.

3-12-1857
Our dearly beloved sister, Miss Louisa Johnson, daughter of Brother J.J. Johnson and Sister Gracy Johnson of Coosa County, Alabama, departed this life on the 7th day of December 1856 in the nineteenth year of her age...

Died at the residence of her father in Macon County on the 2nd day of February last, Miss Elizabeth E. Germany, daughter of G.W. and Lucinda J. Germany, age nineteen years, one month, twenty-three days. In August 1852 Miss G. made a profession of religion and was baptized into the fellowship of the Town Creek Baptist Church by Elder F.H. Moss, the pastor...

3-19-1857
Married on the 12th inst. by Rev. Samuel Henderson, Mr. William E. Coleman of Monroe, Alabama to Miss Mary E. Benson of Macon County, Alabama.

Married on the 4th inst. at the residence of Origon Sibley of Baldwin County, Alabama by Rev. P.E. Collins, Mr. N.R. King of Montevallo, Shelby County, Alabama to Miss Salome E. Sibley.

Married on the 5th of March 1857 in Columbia, South Carolina by Rev. Mr. Prichard, Anderson Holmes of Perry County, Alabama to Mrs. Mary Ann Arthur.

Died at Union Point, Georgia on the 17th of March inst. Mr. LeRoy P. Caldwell of the firm of Baldwin, Star & Co., Clothing Merchants, New York in the thirty-first year of his age. The disease of which he died was tubercular consumption. About two months before his death he decided upon a trip to

## Marriage and Death Notices From The South Western Baptist Newspaper

the milder climate of Florida in the hope that the change would give a favorable turn to the disease. Arriving in Savannah it assumed a more malignant form, thence he removed to Charleston where a brother met him to bestow those kind attentions suggested by the warmest fraternal sympathy. As the disease advanced Mr. C. became impressed with the desire to return to the residence of his parents in Tuskegee... Hearing of his condition, the mother and another brother met him in Augusta Georgia... he begged to continue the journey but upon reaching Union Point, it was discovered he was sinking so fast that further progress was abandoned... His remains were brought to Tuskegee and interred by the Masonic fraternity...

Died on the 13th of January last, Rev. Sam'l Stanton, age sixty-four years... Brother Stanton died away from home and family where he had gone to prepare for removing his family from Columbia, Arkansas...

In memory of Adelia A. West, who died February 11th, age two years, two months, nine days. Burnsville, March 10th.

Died: Little Johnie McConaughy, age five years. Burnsville, March 10th.

Died on Wednesday morning, 11th inst. at Seales' Station, Russell County, Alabama, William Crolius, son of Thaddeus B. and Mary B. Scott, age one year, five months, twenty-six days.

Died in Dale County, Alabama on the 9th of February 1857, Susan Alabama, youngest daughter of Rev. Caswell and Susan Smith, age three years, one month, ten days; after seven days sickness of scarlet fever.

3-26-1857
Married on the 10th inst. in Edgefield District, South Carolina at his residence by the Rev. Iverson I. Brooks, Mr. Ashley C. Wood of Alabama to Miss Margaret Josephine Brooks of South Carolina.

4-2-1857
Died in Cherokee County, Georgia on the 19th of January, A.D. 1857, Deacon William Sanders. The deceased was born January 23rd, 1777. He united with the Baptist Church at Moriah, formerly Oglethorpe, now Madison County, Georgia, about the year 1802, of which church he continued to be a member for about forty years or more and then removed and united with the church at Union in the same county... At the time of his death he was removing from Madison to Gordon County, Georgia; was taken sick on the road on Saturday evening; was carried to the house of a friend where he lingered until Monday morning when he quietly fell asleep... His remains were carried to Gordon County and deposited in the church yard where he expected to become a member if he had lived.

## Marriage and Death Notices From The South Western Baptist Newspaper

4-9-1857

Married on Tuesday, March 31st by the Rev. T.J. Rutledge, Dr. George B. Slaughter to Miss Sidney A.B. Henderson, both of Warrior Stand, Macon County, Alabama.

Married on the 12th ult. by Rev. J.H. Smith, Mr. Lafayette Henderson to Miss Mary Jane Burney, all of Pike County, Alabama

Mrs. M.E. Terrell died on the 1st day of April inst., in the twenty-fourth year of her age, and Mr. Joseph H. Terrell died on the 2nd inst., in his twenty-ninth year; the wife and the husband, and in the evening of the 3rd, they were entombed in the same grave. Mrs. Terrell was the daughter of Wm. and Lucy Terrell of Madison, Georgia... Two little children, one of them an infant of a few months, survive...

4-16-1857

Married on Wednesday morning, 8th April by Rev. A.T.M. Handey, Mr. J.W. Swearingen of Macon County to Miss Sarah M. Kinnebrew of Tallapoosa County, Alabama.

Married on Thursday evening, April 9th by the same, Mr. William B. Salter of Pike County to Miss A.E.L. Lloyd of Macon County, Alabama.

Died at the residence of her son, Warren J. Jordan, in Barbour County, Alabama near Midway on the 28th March 1857, Mrs. Lovicy M. Jordan, wife of Thomas G. Jordan, age sixty-four years, three months, seven days. She connected herself with the Long Creek Baptist Church in Warren County, Georgia November 1816 and continued to be a member of the Baptist Church until her death, at which time she was a member of Mount Zion Church, Macon County, Alabama.

4-23-1857

Miss Mary E., daughter of Gen. George W. Gunn, died in this place on the 15th inst.

4-30-1857

Departed this life April 3rd, 1857 Mrs. Jane Mattison, consort of Benjamin Mattison, Oxford, Alabama, age seventy years, two months, twenty-nine days. The deceased was born in Laurens District, South Carolina, January 4th, 1787; was married February 26th, 1805; moved to Alabama in 1818; professed religion in 1828 and was baptized into the fellowship of the Old Enon Church, Jefferson County...

Died on the 18th of March at the residence of his son-in-law, James Vance, in Bibb County, John A. Woods, age fifty-five years, twelve days. Brother Woods was born in Pendleton District, South Carolina; removed from there to Tennessee with his father when small and from thence to Bibb County, Alabama in 1817. In 1822 he was married to Mary Calfee by whom he had eight children. In 1832 he professed religion and though raised by

## Marriage and Death Notices From The South Western Baptist Newspaper

Presbyterian parents he united with the Baptist Church at Mt. Moriah, Bibb County... Some four or five years ago he removed to Mississippi; shortly after which time he became sorely afflicted and from which he never recovered. Last winter he returned to Bibb County in company with his wife with a view of spending the winter and perhaps the next summer in that region in the hope that it would prove beneficial to his health...

Henry M. Cushman, esq., business editor of the *Charleston Courier*, died in Charleston on the 15th inst.

Maj. Jas. Jackson, formerly professor in Franklin College, died on the 26th ult. in Gainsville, Alabama.

5-7-1857

Married at Notasulga, Alabama on the morning of the 3rd of May 1857 by the Rev. Charles S. Burkes, W.E. Winn, esq. to Miss Mary E. Brawner.

Married on the 5th inst. by Rev. H.E. Taliferro, Robert D. Harvey, esq. of Rome, Georgia to Miss Sarah P. Armstrong of Notasulga, Alabama.

Died at the residence of his brother in Cotton Valley on the 10th of April, Mewton E. Gary, M.D., age twenty-four years...

Mary Eleanor Gunn, daughter of G.W. and Mary A. Gunn, was born in LaFayette, Alabama, April 17th, 1839, and died in Tuskegee, Alabama, April 15th, 1857...

Died near Burnsville, March 29th, Mrs. Jane Whitman, age thirty-one years. She leaves a husband and two lovely little children... an only sister, and aged mother...

Mrs. Eliza Penn, consort of William S. Penn and daughter of James and Rebecca White, died in Cotton Valley, Alabama, April 16th, 1857, in the forty-second year of her age. She was born and reared in Greene County, Georgia where she married in December 1834. The family came to Alabama in 1838 and in 1844 Mrs. Penn joined the Methodist Church. She has left a disconsolate husband and ten children (one an infant)...

Died at her residence near Wedowee in Randolph County, Alabama, Eliza Ann Bowen, in the twenty-sixth year of her age. This devoted lady was born the 7th day of August 1830 in the state of Georgia; and in the year 1848 was converted and became a member of the Baptist Church and from that time she lived an exemplary Christian life to the day of her death which was April 1st, 1857. She has left an affectionate husband and six children...

5-14-1857

Died near Norristown, Arkansas of scarlet fever on the 18th of February last, Mary Susan, youngest daughter of James M. and Susan E. Veazey, age five years, two months, sixteen days. And on the 23rd of February their youngest son, William Walter, age one year, six months, nineteen days, of same disease.

## MARRIAGE AND DEATH NOTICES FROM THE SOUTH WESTERN BAPTIST NEWSPAPER

Died at her late residence in Chambers County, Alabama on the 15th April Mrs. Elizabeth, the wife of Alexander B. Kennedy in the sixty-fifth year of her age. The deceased was a native and for many years a resident of Georgia. Born in 1792... The deceased was the mother of eighty? [this must be eight] children, two of whom had gone before...

Departed this life after a protracted illness of several weeks on the 26th of April 1857, at the residence of her youngest son in Butler County, Alabama, Mrs. Ann Bishop, age seventy-five years. The deceased was born in the state of Virginia and in company with her parents became one of the early settlers of Knox County, Tennessee. In the year 1832, having made a profession of religion, united with the Beaver Dam Baptist Church... Subsequently, she with a few others were organized into a church, called Good Hope, in Talladega Alabama...

Died near Auburn, Alabama, May 6th, 1857 of dysentery, at the residence of her parents, in the ninth year of her age, Anna Martha, eldest daughter of F.M. and Mary T. Reese...

5-21-1857
Died... on the morning of the 6th of May, Lauretta, youngest child of George and France Morgan, in the twenty-first year of her age, after an illness of three weeks... Six days more, on the 12th inst. and the mother followed...Mrs. Francis Morgan, daughter of John and Christiana Irby and consort of George Morgan, was in the sixty-second year of her age...

Departed this life in Macon County, Alabama, May 7th, 1857 after an illness of fifteen days, James Thornton, son of George A. and Martha Ann Thornton, aged four years, six months, fifteen days.

5-28-1857
Married at the residence of the bride's father on Tuesday evening 19th inst. by Rev. H.E. Taliaferro, Mr. Joseph A. Ousley of Bibb County, Georgia to Miss Angeline R., daughter of Wm. Rushing of this county.

Died of scarlet fever on Wednesday 13th inst. Narcissa, daughter of Ira T. and Mary Jordan, age two years, four months, two days.

FERDINAND CLEMENTS: Died on the 21st February last, age fifteen years, six days, at the residence of his father Dr. A Clements, Bibb County, Alabama, after a painful illness of seventeen days, occasioned by the accidental firing of a gun, passing the full charge through, and dreadfully mangling the arm between the shoulder and elbow, which induced inflammation that could not be controlled by medical skill...

6-4-1857
Married at Greenwood on the 12th ult. by Rev. A.T.M. Handy, Mr. E.A. Roberts to Miss M.C. Foy.

## Marriage and Death Notices From The South Western Baptist Newspaper

And on the 26th ult. by the same, Dr. Wm. S. Mabson to Miss Gileam Farley, all of Macon County, Alabama.

On the 21st ult. by Elder Abner R. Callaway of Greenville, California [Georgia?], Mr. J. Mercer Callaway and Miss N. Victoria Hill of LaGrange, Georgia.

Departed this life on Saturday 4th of April 1857 after a protracted illness of four weeks of typhoid fever at the residence of his brother in Chambers County, Alabama, Enoch Calloway Tolbot, third son of John R. and Lucy Tolbot late of Wilkes County, Georgia, in the twenty-second year of his age. The deceased was born in Wilkes County, Georgia...

Died of bloody flux at West Point on the 21st of May 1857, Thomas R., son of Thomas and Margaret J. Roberts, age three years, three months, two days.

Died on the evening of the same day (21st of May), sister Carrie W., consort of Mr. James A. Bass, one of the merchants of this place, of pneumonia after an illness of four days, age thirty years, one month, eleven days...,The husband is comfortless and the three little children are motherless. Sister Bass was the daughter of Eli McMilan, formerly of Green County, Georgia.

Died at his father's residence near Midway, Barbour County, Alabama on Saturday the 9th inst.' Thomas George, eldest son of Ira T. and Mary Jordan, after a short but painful illness of four days, of scarlet fever, age eleven years, five months, seven days...

Departed this life on the 5th day of April 1857 at the residence of her son the Rev. Joseph Bankston, in Coosa County, Alabama, Mrs. Mary Bankston, consort of the late Rev. John Bankston of Gwinnett County, Georgia, in the ninetieth year of her age.

6-11-1857
Sallie Chiles, daughter of Elder Samuel Henderson and Mrs. Eliza Henderson, died June 3rd, 1857, age about two years.

Died in Enon, Alabama on the 1st day of June, Alice Rembert, daughter of Wm. E. and E.T. Dubose, age three years, ten months.

Neil C. Smith departed this life 20th of May 1857, in the forty-sixth year of his age. He was born in South Carolina, Cheraw District, and moved to Tuskegee, Alabama February 1842...

Died on the 15th day of May 1858 at her residence Chunnenuggee, Alabama, Mrs. Mary L. Randal, wife of Henry H. Randal, and daughter of Joseph and Polly Cotton. The deceased was born October 14th, 1823 and when about fourteen years old made a profession of faith... Was baptized into the fellowship of Mount Zion Church, Monroe County, Georgia... Removing to Alabama she became a member of Chunnenuggee Church and continued so until its dissolution in 1854 when she united with Mount Zion Church, Macon County, Alabama... Leaves a husband and five children...

Died at his father's residence in Barbour County on the 17th inst., Thomas J., infant son of Mary and Abram Starke, age one year, five months, fifteen days.

## Marriage and Death Notices From The South Western Baptist Newspaper

John H. Milner was baptized at the age of sixteen years by the Rev. Jesse Mercer and commenced preaching about the year 1828... Died at his residence in Pike County, Georgia the 9th of March 1857, age sixty-four years, seven months, thirteen days... He died in about seven hours after his attack...

6-18-1857
Died on the 13th May 1857, Robt. C. Robison, age one year, twenty-eight days, son of Maj. R.C. and Mrs. Martha Robison of Warrior Stand, Macon County, Alabama.
Departed this life after a protracted illness of many years on the 23rd of May at her residence in Macon County, Alabama, Mrs. F.E. Lloyd, wife of the late W.S. Lloyd...
Miss Almira Strange McCreary, daughter of Joseph H. and Almira McCreary of Conecuh County, Alabama, died in Tuskegee on the night of the 11th day of June 1857 in her seventeenth year. Miss M. entered the Tuskegee (Methodist) Female College last October...
Charlotte Corday Campbell, youngest daughter of John D. and Charlotte Campbell, born December 25th, 1851 and died May 10th, 1857.

6-25-1857
Married by Rev. O. Welch on the 10th of June, Dr. Joseph C. Blake and Miss Caroline V. Scott, daughter of Rev. J.M. Scott, all of Shelby County, Alabama.
Departed this life on the 14th inst., May, daughter of Daniel and Mueidora Say??, age nine years, eight months, seventeen days. This is the fifth and last daughter of these stricken parents, her two older sisters having died near twelve years since at Talladega and her two younger only a few days before, Gem on the 21st day of May, age four years, nineteen days; and Ella on the 25th of the same month, age one year, six months, twenty-one days...
Died on Friday the 5th inst. at her residence in Tuskegee, Alabama, Miss Mary Ann Womack, daughter of the late Wilie and Amelia Womack...
Died in Tuskegee on the 11th inst., little Lizzie, infant daughter of Col. William B. Bowen, age one year, five months. The mother of little Lizzie died in Georgia just ? months before while on a visit to her relations and was brought to Tuskegee for interment.
Died in Columbia, South Carolina on Sunday the 14th inst., Mr. M. S. Kelton, one of the oldest citizens of Tuskegee. Mr. K. leaves a wife and five children...
Died at West Point on Thursday evening the 4th inst. of diarrhea after a short illness, sister Patsy Morris, consort of Mr. Lewis Morris of this place; age fifty-one years...

## Marriage and Death Notices From The South Western Baptist Newspaper

7-2-1857
Died at his residence in Monroe County, Alabama on the 19th inst. of protracted illness, Rev. J.J. Sessions, member and pastor of Concord Church... [see 7-16-1857]
Died on the 11th inst., Edward Callaway, in the seventy-sixth year of his age. The deceased formerly lived near Forsyth, Monroe County, Georgia but at his death was living with his daughter in Macon County, Alabama...
Died in Helicon, Lowndes County, Alabama on the 14th of May last, Mrs. Jane E. Graham, consort of Mr. Duncan Graham, and second daughter of Mr. W.B. Bond of Macon County, Alabama, in her twenty-fourth year, leaving an infant about two weeks old...
Died at the residence of her father, Capt. Levi Jones, in Macon County, Alabama on the 25th May 1857, Mrs. Eliphar Arnold, wife of Anderson Arnold, in the thirty-first year of her age... Leaves husband and five children.
Sister Elizabeth Reed, wife of Brother Benjamin Reed, and daughter of Larkin Stewart, died at the residence of her husband near Demopolis in Marengo County, Alabama on Thursday the 28th day of May 1857, in the forty-third year of her age.

7-16-1857
The Rev. J.J. Sessions is no more. He expired on the 19th of June 1857 at his residence in Monroe County, Alabama, age fifty-two years, two months, sixteen days. He was born in the state of South Carolina on the 3rd of April 1805, emigrated to Alabama in early life and was married in December 1826... The spring of 1833 united with the Bear Creek Baptist Church, Wilcox County, Alabama... [see 7-2-1857]
Married in Columbus, Georgia on the 2nd inst. by Rev. J.H. DeVotie, Mr. Henry Drakeford of Tuskegee to Miss Mary Ann, daughter of G.B. Terry of Columbus.
Departed this life on the morning of the 6th July, sister Nancy Hudson, wife of Isaac Hudson, esq. of Talladega County. Sister Hudson joined the Talladega Church by letter in October 1833. She was afflicted for many years with asthma but was finally taken off by dysentery...
Died at his father's residence in Macon County, Alabama on the 20th day of June 1857, John J. Pierce, infant son of G.J. and S.A. Pierce, age one year, seven months, four days.
Died in Bibb County, Alabama June 7th, Amanda Norwood, daughter of Elizabeth Norwood, age twenty-seven years, six months. Her disease was diarrhea. J.M. Norwood.

7-23-1857
Departed this life at the residence of his father in Perryville, Perry County, Alabama on Saturday the 11th of July 1857 after a short illness, Mr. Jesse G. Cochran, son of the Rev. William L. Cochran, in the eighteenth year of his age. He was born the 8th of September 1839...

## Marriage and Death Notices From The South Western Baptist Newspaper

Departed this life in full assurance of the Christian's hope at 8 o'clock p.m. on the 4th of July last, Mrs. Sabrina S. Holden, consort of Benjamin Holden, esq. of Jackson County, Florida, and the daughter of the late Rev. Hermon Mercer, in the forty-eighth year of her age.

7-30-1857
Died at his father's residence in Tallapoosa County, Alabama on the 9th inst. in the fifteenth year of his age Benjamin T., oldest son of Rev. James M. and Virginia E. Russell, late of Chambers County. The deceased was a regular member of the Central Institute in Coosa County for two years...
Died in Talladega April 2nd, Benjamin Spence, in the sixtieth year of his age.
Died in Talladega April 12th, Nancy Spence, in the twenty-second year of her age.
Since the above was written, sister Spence has left to join her husband and daughter, whose deaths are recorded above, and a son who died some months before...
Died near McKinley, Marengo County, Alabama on the 26th day of June 1857 after a protracted illness, John Jackson, in the seventy-second year of his age. He was born in the state of Virginia on the 30th day of October 1785. He resided a short time in South Carolina then in Kentucky and settled in Alabama Territory in the year 1818 where he resided until his death...Joined the Baptist Church in 1829...

8-6-1857
Rarely if ever has it fallen to the lot of the writer of this to record so painful an affliction as has recently befallen our beloved brother, Thomas Carson, Deacon of Mt. Lebanon Church, Dallas County; as will appear from the following:

First, his infant daughter, Martha Pauline, was taken with cholera infantum and died May 22nd, 1857 after an illness of only four days; age one year, six months, twenty-three days.

Second his next daughter, Laura Sims, was taken with a prevalent epidemic and died May 31st, 1857 after an illness of only six days, age four years, seven months, twenty-seven days.

Lastly his devoted and pious wife was taken ill of the same epidemic and departed this life in the short period of eight days from the time she was taken... Angeline Elizabeth Waldron was born June 4th, 1824 and was married to Deacon Thomas A. Carson, March 4th, 1841 and in August of the same year was baptized into the fellowship of Mt. Lebanon Church, Dallas County, Alabama. She departed this life June 19th, 1857, in the thirty-third year of her age.

## MARRIAGE AND DEATH NOTICES FROM THE SOUTH WESTERN BAPTIST NEWSPAPER

8-13-1857
Died at his residence in Barbour County, Alabama on the 13th of May, Mr. George D. Hodges, in the twenty-third year of his age. Mr. Hodges was born in Harris County, Georgia but had spent most of his life near where he died... He was taken away from hence wither he had gone to attend a course of medical lectures. He succeeded in reaching home where many kind friends and loving hearts awaited his arrival and after long and painful suffering died as above stated.

Died on the 18th day of July at his residence in Barbour County, Alabama, Brother Reuben Thornton, in the fiftieth year of his age, leaving a disconsolate widow and five children, most of them grown... Brother Thornton professed conversion when about fourteen years old... He was baptized into the fellowship of Union Church, Talbot County, Georgia... remaining a member until his removal to Alabama in 1851. He then united with Mt. Zion Church, Macon County...

8-20-1857
Died near Midway, Alabama on the 24th of July last, Mr. James F. Malloy, son of Duncan and Mary Malloy, age nineteen years. The subject of this notice was seized with scarlet fever... He is now in Glory singing hallelujahs with his sisters, Mrs. Bennet and Miss Malloy, who have been there only twelve months...

Mrs. Lucinda J. Germany, wife of G.W. Germany, died in Tuskegee on the 28th of July, in the thirty-seventh year of her age. She had been an exemplary member of the Baptist Church at Town Creek, Alabama for fifteen years. She had been in bad health for many years... She has left behind a husband and children...

8-27-1857
Married on the 4th of August by Rev. C.S. McCloud, Prof. D.W.C. Williams of Mississippi College and Miss Mollie C. Thigpen, both of Clinton, Mississippi.

Married at the residence of Robert Blan on the evening of the 6th inst. by Giles Eaford, esq., Mr. Joshua D. Bostick of Barbour County to Miss Nicey P. Napper, daughter of D. Napper of Henry County, Alabama.

Sister Louisa Hobbs, wife of Brother Wm. Hobbs, Jr., and daughter of our late brother and Deacon Garret Johnston, died at the residence of her husband near Liberty Church, in Talladega County, Alabama on the 27th April 1857 in the twenty-fourth year of her age... left two infant children...

Died on the 21st of last May at her residence in Macon County, Alabama sister Jane Lisenbe, daughter of Silas and Margaret Bryan. Sister Lisenbe was born in Martin County, North Carolina; her parents removed to South Carolina and lived in Marion and Marlboro Districts. She was married to Aaron Lisenbe in the latter District on the 7th of May 1833. They removed to

## Marriage and Death Notices From The South Western Baptist Newspaper

Alabama and settled in Macon County in 1835 where she remained until her death. Sister Lisenbe had been afflicted almost a year... She has left a bereaved husband and five children, three daughters and two sons...

Brother R.J. Marchel departed this life August 7th, 1857. He was about twenty-two years of age... He left his home and friends in Dade County, Georgia about eleven months before his death and came to Butler County, Alabama, some two months after he came to Greenville, Alabama where he united with the Baptist Church and where he closed his earthly career...

9-10-1857
Married on the 30th of August by Rev. W.B. Jones, Mr. James J. Jackson of Atlanta, Georgia to Miss Sarah B. Meriwether of Tuskegee, Alabama.
Died of typhoid fever on the 2nd inst., Sarah Jane, daughter of Mr. and Mrs. Amos Jones of this place, in the eighth year of her age.

9-17-1857
Died on the morning of the 31st of August last, Mr. George W. Lanier, formerly and for several years a citizen of this place. He was born on the 27th of April 1818 and was consequently in the fortieth year of his age...

9-24-1857
Married on the 15th inst. by F.H. Moss, Mr. Barna Ivey to Miss Julia Ann Callaway, all of Macon County.
Married on Thursday evening last, 17th inst. by Rev. Mr. McCarthy, Mr. W.W. Dubose to Miss Emma L. Ivey, both of this county.

10-1-1857
Died, Mrs. Mary Louisa Keitt, wife of Mr. James Keitt, and daughter of Dr. David Johnston of this place. Mrs. Keitt was born in Monroe, Walton County, Georgia, October 26th, 1826. At an early age she was sent to Salem, North Carolina to be educated, where she remained until she completed the course of study... She died at the family residence six miles from Tuskegee, September 8th, 1857... A kind heart stricken husband and two children, sons, one of them quite an infant, a venerable father, brothers, a sister mourn her untimely death...
Died on the 3rd of September last, William Dawsey, son of V.A. and Rebecca Pearson, of congestion of the brain, age seven years, seven months, four days.

10-8-1857
Married on the 22nd September by the Rev. W.G. Conner, Mr. Robert H. Lockhart of Chambers County to Miss Julia E. Adams of Macon County, Alabama.

## Marriage and Death Notices From The South Western Baptist Newspaper

DEAR LITTLE HENRY HORNE is no more! He was next to the youngest child of Brother and Sister D.W. Horne of Orange Hill, Florida, and died suddenly of brain fever on 11th September 1857, age seven years... *Biblical Recorder* (North Carolina) please copy.
Died in Marion on the 19th ult., Bettie R., only child of Shelby and Mary C. King, age thirteen months, six days.
Died at the residence of her mother in Haywood County, Tennessee on the 22nd ult., Mrs. Sarah C. Hatchett, wife of A. Hatchett, esq. of Memphis, Tennessee, and daughter of the late Thomas B. Collier.

10-15-1857
Married on the 1st October by the Rev. J.W. Williams, Mr. James M. Callaway of Harrison County, Texas to Miss Camilla P. Meadors of Chambers County, Alabama.
Married on Thursday evening, 1st inst. by Rev. H.E. Taliaferro, Wm. M. Cooper to Matilda A. Jones, all of Tuskegee.
By the same on Wednesday morning, 7th inst., Geo. E. Kelly to Mrs. Amanda M. Clower, all of Tuskegee.
Married on Thursday the 1st inst. by Rev. S. Henderson, Mr. William W. McGar of Galveston, Texas to Miss Georgia Perry of Macon County, Alabama.
Died, Matilda A. Ivey. She was the eldest of three daughters of Gen. Geo. W. and Mary Ann Gunn all of whom now sleep side by side awaiting the sound of "the trump of God"... Matilda was born in Morgan County, Georgia, February 14th, 1835... Joined the Baptist Church in Tuskegee in the fall of 1851. For several years she was a pupil of the East Alabama Female College; was married to Mr. Malachi Ivey June 28th, 1855. Her health became impaired in the spring of '56 and during the last spring she took measles and has had no health since then. (died 29th September)... The three sisters were: Sarah, Mary and Matilda...
Departed this life at his residence in Autauga County, Alabama on the morning of the 1st of October 1857, Mr. John Lamar in the fifty-ninth year of his age. The subject of this notice was born in the state of Georgia, (county not known to the writer) and brought up in Putnam County till early manhood when he moved to Alabama where he continued to reside (most of the time in Autauga County) till the day of his death. Mr. Lamar joined the Baptist Church in Eatonton, Putnam County, Georgia in 1823...
Jehew Johnston was born December 22nd A.D. 1799 and departed this life August 28th, 1857 in great peace. He was the son of Jehu and Margaret Johnston of South Carolina; was converted and joined the Baptist Church at Bush River Church and was baptized by Rev. H. Rolin of Decatur County, Georgia, where he was well and favorably known as the Georgia Baptist. He removed from thence to Chambers County and from thence to Coosa County, Alabama where he died... He has left a widow and ten children...

## Marriage and Death Notices From The South Western Baptist Newspaper

Died at her residence in Macon County, Alabama on the 11th inst., Mrs. Amy Robertson, age about sixty-seven years. Sister B. made a profession of the religion of Jesus in the summer of 1845 and untied with the Shiloh Baptist Church, Troup County, Georgia...

10-22-1857
Married in the city of Richmond, Virginia by Rev. B. Manly, Jr. on Thursday morning October 8th, 1857, Mr. Geo. L. Wimberley of Edgecombe County, North Carolina to Miss Fanny J. Whitfield, daughter of the late Rev. George W. Whitfield of Gainsville, Alabama.
Married on the 1st of October by Elder F.H. Moss, Mr. Jesse A. Devore to Miss Sarah J. Thomas, all of Macon County, Alabama.
Married on the 6th inst. by the Rev. M.N. Eley, Mr. John B. Martin to Mrs. Susannah Bell, all of Macon County, Alabama.
Adaline M. Bozeman, wife of M. Bozeman, and daughter of E.D. and Eliza M. Perryman, died near Auburn, Alabama, October 13th, 1857. She was the mother of five children...
Ann Eliza, daughter of Ann J. and Jeremiah Dunaway, departed this life on the 22nd of September 1857...
Died in Yanceyville, North Carolina on the morning of October 10th, Mrs. Isabella H. Tobey, wife of Rev. Thomas W. Tobey.

10-29-1857
Married in the city of Selma, October 14th, 1857 by Rev. A.G. McCraw, Mr. Merritt Burns to Miss Eliza L. Law.
Died in LaGrange, Georgia on the 13th inst. N.J. Wyne of Forkland, Greene County, Alabama. He died away from home and family, but among his brethren. His corpse was brought home by Brother H.E. Brooks before his family and friends knew of his decease. May the grace of God sustain his bereaved wife and little daughter.
Died on Thursday morning last in the vicinity of Burnt Corn, Alabama, Susan E., consort of D.W. Harris, and eldest daughter of Sthiel and Emily Lee, age twenty-six years...

11-5-1857
Married on Tuesday evening, October 27th by Rev. Willis B. Jones, Mr. Luther M. Rush to Mrs. Ann E. Breedlove, all of Tuskegee.
On the 14th of October by Rev. J.J. Harris, Mr. Chas. B. Gachet to Miss Mary Josephine Morton, both of Barbour County, Alabama.
Married by Elder A. VanHoose on the 28th ult. in Eufaula, Alabama, Mr. C.H. Perry of Blakely, Georgia to Miss E.C. Willard of Eufaula, Alabama.
By the same on the 29th ult. Elder E.Y. VanHoose to Mrs. Sarah A. Stbinger [Stringer?] both of Clayton, Alabama.

## Marriage and Death Notices From The South Western Baptist Newspaper

Died at the residence of her father, George W. Germany, in Tuskegee on the 8th day of October 1857, Miss Mary L. Germany, age about fourteen years. Miss G. never made an open profession of religion but the death of her mother a few months previously appeared to have very seriously affected her mind.

Frederick Porter died at his residence in Sumter County, Alabama on the 12th of October 1857, age fifty-three years... He was born in Washington County, Georgia; joined the Baptist Church at Eufaula in 1839; married Amelia Talbot; was a member of Columbia Church. He removed to Sumter County in 1851. Belonged to the Livingston Church and at the time of his death was a member of the Jones Creek Church...

Tribute of respect on the death of Henry F. Lake, who died on the 19th inst.

11-12-1857
Married in Montgomery County on Thursday evening, October 15th by Rev. A.T.M. Handy, Mr. Kinchen A. Townsend to Miss Cornelia E. Howard.

And on Thursday morning, October 29th, by the same, Mr. Thomas C. Daniel of Selma to Miss Mary J. Haggerty of Montgomery County.

Died of typhoid fever on the 2nd ult. at his residence near Columbiana, Shelby County, Alabama, J.H. Lawler. He was born 12th July 1829 and joined the Baptist Church at Mt. Zion, Talladega County, Alabama, about the age of fifteen.

Died on the 18th of September last near Orion, Alabama, Mrs. Sarah Jane Park, consort of Mr. R.E. Park, in the thirty-second year of her age, leaving four children, an affectionate husband...

Died in Forsyth County, Georgia on the 2nd of September last, Mrs. Elizabeth Pool, wife of Young P. Pool, in the fifty-third year of her age.

Died in the same county on the 25th day of the same month, Wm. Y. Pool, in the twenty-sixth year of his age. Mr. Pool leaves a wife and two small children...

Died in Cass County, Georgia on the 8th ult., George Washington Pool, in the twenty-third year of his age...

Died in Forsyth County, Georgia on the 10th ult., Mrs. Emily C. Bentley, consort of Jeremiah Bentley, in the thirty-fifth year of her age... The papers at Greenville, South Carolina, *Southern Christian Advocate*, Charleston & Wetumpka, Alabama papers requested by the relatives of the deceased to copy. Vickory's Creek, Georgia; W.D.B.

11-19-1857
Died at the residence of Dr. Willis Wills in Clinton, Alabama, October 5th, 1857, Miss Josephine Maxwell, daughter of Col. Simeon and Elizabeth Maxwell, age about eighteen years.

## Marriage and Death Notices From The South Western Baptist Newspaper

Mrs. Selena Jeter, the subject of this notice was born on the 1st of January 1815 and was the daughter of Joshua and Sarah Haggerty of Montgomery County, Alabama. She was married to Elder James W. Jeter on the 22nd of January 1834 and subsequently removed with her husband to Coosa County and settled ten miles northeast of Wetumpka, a destitute wild society...

Died in Murfreesboro, Tennessee, July 15th, 1857, Miss Anna C. Tharin, daughter of D.C. Tharin, of Lowndes County, Alabama. The subject of this brief notice was born April 7th, 1836... During the last two years of her life, her sufferings were great... Four times with the hope of arresting the fell disease (cancer) did she submit to the surgeon's knife without complaint. As a last expedient she was taken by her father to Dr. January, of Murfreesboro, Tenn...

11-26-1857
Married on the 27th October at Lawrenceville, Gwinnett County, Georgia by Rev. Samuel Henderson, the Rev. W.N. Eley of Union Springs, Macon County, Alabama to Mrs. Emily S. Williams.

Died, Miss Harriet Catharine Coats, which occurred on the 4th of September at the house of her sister, Mrs. Lilly in Enterprise, Mississippi. Her age was just fifteen years, ten months, thirteen days. She was the daughter of our Brother W.W. Coats, a Deacon in the Baptist Church at Gaston, Sumter County, Alabama...

Orange Hill, Florida, November 11th, 1857: In deep distress I have to record the death of our excellent and very dear Brother Duke W. Horne... He breathed his last at 7 1/2 o'clock p.m. on the 4th inst...

12-3-1857
Married on the 22nd of November by U.L. Jones, esq., Mr. John H. Smith of Butler County, Alabama to Mrs. Matilda D. Johnson of Troy, Pike County, Alabama.

Married in Tuskegee, Tuesday, December 1st, at the residence of Dr. J. R. Hand by the Rev. Willis B. Jones, Mr. Thomas B. Dryer of Tuskegee, Alabama to Miss Annie E. Chambliss.

12-10-1857
Married on the 25th of November by J.L. Dagg, D.D., N.K. Davis of Howard College to Miss Ella C. Hunt of Albany, Georgia.

Died in this county on the 14th November 1857 of typhoid fever, James Thomas Robertson, in the thirty-third year of his age... Was baptized by his father Rev. John Robertson. He leaves behind a father, a disconsolate widow and three small children, also brothers and sisters...

Died at his residence in Tuscaloosa County, Alabama after a painful illness of one week, occasioned by severe cold, on Tuesday night the 17th inst., age seventy-three years, sixteen days, Daniel Burgen. He was born in Warren

## Marriage and Death Notices From The South Western Baptist Newspaper

County, Georgia and moved to this county when it was first settled; purchased and improved a farm; raised a respectable family... He leaves an aged wife and many relations...

W.M. Freeman departed this life at his residence in Surry County, North Carolina on 1st November, 1857...

Died at his residence in Shelby County, Alabama on the 22nd of November 1857, James S. Williamson, after protracted suffering... The subject of this notice was born February 25, 1837; united with the Baptist Church at Macedonia, St. Clair County, Alabama... He has left a father and four sisters...

Died at the residence of her husband in Montgomery County, Alabama November 9th, 1857, Mrs. Mary Caffey, wife of B.F. Caffey, in the twenty-fifth year of her age. The deceased was born on the 17th February 1833... She married in December 1852...

Died in Macon County on the 20th November 1857, Adoniram Judson, son of John J. and Martha Jones, age one year, eleven months, four days.

12-17-1857

Married on the 3rd inst. near Pine Level, Montgomery County, Alabama by Elder J.A. Fonville, Mr. Newton Evans to Miss Mary A.R. Dickson.

Married in Tuskegee, Alabama on the 3rd inst. at 4 o'clock by the Rev. Wesley Rush, Col. B.F. Foster of Glennville to Mrs. Martha A. Martin.

Married on the morning of the 3rd inst. by W.N. Hutchins, esq. (at the Perry House in Columbus, Georgia), Milton J. Glaze and Miss Frances Frazier, all of Alabama.

Departed this life on the 12th November 1857 after an illness of ten days, Houston, son of Epheldred and Virlinda Thomas of Coosa County, Alabama, in the sixteenth year of his age. On the 2nd of November he was attacked with pneumonia...

Margaret Simmons, daughter of Dr. Thomas Graves, died on the 28th of November 1857, in the thirty-eighth year of her age... Six children are left...

12-24-1857

Married in this county on the 17th ult. by Elder A.T.M. Handey, Mr. Stephen W. Gardner and Miss Margaret A. Parker.

On the 14th inst. at La Place by the same, Rev. William E. Lloyd and Miss Susan Reid, all of Macon County.

On the 18th inst. at Union Springs by the Rev. Sam'l Henderson, Dr. Wiley D.F. Kelly to Miss Sarah E. Wimberly, all of Macon County.

BRETHREN HENDERSON & TALLAFERRO: As once personal friends of the deceased, you will notice in your widely circulated paper the demise of Mrs. M.E. Lake, late consort of Mr. James Lake, and daughter of the late Col. W.D. and Mrs. L.P. Lovell, and grand-daughter of the late N. and E. Scales, deceased. Departed this life at the residence of her husband (Cave Springs, Georgia) on the 1st of May 1857 after an illness of one month. She was born

## Marriage and Death Notices From The South Western Baptist Newspaper

in Greensborough, Alabama, April 12th, 1823, finished her education in Tuscaloosa, was married in Talladega County, November 30th, 1846. In the winter of 1848, her husband, with Col. Lovell and family, settled at the beautiful and quiet village of C.S...

1-7-1858
Married in Athens, Georgia on Tuesday, December 22nd at the residence of Mr. J.L. Whitman by the Rev. H.H. Parks, Mr. James L. Caldwell of Tuskegee, Alabama to Miss Laura J. Whitman of Athens, Georgia.
Married on Thursday evening the 17th December by Elder A.C. Thomason at the residence of Mrs. Herrin, Mr. John B. Hogan of Bibb County, Alabama to Miss Huldah Herrin of Tuscaloosa County, Alabama.
Married in Clayton, Alabama on the 23rd of December by E.Y. VanHoose, Elder Jesse Robinson of Calhoun County, Georgia to Mrs. Susan K. Cowart of Eufaula, Alabama.
On the 28th of December by the same Mr. Wilson Smart of Texas to Miss Georgiann Warren of Barbour County, Alabama.
Married on the 17th of December by Rev. G. Longmire, Seaborn Moore to Miss Martha J. Mangham, all of Butler County, Alabama.
Martha H. Nicholson, wife of G.W. Nicholson, died near Warrior Stand, 5th December 1857...
Mrs. Sarah Booth died November 13th, 1857. She was the second daughter of Daniel and Mary Dees. She was born in the state of Alabama, Talladega County, in the year 1837. Her father moved to Arkansas, Columbia County in 1850. She was married to Walter Booth in 1854... She had left a husband and child...
Departed this life, Mobile, November 13th, 1857, Rachel R. Borum, daughter of John Grant, esq., and wife of James C. Borum, Deacon of St. Francis Street Baptist Church. The subject of this notice was born May 5th, 1829. She was married to Brother B., February 12, 1846, and united with the church February 10, 1848.

1-28-1858
Departed this life on the 3rd day of September last after an illness of a few hours, Joseph Ray, age eighty-seven years, six months. The subject of this notice was born in the state of Virginia about the year 1770... When he was a small boy his father moved to North Carolina and after a few years to the state of Kentucky... soon afterwards he moved to the state of Tennessee and after a few years residence in Warren County he moved to the state of Alabama and settled in Shelby County; and there united with the church by letter at Hebron; he remained there six years and moved to Coosa valley, and there united by letter with the church at Big Spring; he remained there until the settling of the Creek Indian country; he was an early settler in Talladega County; lived there until about 1834 when he moved to Coosa County and

## Marriage and Death Notices From The South Western Baptist Newspaper

lived there until the year 1848 or '49; after his youngest child of twelve had married he and his wife emigrated to Texas and settled in Smith County near Tyler, and after a residence of five years they moved to Barbour County, Alabama... The deceased has left an aged widow and eleven children...

2-4-1858
Died in Clinton at the residence of her father, W.W. Paschal, on the 13th inst. (1858) after an illness of three weeks, Miss Belle Paschal.
Died in Shelby County, Alabama, January 16th, 1858 after a short but severe attack of pneumonia, Mark A. Cole, in the thirty-eighth year of his age. He professed religion in 1846 and joined the Baptist Church at New Hope, Lincoln County, Georgia where he then resided. In 1852 he removed to Alabama and united himself with the Baptist Church at Spring Creek, Shelby County in which he continued an exemplary member till death severed the connection...
Died at her residence in Perry County, Alabama, Sister Mar?aret Tubb on the 19th of November 1857, the consort of the late Richard Tubb, deceased. The subject of this notice was born in the state of Kentucky and lived to the mature age of sixty-six years. About the year 1817 she embraced the religion of Jesus Christ and she became a member of the Baptist Church...

2-11-1858
Died in the town of Sparta, Alabama, January 28th, 1858, Susan H. Stanly, age twelve days. Little Susan was the fourth child of H.S. & Sarah W. Stanly...
Married on the 3rd of December last by Elder J.T.S. Park, Mr. P.L. Ethridge and Miss Margaret R. Salter, all of Pike County, Alabama.
Married on Thursday the 21st of January by the same, Mr. T.F. Bean and Miss Margaret E. Ethridge, eldest daughter of Malachi Ethridge of Pike County, Alabama.
Married on Tuesday, January 26th, in Farriorville by the same, Mr. L.C. Townsend and Miss Laura F. Williams.

2-18-1858
Married on Tuesday evening the 19th January by Elder Bentley, Mr. Benjamin Walker of Upson County, Georgia to Mrs. Jamima Davis of Crawford County, Georgia.
Married on Thursday morning the 4th February by Elder A.T.M. Handey, Mr. John H. Adams to Miss Martha E. Womack, all of Macon County, Alabama.
Married on Thursday evening, February 11th, by the same, Dr. Bevely W. Walton of Limestone County to Mrs. Fannie Colvard of Macon County, Alabama.
Married in Tuskegee on the 11th inst. by Rev. Mr. Furguson, Mr. H.L. La Plass to Miss M.J. Guatman, all of Tuskegee.

## Marriage and Death Notices From The South Western Baptist Newspaper

WILLIAM GERMANY, Sr. died recently after ten days sickness, in the seventy-fourth year of his age. He was an native of Georgia and removed to Alabama when the Indians inhabited Montgomery County.

3-4-1858
Departed this life, Sister Amanda Ashking, in the thirty-third year of her age.

3-11-1858
Died in Eutaw, Greene County, Alabama, February 12th, Mrs. Martha A. Durham, in the thirty-second year of her age. Sister Durham was born in Greensburg, Kentucky, October 14th, 1825. In April 1848 she came to this town with her late husband...
Reuben Malichi, youngest son of Joseph and Elizabeth Vann, was born July 3rd, 1857; age six months, four days; died January 8th, 1858. He was first attacked by whooping cough, teething commenced soon after and inflammation of the brain ensued...

3-18-1858
Died in Macon County, Alabama on the 12th February 1858 at the residence of her husband, Mr. Samuel Perry, Sister Orra M. Perry, in the forty-second year of her age...
Died in La Place, Alabama on 25 February 1858, Mrs. Mahala Thompson, wife of Mr. Jesse Thompson, in the thirty-ninth year of her age...

3-25-1858
Married on the 19th February 1858 by Rev. James C. Bass, Mr. John B. Dennis to Mary C. Cooper, both of Pike County, Alabama.
Died at his residence in Talladega County, February 18, 1858, Mr. Charles W. Roby, in the fifty-second year of his life. He was born 12th November 1806, and was married to Mrs. Eliza Boswell, March 11th, 1835 since which time he settled five miles south-east of Talladega town... His remains were followed on the 19th February by his friends and relatives to the town of Talladega and interred in the public burying ground with "Masonic Honors." He has left a wife, some orphan children...
Departed this life at Independence, Alabama, February 22nd, Sister Elizabeth Adair, consort of Brother James Adair, in the twentieth year of her age, leaving a husband and a small infant. Sister Adair was the daughter of Madison and Viney Bates. Her father died several years ago after which this beloved sister was taken in care of James and Sarah Nunn...

4-1-1858
Married on the 24th March at her residence in Tuskegee by Rev. S. Henderson, Mr. Thadeus A. Womack of Butler County, Alabama to Miss Attie E. Womack of the former place.

## Marriage and Death Notices From The South Western Baptist Newspaper

Married on Sunday morning, 14th ult. at the residence of Mr. G.W. Arbery (Notasulga, Alabama) by Rev. C.S. Burks, Mr. Anderson W. Arnold and Miss Jane Arbery.

4-15-1858
Died on the morning of the 2nd inst. of pulmonary consumption, Mrs. Sophia Blount Teague, consort of Rev. E.B. Teague, pastor of the Baptist Church, La Grange, Georgia, and daughter of the late Capt. James G. Blount of Tuscaloosa County, Alabama, age thirty-four years. Mrs. Teague was born in Tuscaloosa County, Alabama, December 21st, 1823, baptized by Rev. John A. Hodges into the fellowship of Grant's Creek Baptist Church in the Fall of 1842, married by Rev. Manly to Rev. E.B. Teague on the 15th June 1843. At a very early period in life she was deprived by death of the tender care of a mother. This loss was to a great extent repaired by the kind and generous attention of her relatives, Mr. and Mrs. John S. Bealle, in whose family she was brought up as one of their own children...

4-22-1858
Departed this life on the 9th inst., Sister Susan Farrar, consort of Brother Francis Farrar, daughter of Joel and Media Lee, in the sixtieth year of her age, after a painful and protracted illness... Her afflicted husband, venerable father, with the weight of eighty-six years upon him, a long train of relatives mourn her departure...
Albert Phillips, son of S.G. and C.V. Phillips, departed this life on Monday evening 5th inst., age five years, six months, twenty-seven days, after a severe illness of seven days.
Died at her residence in Autauga County, Alabama, April 6th, 1858, Mrs. Nancy Adair, age sixty-one years, five months, nine days. The deceased ate her breakfast on the morning of death, in her usual health, and went out to attend her domestic business and fell dead in an instant.
Married on the 30th March 1858 by Rev. H.E. Brooks, Jonathan Haralson, esq. of Selma, Alabama to Miss Mattie E., daughter of J.W. Thompson of Muscogee County, Georgia.
Married at the residence of the bride's father, William Burns, by Wm. Nichols, esq. on the 1st April inst., Mr. Lavin Perry to Mrs. Sally A. Cobb, all of Bibb County, Alabama.
Married in the city of Mobile on the 11th inst. by Rev. A.C. Ramsey, Mr. James F. Newberry of Wilcox County, Alabama to Miss Margaret J. Vaughan of Mobile.

4-29-1858
Died near Evergreen, Conecuh County, Alabama on the 1st day of April 1858 Mrs. Margaret Jay, consort of David Jay, in the seventy-first year of her age, leaving behind but two children, a daughter and son, one of whom is

## Marriage and Death Notices From The South Western Baptist Newspaper

responsible for this humble notice. The deceased accompanied my surviving parent to this country from South Carolina in 1818...

Died on the 4th of April 1858 at the residence of Col. Simeon Maxwell, Greene County, Alabama, Drusilla Brown, daughter of Simeon and Elizabeth Maxwell, and wife of Henry Brown, an esteemed Brother and Deacon of Clinton Baptist Church...

5-13-1858

Married on Thursday, 29th April, by the Rev. Sam'l Henderson, Mr. A. Howard of Montgomery, Alabama to Miss Narcissa H. Lewis, daughter of Capt. Lewis of Tuskegee.

Married in Clinton, Green County, Alabama on the 28th April by Rev. S.R. Freeman, Rev. J.R. Webster to Miss Isabella H.L. Higgenbotham.

Married on the evening of the 28th ult. by the Rev. Mr. Peebles, Dr. C.C. Lloyd of Greenville, Alabama and Miss Susan M., daughter of Rev. David Lee of Lowndes County, Alabama.

Married in Montgomery County, Alabama near Orion on the 15th of April by Elder J.A. Fonville, Mr. William J. Frazer and Miss Julia A. Battle.

Married on the 4th inst. in Abbeville, Henry County, by Rev. W.B. Lacy, Mr. E.H. Grouby to Miss Zilpha P.E. Helms.

5-20-1858

Mrs. A.E. Salter, wife of W.B. Salter, and daughter of Rev. W.S. and F.E. Lloyd, deceased, departed this life on the 6th of April at the residence of her husband in Pike County, Alabama in the twenty-fourth year of her age. She was born in South Carolina (Edgefield District); moved with her father's family to this state in 1846... Connected herself with the Cubihatchee Baptist Church in 1855...

Died on Friday the 16th April 1858 at her home in Dallas County, Alabama, Mrs. Sarah A. Hardy, consort of Elder W. Hardy, and daughter of Elijah and Martha Sherrer. She was born in Autauga County, Alabama, December 5th, 1826, joined the Baptist Church at Ashe Creek in Lowndes County in early life, and was married on the 3rd of January 1855. She has left one darling girl, thirteen months old, a kind and affectionate husband...

Mrs. Nancy Tubb died at her residence near Marion, Perry County, Alabama on the 14th of April 1858, in the fifty-third year of her age. Her husband, Richard Tubb, died in the year 1842 and she was left to sustain all the cares and interests of her beloved family...

Thomas Coke Armstrong died of consumption at the residence of Mr. A.W. Hurst, Hickory Grove, Montgomery County, Alabama at 3 o'clock on the morning of the 8th of April last. Brother Armstrong was born on the 29th of March 1825, and at the time of his death was thirty-three years, eleven days old. He has left a wife and one child, father and mother, brothers and sisters...

## Marriage and Death Notices From The South Western Baptist Newspaper

Died at the residence of Col. Thomas Hinkle in the city of Lexington, Missouri of typhus fever on the morning of the 27th of April 1858, in the twentieth year of his age, Francis M. Caldwell, youngest son of James and Mary Caldwell of Tuskegee, Alabama.

5-27-1858
Married by Rev. E.B. Teague on the 11th inst., John A. Foster, President of Brownwood Institute, to Miss Mary M., daughter of Mr. A.H. Borders of La Grange, Georgia.
Married at Scottsboro, Georgia on the 13th inst. by Rev. C.W. Lane, James T. Menefee, esq. to Miss Clara L. Wittisch, both of Tuskegee.
Susan Dorcas, wife of Elder J.C. McDaniel and daughter of James and Sarah Hunter, was born 20th December 1823, married 22nd December 1846, passed away from earth April 9th, 1858. Though born in Pickens, South Carolina she was educated in Carlisle, Pennsylvania. Graduated at Carlisle Female High School. And returning to the scenes of her early childhood was married to J.C. McDaniel (then a minister in the M.E. Church). After a few years residence near Rome, Georgia, she moved with her husband to Alabama. Being ready to go where duty called she with him went to Athens, Montgomery County where she died April 9th, 1858 under very distressing circumstances... Her residence at Athens was not quite four months.... We would bow in submission, while we cannot but regard it a strange and mysterious providence that took her away. A tremendous yet unexpected hurricane about 10 o'clock on the night of the 8th April struck Brother McDaniel's house throwing it several feet off its pillars and unroofing it. Not a scantling, corner-post, window or door was left standing, blowing away much of the timber, overthrowing a chimney with four fire places, destroying furniture, leaving a mass of ruins... Sister McDaniel was entirely covered by the bricks and timbers while the other members of the family were marvelously preserved. The messenger came and became executioner; for she expired in about three and one half hours...
C.J. McConnico died at his residence near Pine Apple in Wilcox County, Alabama on the 8th of May 1858. C.J. McConnio, in the twenty-second year of his age. The deceased was the eldest son of C.T. and Mary McConnico. He was born September 19th, 1836 near Allenton, Wilcox County, Alabama, and raised in the same community. He has left a kind parents, a devoted companion, one little daughter...

6-4-1858
Married on the 26th May, by Rev. Levi Parks at his own residence, Rev. J.S. Abbott to Mrs. Mary C. Seltzer, daughter of Martha and Levi Parks, all of Wilcox County.

## Marriage and Death Notices From The South Western Baptist Newspaper

Died on the 17th ult. of pulmonary consumption, Mr. Joseph K. Walker, son of Joseph and Mary Walker, age twenty-four years. Mr. Walker was born in Dallas County, Alabama, February 21st, 1834, baptized into the fellowship of Town Creek Baptist Church August 21st, 1856, married to Miss M.L. Hardy, February 12th, 1857... He has left an aged and afflicted mother, a young and affectionate wife, brothers and sisters...

Died, Elizabeth Loveless, late consort of Aaron Loveless, who departed this life, November 7th, 1857, age sixty-one years, five months, seventeen days. She embraced the religion of Christ in the twenty-second year of her age in Edgefield District, South Carolina and was baptized into the Baptist Church of Christ at Antioch in said state... Emigrated to Alabama, January 1828, and in '29 joined the Baptist Church at Town Creek in Dallas County by letter. In '34 removed to Lowndes County and joined as before at Bethany Church; and in '54 removed to Conecuh County, and joined Pilgrim's Rest Baptist Church...

Died at his residence in Carroll County, Georgia near Villa Rica on the 6th day of April 1858 at the age of seventy-four years, our beloved Brother Rev. James Reeves... Early in life he gave his heart to God and connected himself with the Baptist Church at Concord, Jasper County, Georgia...

6-17-1858

Married on the 6th last by the Rev. B. Mott, Mr. Dozier Thornton to Miss Sarah S. Lanier, all of this county.

On the 20th ult. at the residence of W.R. Agee, esq. by the Rev. A.J. Lambert of Monroe County, Rev. J.C. Foster of Grove Hill, Clarke County, late of Minden, Louisiana to Miss Josephine M. Megginson, also of Monroe County, and all of Alabama.

James Law died at his residence near Nanafalia, Alabama on Friday, May 21, 1858, age seventy-five years, six months, eleven days.

BROTHER HENDERSON: Please give a place in the *South Western Baptist* as a tribute to our much beloved father, John Davenport, who departed this life Saturday morning, May 8th, 1858, eighty years, eight months, eight days old...

DEATH OF MISS EMMA ADAMS, LA PLACE, ALABAMA. She departed this life Thursday morning, 10th inst., at 6:30 o'clock, disease, typhoid fever.

6-24-1858

Married on the 16th inst. at the residence of the bride's father by Josiah Sanford, esq., Mr. G.R. Dobbs to Miss Sarah Jane Christian, all of Macon County.

Married near Campbellton, Jackson County, Florida on the 15th of June 1858 by Elder William Borum, Nathaniel C. Minchen, esq. and Miss Rebecca E., daughter of Joseph A. and Jane Collier, all of Jackson County, Florida.

## MARRIAGE AND DEATH NOTICES FROM THE SOUTH WESTERN BAPTIST NEWSPAPER

Married on the 17th inst. by Rev. H.E. Brooks, Rev. R.F. Mattison of Selma, Alabama and Miss Ellen E. Brooks of LaGrange, Georgia.

7-1-1858
Departed this life in the city of Eufaula, Alabama on the 18th inst., Deacon Drury Mims, age seventy-five years, five months, two days. Father Mims was born in Edgefield District, South Carolina, January 16th, 1783. In 1830 he moved to Muscogee County, Georgia and Russell County, Alabama in 1837 where he lived until January 1855. Having been bereft of his companion in the Fall of 1854 he sold his property, and dividing most of the proceeds thereof among his children, he selected the house of Thomas A. Brannon of Cusseta, Georgia, who married his second daughter, as his future home. In September last Brother Brannon moved to Eufaula and was soon followed by Brother Mims. He brought a letter from the church in Columbus, Georgia recommending him to the church in this place both as a member and a deacon in good standing and upon the faith of the letter he was received into this church in the two-fold capacity. The deceased was baptized into the fellowship of the Baptist Church in August 1809... He died with what physicians denominate "The Old Man's Apoplexy" which was perhaps hastened by an over exertion to reach home... He had been to Columbus, Georgia on a visit to some friends and for the purpose of enjoying the extraordinary revival which that city had been experiencing for some time past; he remained some two weeks. On the 18th he came down the river on a boat enjoying his usual health. He landed at our wharf about dark and finding no conveyance (the family were expecting him, had sent to the river twice, and were intending to send again when he arrived at home) he attempted to walk home, about 3/4 of a mile, and 1/3 of the way up a steep bluff. He succeeded in walking about 2/3 of the way and finding he could go no further he stopped at the house of a friend who kindly sent him home in a buggy. After reaching home he conversed cheerfully but said he was not well. In a very short time he was taken with violent vomiting and in a few minutes insensibility succeeded. He became only partially rational and that for but a very short period and expired at 1/4 before 11 o'clock p.m., and some two and one half or three hours after reaching home...
Married in Tuskegee, Alabama, 24th June, by Rev. Sam'l Henderson, Mr. John C. Moss to Miss Catharine E., eldest daughter of Col. Jas. W. Echols.

7-15-1858
Married on the 22nd ult. at the residence of the bride's father in Tallapoosa County by the Rev. Jas. M. Russell, Benjamin Walker, Jr. of Thomaston, Georgia to Miss Myra E. Russell.
Married on Thursday the 1st inst. by Rev. C.A. Stanton, Mr. Joseph C. Head and Miss Ann Eliza Cox, second daughter of O.D. Cox, esq., all of Macon County.

## Marriage and Death Notices From The South Western Baptist Newspaper

Died on the 10th of June at the residence of Dr. P. Zimmerman, Eugenia Lloyd, infant daughter of W.B. and Eugenia Salter, age two months, twelve days. Its mother having died when it was but a week old the father is now left alone to experience both the pangs of a husband's and a father's grief.

Died in Harrison County, Texas, May 11th, 1858, Mrs. Jane Hart, in the sixty-second year of her age. She was born in Edgefield District, South Carolina, June 24th, 1796, and was married to Derryl Hart in 1815, to whom she was ever a "help-meet" indeed. She was baptized at Little Stephen's Creek by Brother B. Manly some thirty-four years ago... She removed with her husband to Chambers County, Alabama in 1835 where they reared a numerous and worthy family, eight sons and one daughter. After the death of her husband she removed (January 1857) to Texas.

Died at the residence of her father on the 28th of May last, Miss Mary E. Andrews, after a long painful and lingering illness; age about twenty years... Burnsville, Alabama.

7-22-1858

Married on the morning of the 29th ult. by the Rev. F.C. Lowery, R. Paulding Anderson of Wilcox County to Miss Mary V., daughter of Green E. Jones of Marengo County, all of Alabama.

Died at the residence of Mr. J.O. Long in Autauga County, Alabama of typhoid dysentery, Deacon Littleton Edwards, on the 4th of July 1858. Brother Edwards was born in Edgefield District, South Carolina on the 10th March 1800, moved to Alabama in 1818, was married in 1821 to Miss Linna Lucas of Edgefield District, South Carolina, joined the Baptist Church at Sister Springs in Dallas County, Alabama, August 25th, 1833, from thence he moved to Town Creek, Dallas County and joined the Baptist Church there in 1837... Sister Linna Edwards having died in 1838, leaving five children, Brother Edwards was again married in 1848 to Mrs. Mary Ann Lewis; he leaves a boy and girl orphans by his second marriage...

Died in Wetumpka, Alabama at the house of her son-in-law, Wm. Price, in her eighty-seventh year of her age, Mrs. Lydia George. For about a year she had been unable to get away from home, owing to the effects of a fall from the door-steps. It may be said however, that she died, or rather "fell asleep" under the weight of accumulated years.

Sister G. had been twice married; left a son by her first husband, our esteemed Brother Dorcester, near Prattville, and a daughter by her last, sister Price...

Departed this life on Tuesday morning, June 29th, 1858, Mrs. Sarah Stanton, consort of Deacon William Stanton, age fifty-four years, six months, three days... She embraced religion about the year 1819 or 1820 and was baptized at Elam Church, Jones County, Georgia, by Elder Jacob Watson in 1830...

## Marriage and Death Notices From The South Western Baptist Newspaper

Died on the morning of the 11th inst. at the residence of his parents in Russell County, Alabama, James F., only child of John L. and Adelia Walton, age eleven years, ten months, two days.

7-29-1858
Died in the city of Columbus, Georgia on the 28th of June, Mrs. S.A. Nance. She was born in the state of South Carolina on the 12th of September 1828. She was married to Mr. M.M. Nance on the 17th of March 1846. When she was quite young her parents left South Carolina and became residents of Selma, Alabama...

Died of flux in Rusk County, Texas, John Philip, son of J.C. and Martha A. Shuttleworth. Born in Talladega County, Alabama, January 20, 1855, died June 4, 1858.

Died of whooping cough in Rusk County, Texas, Laura Powell, daughter of Dr. J.M. and Catherine E. Griffin. Born in Coosa County, Alabama, April 10th, 1856, died June 18th, 1858.

As the last tribute of respect it devolves upon me to record the death of our beloved Brother Samuel P. Caffee, who departed this life at his residence in Tuscaloosa County, Alabama, June 30th, 1858, in the forty-sixth year of his age. He has left a kind wife and eleven children...

The subject of this notice, John M. Crowder, died at the residence of his brother, Homer T. Crowder, in Macon County, Alabama, May 18th, 1858, aged sixty-three years... For some years he was a member of the Methodist Church at Oakbo?ery, Alabama... He lived to see the last one of his own family exchange earth's scenes and trials for the unsullied joys of a better land; the last of whom was his daughter Mary. Consumption marked her for its victim...

Judith Tranquila Turner was born February 11th, 1825 in Jackson County, Tennessee. She was married to Stephen Bishop in Talladega County, Alabama the 4th of August 1844. United with the Baptist Church at Wewoka in September 1846 and with her husband moved to Butler County where she departed this life July the 3rd about 8 o'clock in the evening. She had been in a declining state for many years...

Departed this life in the forty-second year of her age, Mrs. Martha Leusueur, consort of Doctor Cary S. Leusueur of Culoden, Georgia, after a long and painful illness. The deceased had repaired to Floyd Springs, Georgia for her health. She had been there but a short time when her debility increased and on the 8th inst. she yielded up her spirit... leaving four children and a husband...

8-5-1858
Married on Wednesday evening the 21st inst. by Rev., C.A. Stanton, Mr. George F. Colquitt of Russell County and Miss Martha J., daughter of Judge Kellam of Macon County, Alabama.

## Marriage and Death Notices From The South Western Baptist Newspaper

Married on the 25th of July 1858 by Elder William Boroum, Joshua S. Johnson, esq. and Miss Nancy L. Bevis, all of Jackson County, Florida.

Died in the city of Eufaula, Alabama on the 14th inst., Mrs. Jane Caroline Morris, age twenty-four years, four months, six days. On the 25th of June 1854, Sister Morris was married to Mr. Richard Morris, whom with one little daughter she has left to mourn this irreparable loss... Was baptized into the fellowship of the Eufaula Baptist Church in the Fall of 1855. Her afflictions were long and severe, she died with consumption...

Died in Greenville, Alabama, July 21st, 1858, Sarah Francis Baldwin, infant daughter of Joseph A. Baldwin and Mrs. M.J. Baldwin, age nine months, twenty-one days.

Died January 16th, 1851, Alfred Kirkland. On the 1st day of February 1852, William D. Kirkland, son of Alfred and Sarah Kirkland. On March 3rd, 1856 Sarah Matilda, daughter of Larkin and Frances E. Watters, and granddaughter of A. and S. Kirkland. On February 23rd, Alfred K., baby of L. and F.E. Watters, and grandson of A. and S. Kirkland. On 1st October 1857, Sarah B. Kirkland, daughter of A. and S. Kirkland, age eighteen years. On 2nd October, Mrs. Sarah Kirkland, late consort of Alfred Kirkland. On 9th December 1857, Georgia M. Berny, wife of T.A. Berny, and daughter of A. and S. Kirkland, and on the 1?th, same month, her infant baby two days old. On the 24th, April 1858, F.E. Watters, wife of L. Watters, and daughter of A. and S. Kirkland.

8-12-1858

Mrs. Samantha N. Sale, wife of Jos. C. Sale of this place, died July 14th, 1858 leaving her husband and four children. She was the daughter of George and Margaret Osborn of Columbus, Georgia and was born on the 6th day of January 1824... (Auburn, Alabama, July 29th, 1858)

Mrs. Sarah M. Everett, consort of M.B. Everett of Daleville, Dale County, Alabama, died at the Coffee Springs in Coffee County on Sunday morning, July 25th, 1858 whither she had gone with her husband and three daughters and several families for health and recreation. She was born August 3rd, 1824; was married in 1841; united herself with the Baptist Church at Hayneville, Houston County, Georgia in 1843. From thence she removed to Orange Hill, Florida and subsequently to Daleville in 1856... She was the daughter of Miles and Margaret Harrell of Georgia. On Friday she had a slight chill, fever ensued, accompanied with diarrhea, both of which continued until her dissolution. She was brought to Daleville on Monday where she was interred...

Our Brother Robert Witherington is no more! On the morning of the 26th May last after a long and protracted illness he fell asleep in Christ. He was born and raised in North Carolina and there married Miss Holland Tillman. He moved to Houston County, Georgia in 1827 where he became a member of

MARRIAGE AND DEATH NOTICES FROM THE SOUTH WESTERN BAPTIST NEWSPAPER

the Baptist Church at Hayneville in 1829... In 1840 he moved to Barbour County, Alabama where he was buried...
Departed this life September 1?th, 1857, Whitney Alexander, son of N.W. and Mariah Pitts, age five years, five months...

8-19-1858
Josephine Elizabeth Swanson, daughter of John and Elizabeth C. Swanson, was born in Morgan County, Georgia on the 21st of January 1839 and died in Tuskegee, Alabama on the 31st of July 1858...
Died July 5th, 1858 at the summer residence of her brother-in-law (Col. Tarrance) in Dallas County, Alabama, Miss Elizabeth Stewart, age fifty-three years, ten months, twenty-two days. (She preferred to live a life of virginity). Sister Lizie was a native of South Carolina...
Died on the 6th inst. in her sixty-third year, Mrs. Charity Graves, wife of Dr. Thomas Graves...

8-26-1858
Died at his residence in this city on the morning of the 2nd inst., James Moncrief, in the forty-ninth year of his age. The deceased was born in the county of Greene in the state of Georgia on the 24th day of November 1809 but lived the greater part of his life in the county and city of Montgomery... He was taken violently ill on Saturday evening the 31st day of July and suffered intensely nearly all the time till Monday morning when he died...
Died at his residence in Bibb County, Alabama on the night of the 23rd of July 1858, Jacob Lightsey of congestion of the liver, in the fortieth year of his age. The deceased was the son of John and Barbary Lightsey and was born in Barnwell District, South Carolina and removed with his parents to Bibb County, Alabama in 1823. His father settled near Centreville, known at that time as the Falls of Cahaba. His father died a few months after he settled in Bibb County leaving a widowed mother and several children... Brother Lightsey leaves a wife and nine children...
Died of croup or bronchitis on the 10th inst., Mitta Guice, eldest child of Elizabeth and Shephard Guice, age three years, eight months, two days.

9-2-1858
Died of flux the 16th day of July 1858, Mrs. Phebe Stallworth, wife of Jackson P. Stallworth, at the residence of Lazarua Carter, her father, near Rural Hill, Conecuh County, Alabama. The deceased was twenty-one years, seven months, ten days old... Was married 13th November 1856. She left her husband, a hapless infant...
Tribute of respect from Ramah Lodge #243, Montgomery County, on the death of James M. Dickey.

## Marriage and Death Notices From The South Western Baptist Newspaper

We learn from the *Forsyth Educational Journal* that Rev. James Carter of Butts County, a venerable Baptist minister, well known in middle Georgia, died at his residence in Butts County on the 24th ult.
Died in Shelby County, Alabama on the 31st October 1857, Alsa M., daughter of Bennett and Elizabeth Davis, age fifteen years...
Died at home in Perry County, August 27th, Mrs. Jane Anne, wife of Jackson C. Curry, age thirty-five years... She was a model sister. Being the eldest of eight children...

9-16-1858
Died at the residence of his father six miles east of Clayton, Barbour County, Alabama, Mr. James L., son of Elder Joel Sims. The subject of this notice was born in Clayton on the 30th of October 1838 and never lived more than six miles from the place of his nativity until the time of his death which took place August 21st, 1858, age nineteen years, nine months, twenty-two days... baptized into the fellowship of Cowikee Church...

9-30-1858
Married on the 19th inst. by Rev. William Davis, Mr. Thos. J. Ray to Mary Adeline, daughter of P.T. Humphries, all of Randolph County, Alabama.
Married by Rev. P.H. Lundy on the 16th inst. in the Baptist Church, Pleasant Hill, Alabama, Mr. Thos E. Williams of Dallas to Miss Lizzie M. Rives of Lowndes County.

10-7-1858
Died on the 22nd of August 1858 after a short illness of twenty-four hours, James Davis Old, son of John W. and Mary Jane Old. Little Jimmy was born the 2nd April 1856, age two years, four months, twenty days. Carroll Parish, Louisiana.
Departed this life September 3rd, 1858 Willie Martin Chasiene Old, son of William W. and Sarah L. Old; born November 25, 1856; age one year, nine months, nine days... Joes Bayou, Carroll Parish, Louisiana.

10-14-1858
Married in La Grange, Georgia, October 5th, 1858 by Rev. Mr. Cunningham, Mr. M.B. Swanson of Tuskegee, Alabama to Miss Anna E. Swanson of La Grange.
At the Baptist Church in Macon, Georgia on the 29th of September by Rev. S. Landrum, the Rev. J.B. Hartwell, Missionary to Shanghai China, and Miss Eliza H. Jewett of Macon, Georgia
Departed this life with typhoid fever in Stewart County, Georgia on the 3rd of October, James L. Cox, in the thirty-third year of his age. For many years he had been the stay of his father's family, cheerfully sacrificing his private interests for their welfare.

MARRIAGE AND DEATH NOTICES FROM THE SOUTH WESTERN BAPTIST NEWSPAPER

10-21-1858
Tribute of respect from Mission Baptist Church, Mobile on the death of B.C.C. Munnerlyn...
Departed this life of a chronic disease in Chambers County, August 30th, 1858, Frances C. Bailey, consort of Allen L. Bailey, in the thirtieth year of her age... leaving a husband and three little children.
Died in Tuskegee, Alabama at the residence of his father on the morning of the 10th inst., Oliver Perry Caldwell, in the thirty-first year of his age. The deceased leaves aged parents, an interesting child, an only sister, and two brothers.
Tribute of respect from Warrior Stand Lodge #115 upon the death of fellow Brother James H. Harris, age about thirty-eight years.

10-28-1858
Married at the residence of the bride's father on Thursday 21st October by Elder A.T.M. Handey, Mr. William W. Adams to Miss Charlotte Jones, all of Macon County.
Died in this city of the prevailing epidemic on the 6th inst., Mrs. Frances S., wife of Robert W. Capers, and daughter of Jas. A. and Sarah F. Branch, age twenty-four years. Sister Capers was born in Dallas County... She leaves a husband and one child...
Matilda Naomi, the first born of Jos. H. and Arsie Park, departed this life at the residence of her parents in Pike County, Alabama on the 29th day of September last, age thirteen years, lacking seven days. Cicero, the last born of this stricken house-hold, died on the 28th of September being four days old.

11-3-1858
COUNTY LINE CHURCH, RUSSELL COUNTY, ALABAMA: The committee appointed to draft resolutions, expressive of the feelings of this church, upon the untimely death of our esteemed Brother James A. Gorham, beg leave to submit the following report: The circumstances connected with the sudden death of Brother Gorham are heart rending in the extreme and it is difficult to comprehend the mysterious dispensation of Providence which removed him from this sphere of action. The facts connected with the melancholy affair according to the evidence before the jury of inquest, in the presence of the writers are about this: That on Thursday evening, 19th August, Abner and James Nance attacked and murdered Brother Gorham in a most unfeeling manner. It appears that Brother Gorham, as overseer of one of the public roads, returned the above named young men to the magistrate for non-performance of road duty. The parties met at the house of a neighbor, when a dispute arose concerning the road working and returning of defaulters. During the altercation Abner Nance gave Brother Gorham the lie with an oath. Declaring that he would suffer their abuse no longer he attempted to resent

the insult, whereupon the assailants attacked him with open knives and inflicted three wounds upon his person, two of which either would have proved fatal. Surgical aid was summoned and soon arrived at the scene of distress and suffering but our unfortunate Brother sank rapidly and died in about an hour and a half after the rencounter... He was interred in County Line Burying Ground... a wife and eight children.
Died on the 28th of April 1858 in Pike County, Rufus A. Judson, son of Guilford and Catharine Burney, age ten months, twenty-eight days; and Sema Docia Ida, their daughter, died August 27th, 1858, age ten months and twenty days. [???]

11-11-1858
Married on the 12th October at Helicon, Lowndes County, Alabama by Elder J.A. Fonville, Mr. G.M. Jordan to Miss Julia A. Bonds.
At Hickory Grove, Alabama on the 13th of October by Elder J.A. Fonville, Dr. C.W. Powell to Miss M.L. Moncrief.
By the same and at the same time and place, Mr. G.M. Powell to Miss J.A. Moncrief.
Married on the 27th of October at the residence of Mr. Jesse Holmes by Rev. J.S. Abbott, Mr. David W. Melton of Selma, Alabama to Miss Ann E. Holmes of Dallas County, Alabama.
Married in the city of Eufaula, Alabama on the 28th of October 1858 by Elder A. VanHoose, Elder J.S. Paullin to Miss Ann H. Brannon, all of Eufaula, Alabama.
Died in Keachi, De Soto Parish, Louisiana, September 10, 1858, Mr. James Drayton Darby, age forty-eight years. The subject of this notice was born in Newberry District, South Carolina, November 1810 where he resided until twelve years ago. He then removed to Lauderdale County, Alabama from thence to Yalobusha County, Mississippi, which place he soon left for Lafayette County. In 1845 he removed to Caddo Parish, Louisiana from thence to Keachi where he resided until his death. He has left a wife and four children...
Died, August 30th at her residence in Chambers County, Alabama, Mrs. Francis C. Bailey, daughter of Thomas and Mildred Steed, and consort of Allen L. Bailey. She was born December 21st, 1825... She leaves a husband and three small children...

11-18-1858
Married on the 21st of October by E.Y. VanHoose, Mr. Thomas J. Coleman to Miss Mary V. Tarver, both of Barbour County.
On the 2nd of November by W.B. Jones, R.E. Covington of Uchee, Alabama to Mrs. Sarah A. Eady of Tuskegee.

## Marriage and Death Notices From The South Western Baptist Newspaper

On the 31st ult. at the residence of the bride's mother by Rev. J.W. Williams, Mr. Samuel W. Harkness to Miss North Carolina Frederick, all of Chambers County, Alabama.

On the 10th November by W.B. Atkinson, Mr. Malachi Ivey of Glennville, Alabama to Miss Samantha Dendy of Hamilton, Georgia.

Departed this life in Ocktibbeha County, Mississippi on the 13th of October 1858, George Gales Foster, second son of Arthur and Elizabeth Foster, age nine years and four months. Little George was born in Tuscaloosa County, Alabama on the 19th of May 1849 and when quite young moved with his parents to Western Texas where he spent the greater part of his short existence...

Died at his residence in Macon County, Alabama near Hardaway on the 1st day of October 1858, in his fifty-eighth year, Brother James R. Kendrick. The deceased came to his death by a distressing casualty. In passing around some horses that were driven to his gate for him to see, one of them kicked him in such a way as to dislocate his neck and cause immediate death. Brother Kendrick had been a member of the Mt. Zion Church about five years... leaves a wife and six children...

Died at his residence in Glennville, Barbour County, Alabama on the 8th October after a long and painful illness, Wm. Curry, in the fiftieth year of his age. He was the eldest son of Lewis and Sarah Curry of Edgefield District, South Carolina. He came to the eastern part of Alabama a few years since and finally settled in Barbour County... He leaves his wife and one son... The *Edgefield (South Carolina) Advertiser* will please copy.

11-25-1858
Married on Thursday the 18th inst. by Rev. C.A. Stanton, Mr. George W. Phillips and Miss Georgia Ann Trawick, all of Macon County.

Died in Chambers County, Alabama on the 7th September 1858, Victoria A., youngest daughter of William P. and Isabella Allen, age nineteen years, twenty-five days...

12-9-1858
Married on Tuesday morning the 30th ult. at the residence of the bride's father in Tuskegee by the Rev. Sam'l Henderson, Dr. U.R. Jones to Miss Mollie C. Chilton, daughter of the Hon. W.P. Chilton.

Married at the residence of the bride's father in Pike County, Alabama by Rev. J.T.S. Park on Tuesday the 2nd inst., Mr. Rob't J. Cogburn and Miss Cynthia A., daughter of Henry B. Thomas.

Married at the residence of the bride's father in Perry County, Alabama on the 18th November by Rev. Levi Parks, Mr. George B. Holmes of Montgomery to Miss Mary C. Talbert, daughter of Gen. E.G. Talbert.

## MARRIAGE AND DEATH NOTICES FROM THE SOUTH WESTERN BAPTIST NEWSPAPER

12-16-1858
Departed this life in the twenty-eighth year of her age, Mrs. Sarah Fuller, consort of William Fuller, and daughter of Joshua and Martha Adams, all of Chambers County, Alabama... Her disease was brief and terminated her existence in a few days. She leaves a husband and five children...
Died at the residence of Rev. John Talbert in Perry County, Alabama on the 19th of November, his son, Edgar Jackson Talbert, in the thirty-first year of his age. He had been a consistent member of the Baptist Church at Bethel, Marengo County for nearly two years... He had no family but resided with his father...
Tribute of Respect from the Good Hope Baptist Church of Christ, Coosa County, Alabama, November 1858 upon the death of Drury Harrington, who died on Monday night the 8th inst. after a protracted and most painful illness... He was born in Union District, South Carolina on the 4th of March 1790; removed to the state of Georgia about the year 1815 or '16... united with the Salem Baptist Church in Fayette County, Georgia in the Fall of 1826. Subsequently removed to Alabama, was chosen and ordained Deacon. Licensed as a Minister of the Gospel by the County Line Baptist Church in Russell County, Alabama...

12-23-1858
Married at the residence of Dr. H.A. Howard of Tuskegee on the 13th inst. by the Rev. Sam'l Henderson, the Rev. Thomas W. Tobey, late of North Carolina, to Mrs. Hattie A. Howard. The party immediatly left Tuskegee for Sumterville, Alabama where Brother Tobey has been called to take charge of the Baptist Church.
Married on the evening of the 2nd inst. by Rev. W. Wilkes, Mr. Jas. A. Gibson of Dallas and Miss Rebecca J. Peeples of Autauga County, Alabama.
On the 9th inst. at the residence of the bride's father near Loachapoka by the Rev. Sam'l Henderson, Mr. Randolph M. Phillips to Miss Martha E. Stroud.
Married at the residence of Mrs. Eliza Caffee, Tuscaloosa County, on the 10th of December by Elder A.C. Thomason, Dr. James W. Acker to Miss Sarah Jane Caffee.
By the same on the 12th inst. Mr. Samuel H. Curry to Miss Delilah Croft, both of Bibb County, Alabama.
John T. Faulkner is dead. He died near El Dorado, Arkansas the 13th of November 1858. He was the son of John M. and Emily A. Faulkner and was born Jan 10th, 1836. Brother Faulkner joined the Missionary Baptist Church at Ed Dorado, Arkansas; was baptized 30th of July 1858. Brother Faulkner has left many friends to mourn his loss, his mother, his kind step-father, brothers and sisters...

## Marriage and Death Notices From The South Western Baptist Newspaper

Died at his residence in Montgomery County on Tuesday morning, 30th November 1858 of pneumonia, Mr. John W. Ray, in the sixty-eighth year of his age. The deceased was amongst the oldest settlers on Montgomery County having removed from his native state (Georgia) to Alabama when a young man... In 1848 he made a public profession of faith in the Redeemer and was baptized into the fellowship of the Antioch Baptist Church... He leaves behind him an aged companion, six children...

Elder Joseph J. Battle departed this life the 8th of December 1858 at his residence in Marion County, Georgia, in the seventy-third year of his age. He was baptized into the fellowship of Rocky Creek Baptist Church, Lawrence County by Elder John Ross in the year 1825. A few years after he moved to Upson County and united with Bethlehem Church where he was licensed to preach and where he was soon after ordained to the work of the ministry by Elders John Hamrick, Jacob King, and John Ross, on the 3rd day of June 1831. In January 1835 he moved to Marion County... He has left a disconsolate wife and eight surviving children...

Died in Macon, Mississippi, October 29th, 1858 at the residence of her father, E.T. Bush, Mrs. Celestia A., wife of N.H. Harrison, in the nineteenth year of her age, leaving an infant ten days old.

1-6-1859
Married on the 23rd December 1858 at the residence of the bride's mother near Society Hill, Macon County, Alabama by Rev. Sam'l Henderson, Mr. A.B. McPherson of Lowndes County to Miss Mary A. Canady.

Married on the 16th December by Rev. C.A. Stanton at the residence of the bride's father in Tallapoosa County, Mr. Lewis Wright of Macon County to Miss Lucy Ann Middlebrooks.

Married on the 21st of December 1858 at the residence of the bride's mother (Mrs. Mariah Frederick) by the Rev. J.W. Williams, Mr. John Vernon to Miss Frances Frederick, all of Chambers County, Alabama.

Married on the 15th December by Rev. J.E. Bell, Mr. Wm. H. Wright of Tuskegee to Miss Lucy A. Carter, daughter of Mr. Alfred Carter, of Butler County, Alabama.

Married on the 16th of December 1858 at the bride's father's (H. Williams) near Coffeyville by Rev. J.C. Foster, Hon. Jas. J. Goode to Miss Caroline S. Williams, all of Clarke County, Alabama.

Married on Thursday evening, 23rd ult. by Rev. C.A. Stanton, Mr. J.W. Moon of Louisiana and Miss Jane L. Seals of Macon County, Alabama.

Married on the 15th ult. near Dadeville at the residence of Mr. Allan Bryan by Rev. Wm. P. Bryan, Mr. M.B. Everett to Miss Mary E. Bryan of Russell County, Alabama.

MARRIAGE AND DEATH NOTICES FROM THE SOUTH WESTERN BAPTIST NEWSPAPER

Died at the residence of R.J. Allen in St. Clair County, Alabama on the evening of the 21st October 1858, Dr. W. Clayton Neal, eldest son of Joel C. and Louisa Neal, of Chattooga County, Georgia, age about twenty-seven years. Dr. Neal was baptized into the fellowship of Mount Harmony Baptist Church in Chattooga County, Georgia in 1850 by the Rev. Wm. Newton of Cave Spring... Dr. Neal came to this county some four years ago, united with the Coosa Valley Baptist Church and commenced the practice of medicine... He was taken with the flux and was sick twenty-four days...

Died on the 17th inst. at the residence of her father, Capt. Wilson Ashley, in Conecuh County, Alabama, Mrs. Susan J. Jones, after a protracted illness of five months, age thirty-one years. Mrs. Jones was the widow of Sanford Jones to whom she was married about ten years ago in company with whom she removed immediately to Louisiana. Mr. Jones died in less than a year after their marriage since which time she has resided with her father in Alabama... She leaves a little daughter about eight years old...

Jeremiah T. Perry, son of E.N. and Rebecca Perry, was born on the 27th of July, A.D., 1838 in Talbot County, Georgia and joined the Calebee Baptist Church in Macon County, Alabama on the 2nd day of September 1849... He died of pneumonia, November 21st, 1858, in the twenty-first year of his age... Also on the 27th of November Edward N., consort of Rebecca Perry, fell a victim of the same disease. He was born in Warren County, Georgia, February 23rd, 1806. Sometime in 1829 he joined the Williams' Creek Baptist Church... He moved to Macon County, Alabama in the year 1845...

1-13-1859

Married on the 28th ult. by Rev. A. Small, Mr. Isaac M. Ford to Miss S.A.R. Brodnax, all of this place.

Married on the 28th December at the residence of Mr. N. Long by Elder E.Y. VanHoose, Mr. Edward N. Brown to Miss Annie E. Long, all of Barbour County, Alabama.

Died in Panola County, Mississippi, November 21, 1858, William Bennett, son of Julia A., formerly of Lowndes County, Alabama and Bennett Bowden, age three months, twelve days.

Died at Cross Keys on Tuesday 28th December last after a short illness, Toliver, son of A.T.M. and Sarah J. Handey, age two years, one month, twenty-one days.

Departed this life on the 23rd of December 1858 at the City Hotel, Orleans, Mrs. Margie Reynolds. She was the only daughter of Dr. Reuben and J.P. Reynolds of Monroe County, Mississippi... She professed faith in the precious Savior and was immersed with her husband, Thomas Reynolds, by the writer of this poor tribute to her memory seven years ago. Disease of a pulmonary cast had been preying upon her delicate constitution for several years until it developed about the first of September, awakened serious fears with her relatives and friends. She declined so rapidly it was thought best to remove

## Marriage and Death Notices From The South Western Baptist Newspaper

her from her home in Talladega County, Alabama to New Orleans for the benefit of the most skillful physicians of the South...

1-20-1859
Married on Tuesday the 28th December by G.C. Elford, Dr. B.C. Bennett to Mrs. Amanda Huey, youngest daughter of Adam Grubbs, all of Louisville, Barbour County, Alabama.
Died on the 2nd of December 1858, William Whiting Adams. He was born October 21st, 1836 and consequently at the time of his death was a little over twenty-two years of age. He was married 21st of October 1858. Thus leaving beside his parents, brothers and sisters, a young widow to mourn his early death having been married only about six weeks. He was on his way to a new country and was stopped by disease in the city of New Orleans... was baptized into the fellowship of the Ebinezer Baptist Church in this (Macon) County...
Departed this life in Montgomery County, Alabama on the ??? of December 1858, Sister Mahulda Mathis... [this issue was severely damaged]

1-27-1859
Married by Rev. F.H. Moss on the 6th day of January 1859, Mr. Francis M. Nuckolls of Macon County, Alabama to Miss Martha Orum of Montgomery County.
Also by the same on the 13th day of January 1859, Mr. Wm. Turnipseed of Montgomery County, Alabama to Miss Isabella B. Beverly of Macon County.
Died at Portersville, November 29th, 1858, Mrs. Elizabeth Griffing, consort of Deacon Hiram Griffing of Mobile, in the forty-ninth year of her age. Elizabeth Howe (her maiden name) was born October 9th, 1810, married in July 1830, and united with the first Baptist Church in Hartford, Connecticut in the summer of 1831. In November 1835, twenty-three years ago, she with her husband removed to Mobile where she continued to reside until a few months previous to her departure from earth!...
Departed this life on the 24th December 1858 at the residence of her father, Tuscaloosa County, Alabama, Miss Elizabeth Ray, in her nineteenth year... Three days previous to the death above recorded the mother of the deceased, Mrs. Cynthia Ray, consort of James Ray, was taken violently ill and after unusual and almost unparalleled suffering departed this life on the 3rd day of January inst., leaving a husband, son and daughter, the only surviving members of the family, having previously buried eight children. Mrs. Ray was between forty-five and fifty years of age...

2-3-1859
Married on Thursday night, 20th January, at the residence of her father (Wm. F. Samford) near Auburn, Alabama by Rev. A. A. Lipscomb, D.D., Mr. Thomas D. Fullilove of Louisiana to Miss Elizabeth J. Samford.

## MARRIAGE AND DEATH NOTICES FROM THE SOUTH WESTERN BAPTIST NEWSPAPER

Married in Tuskegee on the 27th January ult. by Rev. Sam'l Henderson, Mr. Eldred W. Hardy of Lowndes County to Miss Sarah E. Jones, daughter of Rev. W.B. Jones.

Married in the First Baptist Church, Montgomery, Alabama on the evening of the 27th January, ult. by Rev. I.T. Tichenor, Allen Glover of Greene to Miss Kate Molton of Montgomery.

Married on the 28th of January at the residence of the bride's mother, James R. Monk of Homer, Louisiana to Miss Mary G. Robertson of Chambers County, Alabama.

Married on Tuesday evening 25th of January 1859 at the residence of the bride's father in Chambers County by Rev. C.A. Stanton, Mr. William W. Thomas of Macon County and Miss Laura Lovonia Cotton.

Died at his residence in Conecuh County, Alabama on Tuesday, 4th January 1859, Mr. Mortimore Boulware, in the fifty-first year of his age. The deceased was one of the early settlers of this county. In 1834 he removed from his native state (Virginia) to Alabama where he married and followed the pursuits of agriculture to the close of his life.

2-10-1859

Died in Perry County, Alabama on the 28th of January 1859, Mrs. Haran Lee, consort of David Lee, in the fifty-seventh year of her age.

Died at the residence of his aunt Mrs. M. Hill in Clarke County, December 25th, 1858, John L. Megginson, age twenty-eight years. A member of a large family he had seen through still in early manhood, parents, three brothers and a sister, cut down before himself...

Married on the 22nd day of December near Hickory Grove, Alabama by Elder J.A. Fonville, Mr. J.M. Moncrief and Miss Sallie E. Turner, daughter of Dr. J. Turner.

Married in Russell County, Alabama on the 9th inst. by Rev. J.H. DeVotie, Dr. William W. Broadhurst, ?? Carolina to Miss Ann Eliza Ware, eldest daughter of Rev. B.M. Ware of Russell County, Alabama.

2-17-1859

Married on the 8th inst. in Loachapoka, Alabama by the Rev. Sam'l Henderson, Mr. John Nelms to Miss Mary Havis, all of Macon County.

Married on the evening of the 8th inst. by Rev. B. ???, Mr. Wm. B. Arant of Tallapoosa County and Miss Amanda O'Neal of Macon County.

Married on the 26th January at the residence of the bride's father by the Rev. David Lee, Mr. John F. Lloyd of Butler and Miss Mary E. Lee of Lowndes County, Alabama.

Departed this life on Tuesday evening the 17th January at the residence of her father, Mr. Geo. H. Taylor, near Long Cane, Troup County, Georgia of pulmonary consumption after a distressing and protracted illness, Mrs. Mary E. Matthews, consort of Mr. John J. Matthews of West Point...

## MARRIAGE AND DEATH NOTICES FROM THE SOUTH WESTERN BAPTIST NEWSPAPER

Died at the residence of Col. M.R. Brasfield near Forkland, Greene County, on the 9th inst. Sina, daughter of Mrs. Jane Brasfield, in the tenth year of her age.

3-4-1859
Died at his residence in Bibb County, Alabama of bronchitis on the 3rd of December last, Rev. Allen Brassell, age forty-eight years and one day. The subject of this notice emigrated at an early period of his life with his father from Georgia and settled in Montgomery County, Alabama. From thence he removed to Shelby County, Alabama. There he obtained religion, joined Bethesda Church, remained therein a regular, consistent member some two or three years. At this time he removed to Bibb County, joined Antioch Church, and was therein liberated to preach. Shortly afterwards moved his membership with his family to Enon Church.... His wife, an only daughter, and one grandchild, are among the bereaved...
H.L. Ray died at his residence in Lowndes County on the 6th inst. of pneumonia, age about thirty-four years. Brother Ray was born in Montgomery County in 1825... Was married to Miss Eliza Judkin, daughter of Thos. J. Judkin, in 1840. Removed to Lowndes County in 1854; and united with the Hopewell Baptist Church...
Mary Iola, the first born of William W. and Sarah L. Old, departed this life at the residence of her parents in Carroll Parish, Louisiana on the 1st day of November 1858, age five years, eleven months, sixteen days.
Deacon Edward Birdsong was born in Oglethorpe County, Georgia, May 10th, 1804. Was baptized by Elder Jacob King in 1831 and ordained Deacon in August 1842. On the 26th day of January 1859 he was seized with apoplexy and expired in a few hours, in the fifty-fifth year of his age.

3-10-1859
Married by the Rev. F.H. Moss on the 25th of February, Mr. W.C. W(i)lson of Dale County, Alabama to Miss Ardelia S. Battle, daughter of W.W. Battle of Macon County.
Married on the 15th February by Rev. J.J. Harris at the residence of Thomas J. Ivey, John M. Linton of Pike County to Miss Harriett C. Ivey of Macon County.
Ida Stallworth died at the residence of Capt. Wm. Green, Conecuh County, Alabama. Ida Stallworth was born the 8th day of May 1858, and died 4th January 1859... Her mother was removed from her by the resistless hand of death 16th July last... Little Ida was the only child of Jackson P. Stallworth...
Mrs. Sarah Hines, consort of Lieut. Isaac Hines, died at the residence of her husband near Burnt Corn, Conecuh County, Alabama, February 7th, 1859, age forty-four years. The deceased was born in South Carolina; moved to Georgia, remained there two years and from thence to this state... an affectionate wife, a devoted mother and step-mother...

## MARRIAGE AND DEATH NOTICES FROM THE SOUTH WESTERN BAPTIST NEWSPAPER

Died on the 25th day of January, Maria Francis, daughter of Wingfield W. and Jane E. Smith of Dale County, Alabama, age eleven years, ten months. Deceased came to her death under the most awful circumstances. On the morning of the 24th she arose early and went, accompanied by her younger brother to milk the cows, and the weather being extremely cold. She carried some fire and after she had build up her fire her little brother says she was standing with her back to it to warm and he discovered her dress had caught fire, and him and her tried to extinguish it, but they soon found that it burned still more rapid, and they commenced crying for help, and her father heard the shrieks of pity, and knew there was something wrong; he rushed to the door and by that time the flames were rising above her head and he could discover nothing but the flames, except her hands, either reaching out for help or trying to put out the fire, her father could not decide which. He immediately caught a bucket of water and when he reached the place where she was she had fallen and by the aid of the water he extinguished the fire; but it availed nothing for after suffering the most excruciating pain that human could endure, for about twenty-four hours, she expired. Skipperville, 2 February 1859.

At a monthly meeting, February 1859, of the Salem Baptist Church of Christ, Pike County, Alabama... Tribute of respect upon the death of John H. Smith on Thursday the 13th of January last, with congestive fever... He was born in this county, March 22, 1828...

3-17-1859
Died at his residence in Dallas County, 2nd of February 1859 Thomas L. Traylor, son of Joel and Anna Traylor, age thirty-one years, three months, fifteen days.

3-24-1859
CENTRAL INSTITUTE, MARCH 11th, 1859: My mother Mrs. M.T. Wood died on the 4th inst. at my house of cancer of the tongue and throat. She was baptized more than forty years ago by Elder Isaac Suttle and maintained her connection with the Baptist Church until her death. W.M. Lindsey.

Died on the 9th inst. at his residence in Harris County, Georgia, William Copeland, Sen., in the eighty-second year of his age. He was born on the 4th day of October in the year 1777 in the state of Virginia. His father moved to Georgia during the year 1796 and settled in Clark County on the Oconee River near Skullshoals where he remained until the year 1819 when he removed to Morgan County near Madison, where he remained until the year 1829... In the year 1829 he removed to Harris County where he remained until his death. Hamilton, Georgia, March 10, 1859.

## Marriage and Death Notices From The South Western Baptist Newspaper

3-31-1859
Married on the 17th inst. by Rev. W. Menefee, Jas. A.H. Granberry to Miss Susan, daughter of Joseph Wilson, all of Cotton Valley, Macon County, Alabama.
Married on the 3rd inst. by the Rev. Geo. W. Purifoy at the residence of the bride's father, E.D. Hendon of Newbern, Alabama to Miss Sue W. Duskin, daughter of William Duskin of Orange County, North Carolina.
Died, March 7th Mobile, Alabama after a brief illness, Rev. Asa Chaddick, age near ninety... He served in the war of 1812...
Died at the late residence of his mother near Centerville, Bibb County, Alabama on the 27th day of February 1859 of pneumonia, John D. Lightsey, age nineteen years, eight days... his father died in July last...

4-7-1859
Died at the family residence in Clarke County, February 19th, 1859, Elder Hiram Creighton, age sixty-three years. The subject of this notice was born in South Carolina in 1795; removed to Clarke County, Alabama about 1815; was baptized and united with the Horeb Baptist Church in 1827 and was ordained in 1833...

4-14-1859
Died in Marion, Alabama on the morning of March 29th, Helen Maria, wife of Rev. Wm. H. McIntosh, and daughter of Rev. Lewis Colby.

4-21-1859
Died near Notasulga on 1st of April our sister and mother in Israel, Mrs. Rebecca Fielder, daughter of George and Rebecca Notan [Nolan?]. She was born in South Carolina, 16th November 1803, moved to Morgan County in 1812, married Terrell Fielder, October 1820, baptist at Holler Springs Church 1824, moved to Meriwether County, Georgia 18?0, and came to Tallapoosa County in 1851, age fifty-five years, eight months, fifteen days...
Deacon David Conington: This servant of the Lord died at his residence in Russell County, Alabama on the 12th day of November last, in the sixty-fifth year of his age, after a protracted attack of paralysis...

4-28-1859
Married at Lowndesboro on Thursday the 14th inst. by Rev. J.C. Davis, Dr. P.N. Cilley and Miss Sallie B. Whitman, both of Lowndesboro.
Tribute of respect on the death of E. Williams.
Died at the residence of his son in Barbour County, Alabama on the 30th of March, Samuel C. Stark, age eighty-one years, seven months, eighteen days.
Departed this life March 3rd, 1859 at the residence of her grandfather in Polk County, Texas, Mary Willie, only child of K.H. and J.E. Lockhard, age six months.

## Marriage and Death Notices From The South Western Baptist Newspaper

Died at his residence in Enon, Macon County, Alabama of apoplexy, Maj. George Greer, in the sixty-third year of his age.

William M., eldest son of James and Martha E. McGee, was born May 17th, 1841, and died at Chunnenuggee, Alabama, December 13th, 1858.

5-12-1859
Died at the residence of her ???, in Tallapoosa County, Alabama, on the 3??? of April 1859, Mrs. Elizabeth Wyatt, consort of William Wyatt, deceased, in her eightieth year. She was baptized into the fellowship of the old ??? Baptist Church, Henry County, Georgia in the year 1828...

5-19-1859
Married on Tuesday morning, 10th inst., at the residence of the bride's father by Elder ?T.M. Handey, Mr. Julius W. Rast of Lowndes to Miss Augusta Zimmerman of Montgomery, County.

Died at her residence in Conecuh County, Alabama on the 13th March 1859 Mrs. Pollie A. Travis, in the sixty-ninth year of her age. The deceased was the widow of the late lamented Rev. Alexander Travis and a native of South Carolina. In company with her husband she came to Alabama amongst the earliest settlers in 1817...

DEATH OF DR. H.A. THORNTON: This estimable gentleman so long and so favorably known in this section of the country expired in this city on the night of the 14th of April after a lingering and painful illness of two or more months... (*Columbus Enquirer*)

Tribute of respect on the death of Mitchell Bennett who departed this life in his seventy-fifth year on the 18th day of April 1859... Concord Church, Russell County, Alabama.

Tribute of respect on the death of Hughes Conway, who departed this life on the 2nd of April, in his twenty-eighth year... Concord Church, Russell County, Alabama.

5-26-1859
Mrs. Mary Cornelia Talbert Holmes, wife of Mr. George B. Holmes, and daughter of Gen. E.G. and Mrs. Emily D. Talbert, departed this life at the residence of her husband in the city of Montgomery, Alabama on the 2nd of May 1859, in the nineteenth year of her age. She was born in Perry County on the 15th of February 1841... She was married to Mr. Holmes in November last...

Died of consumption, May 2nd, 1859 in Fredonia, Alabama, Brother Jonathan L. Eberheart. He was born in Troup County, Georgia, February 8th, 1835...

Died at her residence near Pleasant Hill, Sister Hardy, wife of Brother Freeman Hardy, May 17th, after an illness of nearly four months, originating from a severe spell of typhoid fever. She passed her life from an early age to the good old age of fifty-eight...

## MARRIAGE AND DEATH NOTICES FROM THE SOUTH WESTERN BAPTIST NEWSPAPER

6-2-1859
Died on the 2nd day of March, Dr. C. [or O] B. Dill at the residence of his brother-in-law, Mr. G.W. Campbell, in Tuskegee after an illness of more than two months, in his thirty-ninth year. Dr. Dill was attacked in the month of December last with apoplexy and never fully recovered from it. He leaves a wife and six children... joined the Baptist Church in the city of Augusta, Georgia... He had been living in Alabama some eight or ten years...
On the 21st of May, little Jesse, son of John and Elizabeth C. Swanson, died in Tuskegee, age eleven years, two months...

6-16-1859
Died at her residence near Pleasant Hill, Sister Dorse; expired, after an illness of four or five days, from dysentery...
At his father's residence in Pleasant Hill, Frank Quarles died of scarlet fever, after an illness of eight days. He was in the thirteenth year of his age...
Died on Thursday the 2nd day of June at his residence in Marengo County, Alabama, Col. James B. Craighead, in the sixty-second year of his age. The subject of this notice was a native of Tennessee. He practiced law successfully for several years in Huntsville and Mobile...
Died at his residence in Perry County, Alabama on the 15th of May 1859, William Chapman, in the fifty-first year of his age...

6-23-1859
Married on Tuesday morning the 14th inst. at the residence of George B. Nuckolls, esq. by the Rev. Samuel Henderson, Mr. John Randolph Griffin of Chambers County to Miss Otillia Macon Nuckolls of this place.
Died at her residence in Macon County, Alabama, May 12th, 1859, Mrs. Ann M. Treutlen, in her sixty-fourth year... united with the Baptist Church in Effingham County, Georgia, more than twenty-five years ago... Glenville, Alabama, June 8, 1859.

6-30-1859
Died on Wednesday morning, June 22nd, at half past one in the morning in this city, Miss Mattie M., daughter of R.G. and Nancy Walker, age nineteen years, seven months, three days...
The subject of this notice, Mrs. Katharine D. Swanson, died in Auburn, Alabama, May 30th, 1859. She was the youngest daughter of Augustus G.C. and Elizabeth W. Mitchell, and was married to Patrick H. Swanson, 23 July 1850... received into the fellowship of the Baptist Church at Chalybee, Macon County, Alabama...

## Marriage and Death Notices From The South Western Baptist Newspaper

7-14-1859

Married on Sabbath morning, June 26th at 10 o'clock by Rev. W. Wilkes at the house of the bride's mother, D.T. Vincent and G. Alabama McGee, all of Perry County, Alabama.

Died at the residence of Mr. Fielden L. Ellis, Lowndes County, Alabama on the night of the 22nd of June last about 12 o'clock, Miss Sarah J. Ellis, daughter of Mr. Thomas M. Ellis of Bibb County, Georgia. The subject of this notice was born August 27th, 1840. Baptized into the fellowship of the Baptist Church Macon, Georgia by Elder Sylvanus Landrum, May 1854; age eighteen years, nine months, twenty-five days. She came on a visit to Alabama in February last and expected to return to her father's residence in Georgia in this month...

Died in Russell County, Alabama on the 24th of June, John White, Sr., in the eighty-eighth year of his age. He was a native of South Carolina, born in Kershaw (District). He was baptized into the fellowship of the Uchee Grove Baptist Church in 1854.

Died on the 23rd ult. at the residence of her father in Perry County, Mrs. F.C. Crow, relict of the late J.M. Crow, and daughter of G. and E. Hopper. The subject of this notice was baptized by the hand that pen's this account, at the age of eleven into the fellowship of the Ocmulgee church... three children.

Died at the residence of his mother in La Place, Macon County, Alabama June 17th, 1859, Mr. James L. Roberts, in the twenty-first year of his age...

7-21-1859

Married on the evening of the 13th inst. by Rev. J.F. Bledsoe, Mr. James M'Guire of Pike County, Alabama to Mrs. A. B. Wright of LaFayette, Alabama.

Departed this life on the 18th of April 1859 of pulmonary apoplexy at the residence of her daughter, Mrs. J.A. Holland, Oxford, Calhoun County, Alabama, Mrs. Nancy Bush, relict of John Bush, age sixty-nine years. The subject of this notice was the daughter of Edmund and Elizabeth King and was born in Halifax County, Virginia, July 14th, 1789. She married in Greene County, Georgia, 1804, and joined the Baptist Church at Grove Level, Franklin County, Georgia in 1833. She removed with her husband to Alabama in 1836 and resided there until her demise... Several children and a large circle of friends and acquaintances are left to mourn her loss...

Died at the residence of her husband in Shelby County, Alabama, Mrs. Grace Ann Posey. The deceased was born in Charles County, Maryland, October 8th, 1798, moved to Alabama in the spring of 1838, was married to Wm. E. Posey, December 16th, 1838, embraced religion and was baptized into the fellowship of the Big Spring Church, July 10th, 1844, lived a consistent member thereof until her death July 4th, 1859.

## MARRIAGE AND DEATH NOTICES FROM THE SOUTH WESTERN BAPTIST NEWSPAPER

7-28-1859
It becomes our painful duty to announce the death of Simeon Goolsby, former probate judge of this county, which took place at his late residence 1? from this place on the 10th inst., at fifty minutes past 7 o'clock a.m. Judge Goolsby was born in Oglethorpe County, Georgia on the 30th May 1802... He removed to Alabama in 1835 and settled in this county... (*Tallapoosa Times*)
Died at her father's residence near Midway in Montgomery County, Alabama, F.E. Crow, daughter of James and E.A. Crow, on the 7th inst., age seventeen years, seven months, nineteen days.
Died at the residence of her mother, Mrs. Martha J. Lide, seven miles east of Camden on the 21st of June 1859, Miss Sallie E. Lide, age eighteen years, formerly of Carlowville, Alabama.

8-4-1859
Died in Smith County, Mississippi on the 4th day of July 1859, Hance Dunklin Hardy, in the twenty-sixth year of his age. The deceased was born in Lowndes County, Alabama, August 3rd, 1833; united herself with the Old Town Creek Baptist Church in the Summer of 1850...
Tribute of Respect from Female Academy, Cotton Valley, Alabama, July 20th, 1859 on the death of Sarah Perkins, age nine years.

8-11-1859
Married on the 4th of August 1859 by the Rev. ?H. Moss, Mr. Henry R. Slaughter to Miss Sallie A. Martin, all of Macon County.
Departed this life on Saturday morning, 30th July, after an illness of nearly two weeks, Emma Isabella, daughter of Jonathan and Nancy Covington...
Died of typhoid fever June 22nd, 1859 at the residence of her father (E.B. Adams) in Polk County, Texas, Mrs. Julia E., consort of Robert H. Lockhart. The subject of this notice was born on the 15th of March 1838 and in her twelfth year joined the Baptist Church at Ebenezer, Macon County, Alabama. She was married on the 22nd September 1857 and in November 1858 emigrated with her husband to Texas where they resided until her death...
Died of typhoid fever on the 28th of June 1859 at the residence of her father near Clopton, Alabama, Miss Elizabeth Bolger, in the twenty-fifth year of her age...
Tribute of respect on the death of Sarenia Kelly from New Providence Church. The subject of this notice was born on the 13th day of December 1817 and was baptized in 1841 by John McKinzy into the fellowship of the Baptist Church of Christ in Dooly County, Georgia. She afterwards removed to Alabama, Coffee County, and there united with the church at New Providence where she remained a good and pious member until the day of her death which took place on the 8th of May 1859.

## Marriage and Death Notices From The South Western Baptist Newspaper

8-18-1859

Married in Rome, Georgia, August 9th by Rev. Wm. M. Crumly, Col. M. Tatum of Alabama to Miss Eliza W. Walker.

David P. Nuckolls, son of Geo. B. Nuckolls, died at his father's residence in Tuskegee on Thursday the 4th day of August, inst. of a wound received from a pistol shot on Tuesday the 2nd. He was born in Hall County, Georgia, 3rd September 1836 and was therefore at the time of his death in his twenty-third year. Mr. Nuckolls was murdered by an unseen and yet unknown hand while engaged in a personal rencounter with another man. He had been wild and wayward but for some months past had exhibited flattering signs of reformation... Mr. Nuckolls lived about sixty hours after he was shot...

Died in Burnsville at the residence of her father July 24th, 1859, age ten years, ten months... Harriet McConaughy.

9-1-1859

Died at his residence in Russell County, Alabama on the 18th day of April 1859, Rev. Mitchell Bennett, wanting three days of being seventy-five years old. The subject of this notice was born in Virginia on the 21st of April 1784. He emigrated to Pendleton District, South Carolina when very young... He removed to Jackson County, Georgia about the year 1810...

Died in Eufaula, Alabama on the 15th inst. and in the twenty-first year of her age, Annie Helen, consort of Rev. J. Stratton Paullin, and eldest daughter of Capt. William B. Brannon...

9-8-1859

Married on the 28th of August by Rev. A.G. McCraw, Mr. J.F. McAdams and Miss Sarah J. Crow, daughter of J.W.W. Crow, all of Perry County.

Died on the 22nd of August 1859 at the residence of Col. J.C. Rupert on the eastern shore of Mobile Bay, John Rolfe, son of M. and Susan Threefoot, age one year, nine months. The body was brought to the city of Mobile (where its parents reside) for interment.

Died August 3rd, 1859 at the residence of her father in Jackson County, Alabama, Cyrena Caroline Rice, wife of Dr. Francisco Rice, and daughter of R.H. and Elizabeth Taliaferro. She was born November 19th, 1831, professed faith in Christ about the 20th of August 1847 at Salem Campground, Tennessee; was married to Dr. Francisco Rice, September 30th of the same year... She leaves a husband and three children... [see below]

Died, July 16th, 1859, Montillius Fernando, infant son of Cyrena C. Rice; age one month, nine days. [see above]

Died on the 15th of August in Perry County at the residence of her son Col. O.H. Perry, Mrs. Mary, relict of Britton Perry. The subject of this notice was the eldest daughter of Joseph Dennis of Jones County, Georgia. She was baptized in 1815 by Elijah Mosely into the fellowship of the Rooty Creek Church in Hancock County. In 1819 she removed with her husband and

## Marriage and Death Notices From The South Western Baptist Newspaper

family to Alabama and united with the Baptist Church at Beard's meeting house. After a residence of two years in that place the family removed to Perry County near Ocmulgee Church...
Died at his residence in Dale County, Alabama on the 28th of July 1859, Jas. K. Aldridge, Sr. He was born in Columbia County, Georgia 18th of March 1798, and was at the time of his death in the sixty-second year. Brother A. was the eldest son of the late Reuben Aldridge. He attached himself to the Baptist Church at Talbotton, Georgia in the winter of 1830 and was baptized by Rev. William Henderson of Monroe County, Georgia...He has left a kind wife and seven children, all grown...
Died in the thirty-fifth year of her age at the residence of H. M. Vann in Russell County, Alabama, Mrs. Sarah A. Vann, relict of Abner H. Vann, and daughter of Elizabeth and Andrew Mayes. She has left five children, three of her own and two step-children...
Died on the 19th of June, in her thirty-second year after an illness of two days at her residence in Macon County, Alabama, Mrs. Frances M. Benton, wife of G.C. Benton, and daughter of Sandy and Lucy Stallings, deceased. She was born in Jasper County, Georgia and was raised in Muscogee County...

9-15-1859
Died at Tuskegee, Alabama May the 26th... Mrs. Nancy E. Bryan, wife of Geo. Bryan. Mrs. B. was born March 4th, 18??...
Died on typhoid fever in the city of ???? on the 27th of June at 11 p.m., Sister Nancy Caroline Mathews, age thirty-two years, five months, fifteen days... her body lies beneath the cold sod in the grave yard in Tuscaloosa... The subject of this notice was born on the 12th of January 1827; married to Brother Littleton Mathews on the 20th February 1845, who died on the 5th November 1857...
Died at the residence of her husband in Barbour County, Alabama on the 16th of August 1859, Mrs. J.J. Lawson. Mrs. Lawson was born September 29th, 1836 in Effingham County, Georgia and at the time of her death was aged twenty-two years, twenty-two months, seventeen days. July 16th, 1857 she was married to Mr. A.B. Lawson and shortly thereafter moved to Barbour County, Alabama... leaves a husband, an infant only seven weeks old...
Departed this life, Mollie Foster, orphan daughter of J. Hardy Foster, on the 26th of August last at the residence of J.L.S. Foster of Oktibbeha County, Mississippi. Little Mollie was born in Alabama, Tuscaloosa County, on the 16th of September 1853...

9-22-1859
Married on the 13th inst. by Rev. B.T. Smith, Rev. James W. Jeter to Miss Caroline R. Boyd, all of Central Institute, Alabama.

## Marriage and Death Notices From The South Western Baptist Newspaper

Died in the county of Russell on the 21st day of August last, Miss Martha P. Douglass. Sister Martha was born in Middlebury, Vermont on the 3rd day of April 1797 and united with the Presbyterian Church when she was about fourteen years of age... removed to the state of Georgia in the year 1830... her remains rest in the Baptist Church yard at Union Grove, Russell County...
(Montgomery, Alabama, September 14th, 1859)
Sallie Elizabeth, only daughter of W. George and Mary L. Brewer, was born on the 12th of October 1857, and died on the 28th of August 1859.

10-6-1859
Married, on the 25th September 1859 near Chandler's Springs by Rev. F.M. Law, James W. Graves to Miss Mary E. Brassell, all of Talladega County.
Tribute of respect from Concord Church, Russell County, on the death of Wilson Duke.
Tribute of respect from the First Baptist Church, Montgomery, on the death of Dr. A.B. McWhorter, Senior Deacon of this church.

10-13-1859
Married at the bride's father's near Notasulga, Macon County, Alabama on Tuesday evening the 4th inst. by the Rev. C.T. Burks, Mr. Wm. H. Crawford of Cuthbert, Georgia to Miss C.A. Callaway.
Died in Abbeville, Henry County, Alabama on the 17th of September 1859; Mrs. Selina Matthews, wife of L.B. Matthews, age about thirty-seven years. This excellent sister was baptized into the fellowship of the Piney Grove (Georgia) Baptist Church, 3rd September 1851...
Died on the 14th of September 1859, Sarah Louisa, second daughter of Arthur and Elizabeth A. Foster of Oktibbeha County, Mississippi, age five years, minus two days.
Also on the 22nd September, Emilie Lucy, second daughter of J. Hardy Foster, age three years, eight months.

10-20-1859
Married on Thursday on the 13th in La Place by the Rev. Samuel Henderson, Mr. Andrew J. Bagget to Mrs. Sarah Ann Foscue, all of Macon County, Alabama.
Departed this life on the 3rd inst., Zennie Ware Molton, daughter of Thos J. and Mary W. Molton, not quite six years of age. She had ulcerated sore throat and croup and lingered a week...
Died in Selma, September 30th, Bethel M., only son of Rev. F.M. and Mrs. Kate Law, age nine months.

## Marriage and Death Notices From The South Western Baptist Newspaper

10-27-1859
Married on the 12th inst. in the Methodist Church in Wetumpka, Alabama by Rev. Platt Stout, Mr. Henry H. Ware of Selma and Miss Idna Williams of that city.
Married in Troup County, Georgia on the 11th inst. at the residence of the bride's father by Rev. C.M. Irwin, Mr. Hunter C. Pope of Washington, Wilkes County to Miss Beatrice E. Hill, eldest daughter of Hon. E.Y. Hill.
Died with typhoid fever at the residence of Jacob Griffis, Autauga County, Alabama, September 29th, 1859 Joseph Green, son of Farmer and Nancy Adair, in his seventeenth year...
Died at the house of their father in Conecuh County, Alabama, September 6th, Emma R. Snowden, in the fifth year of her age; September 7th, Lilly Amanda Snowden in the thirteenth year of her age; September 8, Eliza N. Snowden in the tenth year of her age; September 9th, Frances Snowden, age four months...
Died at his residence in Russell County on the 16th of September 1859, Deacon Joseph M. Vann, in the fifty-first year of his age.

11-3-1859
Married on Tuesday morning, October ??? at the residence of Wm. Parmer in Montgomery County by the Rev. C.A. Stanton, Mr. Thomas E. Thomas of Macon County and Miss Mariah Louisa Parmer.
By the same on Thursday evening, October 20th at the residence of Pleastant Ma???, Mr. John A. Thomas and Miss Eliza J. Horne, all of Macon County.
Died in Columbus, Georgia on Sunday the 16th after a short illness of croup, Willie Elias, youngest daughter of Wm. E. and Elizabeth T. DuBose of Enon, Alabama, age three years, two months.
Died after several years extreme affliction at his residence in Coosa County, Alabama on the morning of the 17th of October 1859, Alfred B. Gary, age fifty-seven years, one month, twelve days...
Barnett Cody departed this life at his residence in Henry County, Alabama on the 13th day of October 1859. Brother Cody was born on the 17th day of January 1792 in Warren County, Georgia. He was married in the year 1813 to Sinai McCormick who survives him. Removed to Early County, Georgia in the year ???? where he was baptized into the fellowship of the church at Blakely, and made his earthly residence from 1819 till his death in Alabama. Of his five children, but one, Elder Edmund Cody, survives him...
Died in Tuscaloosa County, Alabama, October 11th, 1819, little Charlie, infant son of William and Louisa Clark, was born May 11th, 1859, age five months... On the second day after his death, his little body was brought to Bibb County, Alabama, to the graveyard near his grandfather's, where it was deposited there to sleep with two aunts, and three little cousins...

## Marriage and Death Notices From The South Western Baptist Newspaper

11-10-1859

Married in Siloam, Mississippi on the 13th of October by W.L. Foster, Mr. J.G. Montgomery and Miss Sallie K. Foster at the residence of her father, J.L.T. Foster, Ock. County, Mississippi.

Married on the 18th ult. by Rev. Mr. Welch, Mr. Albert J. Crumpler of Coosa County to Miss Bettie Ann, daughter of Wm. A. Morris of Talladega County.

Married on the morning of the 27th ult. by Rev. W.H. McIntosh, Mr. B.H. Crumpton of Dallas County to Miss Sallie C. Armstrong of Marion.

About eight miles southeast from Andalusia on Thursday, October 27th were married at the residence of B.B. Bass by G.A. Snowden, Judge of Probate, James Teel to Nancy Bass, William Teel to Mary Bass, Wilson Bass to Jane Teel. James, William and Jane Teel, all sons and daughter of John and Anna Teel; Wilson, Nancy and Mary Bass, all son and daughters of B.B. and Elizabeth Bass; all of Covington County, Alabama.

Died in Talladega County on the 7th day of October 1859, Thomas C. Wood after an illness of eighteen days. He was born in Greenville District, South Carolina on the 11 day of April 1819 but when quite young emigrated with his father to Jefferson County in this state... In 1847 he was married to Miss Nancy Truss and in 1848 they settled in Talladega County...

Departed this life on the 24th of October 1859, Mrs. Nancy Gafford, consort of Joseph M. Gafford of Greenville, Alabama. Her age was twenty-eight years, one month, fifteen days...

Died at his father's residence in Montgomery County, October 26th, 1859 of typhoid fever, Samuel Calhoun, the son of George W. and Frances Marshall, age sixteen years, eight months, nine days. The subject of this notice was a student of the Central Institute of Coosa County...

Died in Crawford, Alabama on the 19th day of October, Mrs. Hannah L. Calhoun, in the forty-sixth year of her age...

Tribute of respect on the death of D.F. Dean.

11-17-1859

Died, October 25th in Memphis, Tennessee at the residence of Col. J.M. Gonder, Mrs. Geraldine, wife of Mark F. Gonder of Louisiana and daughter of Rev. P.H. Lundy of Alabama... She requested to be buried near her Alabama home and where the friends of her childhood lived...

Died at his residence in Dallas County, Alabama, October 7, 1859 of a complication of disease of which rheumatism was the principal, Brother Elbert J. Hardy. He was born 25th July 1817, married to Miss Rebecca E. Watts on the last day of August 1843 and joined the Baptist Church at Town Creek, November 18th, 1837...

## Marriage and Death Notices From The South Western Baptist Newspaper

11-24-1859
Married in Glenville at the residence of the bride's mother by Elder E.Y. VanHoose, Mr. Warren W. Goolsbie and Miss Cynthia A. Evans, all of Barbour County, Alabama.
Also by the same near Glenville at the residence of Mrs. Cobb, Mr. Alexander Johnson and Miss Nancy A.S.S. Cobb, all of Barbour County, Alabama.
Died at his residence in this city on the 13th inst. William Larkins, in the seventy-ninth year of his age. The deceased was born in the county of New Hanover, North Carolina in the month of January 1778 and removed to this (Montgomery) County in the year 1819. In 1828 or '29 was baptized into the fellowship of the Baptist Church at Elim...
Died at the residence of E.H. Kinnebrew, (Louisiana) James A. Browning on the 3rd day of September 1859 of a congestive chill. He was born in the year 1837.
Died at the residence of her mother near Hardaway, Macon County, Alabama, Buenna, youngest daughter of J.R. Kindrick, deceased, and Mrs. N.S. Kindrick on the ? day of October last, age twelve years, four months...

12-1-1859
Died at the White Sulphur Spring in Meriwether County, Georgia on the 4th of October 1859 of typhoid fever, Mr. Moses Cox, in the twenty-seventh year of his age. He was born in Jones County, Georgia and in early life with his parents moved to Alabama. His health had been somewhat impaired and in the hope of regaining it he left Clayton, his residence, and went to the Springs, but instead of realizing the desired object the fell monster found him there and after a painful illness of some two months, he fell a victim to the grim monster death... He was a lawyer by profession...
Died in Tuskegee on the 15th November inst., Kate, only child of Wm. A. and Mary Jane Pinckard, age three years, two months, sixteen days...

12-8-1859
Married at the residence of the bride's mother, Col. J.C. Lewis of Russell County to Miss Eliza J. Kendrick of Macon County.
Married on the 1st inst. near Notasulga by A.P. Roberts esq., Mr. N.M. Bayzer to Miss Louisa D. Jackson, all of this county.
Died in this city on the 26th ult., Mrs. Ann Goram at the advanced aged of eighty-six years. The deceased was born in Tyrrell County, North Carolina the 25th September 1773 where she continued to reside up to the year 1852 when she removed to this place, where she resided up to the period of her death. Mrs. Goram had been a member of the Baptist Church about forty-five years, having been baptized into the fellowship of the Baptist Church at Edenton in the state of North Carolina by the Rev. Martin Ross, and upon her removal to this place in 1832(?) she united with the Baptist Church in which she lived...

## Marriage and Death Notices From The South Western Baptist Newspaper

Tribute of respect upon the death of Seaborn Williams from the members of the Tuskegee Bar...

12-15-1859
Married in the city of Eufaula on the 29th ult. by Rev. J.E. Dawson, Mr. Junius K. Battle of Tuskegee to Miss Sallie B. Hunter of Eufaula.
Married at La Place, Alabama on Tuesday morning, 6th inst., by Elder A.T.M. Handey, Mr. John A. Floyd and Miss M. Angella Greenwood.
Married by Rev. Andrew A. Lipscomb at the residence of the bride's mother in Tuskegee, Alabama on Thursday 8th inst. Col. Edward W. Pou, of Talbotton, Georgia to Miss Anna M. Smith.
Married on Wednesday evening the 7th inst. by Rev. C.S. Burks at the residence of the bride's mother, Mr. Wm. R. Collins of Georgia to Miss Elizabeth A. Williamson of Tallapoosa, County.
One of our most beloved, benevolent and patriotic men of the age has been cut off in the meridian of his activity and his usefulness, Seaborn Williams is no more! He was a native of Edgefield District, South Carolina and began life with meager means and limited advantages, never having gone to school more than three months; added to these the misfortune of a burn in childhood upon his left arm and breast, which enfeebled his constitution forever, and entailed upon him the bitter pangs of unutterable suffering. Such were the early advantages of one who selected the intricate profession of the law as his future avocation and by his assiduous efforts and diligent application, made himself one of the profoundest lawyers in East Alabama. He first located at La Fayette in Chambers County, Alabama, thence removed to Wedowee in Randolph County where he was very unfortunate and left that place very discouraged in search of a location; was attacked by sickness and compelled to stop at Tuskegee; upon his recovery he was so well pleased with this village that he permanently located here and commenced the practice of his profession...
Died at her residence in Monroe County, Alabama, Mrs. Claressa Coleman, the wife of James Coleman, deceased, in the sixty-sixth year of her age. Sister Coleman was born in Darlington District, South Carolina... She afterwards removed to Alabama, Monroe County, where she became a member of the Mount Pleasant Baptist Church...

12-22-1859
Married on Wednesday, November 16th, at the residence of the bride's father by Rev. David Lee, Mr. Robert McCall and Miss Melissa R. Robertson, all of Lowndes County.
Married on the 23rd ult. at the residence of the bride's father in Selma, Alabama by Rev. N.L. DeVotie, Mr. Henry G. Noble and Miss Sarah A. Melton, all of Selma.

## Marriage and Death Notices From The South Western Baptist Newspaper

In LaGrange, Georgia at the Simms House on the 8th inst. by the Rev. Mr. Cunningham, Dr. William S. Harris to Miss Matt. Edwards, all of Tuskegee.
At the residence of the bride's mother in Meriwether County, Georgia on the 15th inst. by E.B. Teague, Mr. C.M. Amoss of Tuskegee, Alabama to Miss Georgia F. Pyron.
Died at Spring Ridge, Louisiana on the 23rd ult. of typhoid fever, Jesse Williams, son of Elder Jordan Williams of Talladega County, Alabama.
Died in Chambers County, Alabama on the 20th September 1859, Sister Isabella Allen, consort of Brother William P. Allen, in the sixty-third year of her age... united with the Presbyterian Church in the early part of her life and continued an exemplary member of said church until the year 1838 when she united with the Baptist Church at Liberty on the 20th September. From that time to the day of her death (which was twenty-one years) she was truly a mother of the church... She was the mother of ten children, forty-six grandchildren and three great-grandchildren...
Died, December 4th, 1859 at the residence of his son-in-law, (Thomas Harvies) at Oak Hill, Wilcox County, Alabama, Rev. J.G. Collins, a Baptist minister, in the fifty-ninth year of his age. He was born in Edgefield District, South Carolina, June the 1st, 1801. He removed from South Carolina to Georgia and from thence to Mississippi when quite young, and embraced the religion of Christ in his twentieth year in Wayne County, Mississippi... He was married to Miss Mary Ann King, January 27th, 1825... Brother Collins leaves behind him a bereaved companion, two sons, a daughter...

1-5-1860
Married in Tuskegee on the 1st day of January 1860 by the Rev. Samuel Henderson, L.A. Abercrombie of Huntsville, Texas to Miss Livinia Chilton, eldest daughter of Hon. W.P. Chilton.
At the residence of W.B. Wynn in Gadsden, Alabama by Rev. S.R. Hood on the evening of the 7th November 1859 Rev. W.C. Boone to Miss M.E. Watson.
At the bride's father's in Andalusia, Alabama, December 22, 1859 by G.A. Snowden, Judge of Probate, Dr. Jas. H. Puriroy to Joicey Ann Riley, all of Covington County.
On the 20th December 1859 at the residence of Col. T.V. Rutherford (Chunnenuggee) by W.H. Ellison, D.D., Mr. H.W. Battle to Miss M.E. Moore, both of Macon County, Alabama.
By Elder F.H. Moss on 22nd December at the residence of Rev. P.M. Callaway, Macon County, Alabama, Dr. Aaron Witherington of Barbour County to Miss Ada Callaway.
On Wednesday evening, December 21st, at the residence of Col. R.R. Moseley, Monroe County, Alabama by Elder W.C. Morrow, Elder Z.G. Henderson of Pensacola, Florida and Miss Mattie H. Stearns of Swanton.

## Marriage and Death Notices From The South Western Baptist Newspaper

On the 22nd December by Rev. H.E. Taliaferro, Rev. John Robertson of Montgomery County to Mrs. Elizabeth Baker of Tuskegee, Alabama.

DIED: Mrs. Elizabeth Armstrong, she fell asleep in Jesus in Notasulga, Alabama, December 10th, 1859, in her eighty-sixth year. She was born in Chatham County, Georgia and was baptized by Rev. Henry Holcomb in Savanna, Georgia upwards of sixty years ago. She was a widow, Mrs. Butler, when she was baptized and soon there after married James Armstrong. In a few years after this marriage they removed to Wilkes County, Georgia where her husband became a distinguished Baptist minister and "finished his course" in 1835... Her remains were sent to the old homestead in Wilkes County, Georgia owned by her eldest son, Francis Armstrong...

Died at the residence of his father in Montgomery County, Alabama on the 26th day of October 1859, Samuel C., son of George and Sarah Marshall, age sixteen years, eight months, nine days...

Died at the residence of R.F. Owen in Pike County, Alabama on the 1st inst., Spurgeon, infant son and only heir of Elder J.J. and Dora Webb, age one month, sixteen days...

1-19-1860

Married on Thursday evening, December 8th, at the residence of P. Philips in Tuscaloosa County, Alabama, by the Rev. Charles Bain, Mr. J.N. Philips to Miss Mary E. Philips.

On Wednesday morning, December 14th, at the residence of Daniel Holly in Green County, Alabama by the Rev. Charles Bain, the Rev. S.D. Rogers of Mississippi to Mrs. J.C. Easley of Texas.

On the 10th of December by the Rev. Charles Bain, Mr. John J. Stuckney to Miss Laura A. Walker, all of Pickens County, Alabama.

On the 22nd of December by the Rev. Charles Bain, Mr. W.S. Hatter to Miss Tranquilla Thompson, all of Green County, Alabama.

On the 29th of December by Elder Charles Bain, Mr. Robert L. Belsher to Miss Julia A. Sugo.

On the night of the 3rd January 1860 in the city of Eufaula, Alabama by Elder A. VanHoose, Mr. Reuben F. Kobb and Miss M. Callie Cargile.

On the 28th ult. at the residence of the bride's mother near Camden, Arkansas by Rev. T.G. Freeman, Mr. Joseph W. Hale of Montgomery to Miss Maggie H. Lide.

Married on Tuesday evening, December 27th, by Rev. C.C. Willis, William A. Dunklin of Selma, Alabama to Miss Jennie A. Thompson of Muscogee County, Georgia.

On Wednesday morning, December 28th, at the residence of Pleasant Macon by Rev. C.A. Stanton, Mr. George A. Beck of South Carolina and Miss Charlotte M. Horn of Macon County.

By the same on Sabbath morning, January 1st, Mr. Clinton E. Harrell and Miss Susan A. Pettigrew, all of Macon County.

## Marriage and Death Notices From The South Western Baptist Newspaper

Married on the 3rd inst. at the residence of Mr. James Askew by Rev. J.W. Williams, Mr. Pleatus O. Whitlaker of Georgia to Miss Elizabeth Askew of Chambers County, Alabama.

On the 3rd inst. at the residence of the bride's mother, Chambers County, Alabama by Rev. J.W. Williams, Mr. Houston L. Griffen of Russell County to Miss Elizabeth Amanda Summers.

Died in Tuskegee on the 6th December 1859, Mrs. Mary Drakeford, in the forty-third year of her age. She was born in Covington County, Alabama, I believe...

It becomes our painful duty to announce the death of our beloved Brother Cunningham Wilson which occurred the 24th of December 1859. The disease which took him off was an affliction of the heart. He was born in Pendleton District, South Carolina and moved to Alabama in 1817; and was sixty-two years old. The subject of this notice was one of the first settlers of Talladega County... Kingston, Talladega County, Alabama.

Died at his father's residence in Butler County, Alabama, Furman Williams, son of Allen J. and Rebecca S. Mims. His demise occurred the 27th December last... He had just entered on his twenty-first year.

Died near Chunnenuggee, Macon County, on the 16th of October 1859, little Johnnie C. Baker, a son of John and Iphigenia Baker, after an illness of five weeks, age one year, seven months, fifteen days...

1-26-1860

Died on the morning of the 13th inst. at Bradford, Alabama, Mary Morgan Chilton, eldest daughter of Mr. and Mrs. Thomas G. Chilton, age two years, eight months.

Died in Russell County, Alabama on the 2nd day of November 1859, Mrs. Elizabeth Johnson, relic of the Laban S. Johnson, Jr., in the twenty-eighth year of her age, leaving two children...

Tribute of respect upon the death of Brother Morgan H. Riley, who died at his residence near Andalusia, Alabama on the 2nd day of January 1860.

Married in La Grange, Georgia on the 27th ult. at the residence of Mr. P.H. Greene by Rev. E.B. Teague, Mr. Wiley F. Jones and Miss Frances Fitzpatrick, all of La Grange.

In Tuskegee at the residence of the bride's uncle, Judge Dougherty, on the 11th inst. by the Rev. J.M. Mitchell, Mr. William F. Lee and Miss Susan R. Lloyd, both of Pensacola, Florida.

In New Orleans on the 12th inst. by the Rev. Arthur M. Small, R.H. Abercrombie and Miss Fannie Gary, all of Tuskegee, Alabama.

2-2-1860

Married in Montgomery County, Alabama at the house of Mr. R. Barnet by Elder J.A. Fonville, Mr. H.T. Clarke of Pine Level to Miss E.T. Locke, daughter of Judge Locke.

## MARRIAGE AND DEATH NOTICES FROM THE SOUTH WESTERN BAPTIST NEWSPAPER

Married on the 17th January, ult. by the Rev. Sam'l Henderson, Mr. Abner P. Hoffman of Macon County to Miss Mary M. Evans of Forsyth, Georgia.

Mt. Olive, Alabama January 13th, 1860: Dr. A.J. Kaukle of this place (Mt. Olive) was looking in the muzzle of a rifle gun, counting, the rifles, and by some unknown accident the gun went off and killed him, the ball entered his head near his right eye and passed back near the top of his head and lodged. He survived some fifteen hours, this happened on Saturday the 7th inst. and he was buried on Monday at this place, Mt. Olive... The doctor was born and raised near this place... He courted a Miss Louisa Harwell and was married to her in his nineteenth year... he lived a married life four years, and was snatched away from his loving wife and darling son...

Departed this life on the 27th of December last, Anna Matilda, daughter of J.C. and Julia A. Cooper, age three years, eleven months...

James Alexander Varner, son of William Varner, died at his father's residence in Tuskegee on the 11th of January 1860, in the twenty-first year of his age of inflammation of the brain. His illness was short, lasting not more than twelve hours...

Died in Tuskegee on the 27th ult., Mary Lewis, daughter of the late Dr. Jacob Lewis, in her tenth year.

2-9-1860

Married at the residence of Wm. Smith on the 28th of December by Rev.J.J. Harris, James Hammett to Matilda J. Smith, all of Macon County.

At the residence of Mr. Dickenson by Rev. J.J. Harris on the 15th of January, S.J. English to Miss M. Boswell, all of Pike County.

Died on the 26th of January of typhoid fever, Horatio B. Stark, age eighteen years, eleven days. He was the youngest son of B.W. and Nancy M. Stark.

Died in Macon County, Alabama on the 23rd of January 1860, Little Berry Crittenden, son of Ben. F. and Lizzie Crittenden, age three years, ten months, twelve days...

Tribute of respect from the Baptist Church in Clinton, Greene County, Alabama on the death of Rev. James R. Webster. He died on the 12th inst. at 5 o'clock p.m.

2-16-1860

Married on Wednesday evening the 15th of January 1860 at the house of Rev. John Howell in Taylor County, Georgia by Elder S.W. Du?ham, Mr. William Walker to Miss Emma Howell.

Married at the house of T. McGee in Taylor County, Georgia on the 23rd December 1859 by the Rev. John Howell, Mr. John A. Sanders to Miss Anna C. McGee.

Married on the 1st of February at the residence of Mr. Edward Garland by Elder E.Y. VanHoose, Mr. John M. Curry to Miss Emma L. Garland, all of Glenville, Alabama.

## Marriage and Death Notices From The South Western Baptist Newspaper

Married on the 31st January 1860 at the residence of Mr. S.S. Gullett by Elder J.D. Kendrick, Mr. William Jarvers of Georgia and Miss Leacy Riley of Wilcox County, Alabama.

Married at the residence of the bride's father in Shelby County, Alabama on the 2nd of February 1860 by Rev. T.J. Freeman, Mr. R.B. Priest, of Mount Olive, Alabama to Miss Elmira ? Cobb...

Died at his residence in Orion, Pike County, Alabama on the 28th day of January last, John Park; having since the 26th of December last entered his seventy-fourth year. He was a native of Prince Edward County, Virginia but was brought up principally in Greene County, Georgia where he lived for forty years...

Died at the residence of his son in Monroe County, Alabama, December 30th, 1859, Robert Lambert, a Deacon in the Claiborne Baptist Church. Brother Lambert was born in Burk County, Georgia in 1770, joined the Baptist Church in 1812, moved to Monroe County, Alabama in 1816 and joined the Claiborne Church...

Died in this county at the residence of Rev. J.M. Newman on the 30th November last, Mrs. Margaret Pool, in the eighty-ninth year of her age. She made a public profession of religion in 1845 and united with the Baptist Church in the city of Montgomery... She had survived nearly all the members of a numerous family...

Died at Cherokee Bayou, Rusk County, Texas, January 18th, 1860 of inflammation of the bowels, Allen Taylor, son of Allen and Maria Gibson. The subject of this notice was born in Talladega County, Alabama, July 3rd, 1846.

Departed this life on the 29th January at his residence in Barbour County, Alabama after a very short illness, Buckner Bass, in the seventieth year of his age.

Died at the residence of her husband, Willis Willingham, in Foster's Settlement, Tuscaloosa County, Alabama, December 18th, 1859, Mrs. Martha Willingham. For many years her health had not been good. She joined the Grant's Creek Baptist Church of Christ... She was taken sick Saturday, December 10th...

2-23-1860

John Hodges Drake, Sr. died in Auburn, Alabama on Sunday the 11th day of December 1859, in the ninety-third year of his age. The deceased retained his health and physical powers in an uncommon degree until the 1st day of December 1858 when he had the misfortune to receive a fall by which two of his ribs were fractured and his system, generally, so shocked as to render him entirely helpless for the remained of his life... John Hodges Drake was born in Edgecombe (now Nash) County, North Carolina, January 29th, 1767. Although he was too young to take part in the struggle for Independence he was reared in "the days that tried men's soul's" and with the example of his father and elder brothers, who periled their lives in the cause, he early

## Marriage and Death Notices From The South Western Baptist Newspaper

imbibed those principles of patriotism and love of right and justice, that characterized his life. The writer has often heard him recount many stirring incidents of revolutionary times and loved to see his noble countenance lit up with the fire of patriotism as he would relate them. One incident especially of which he was an eye witness, seemed to warm his whole soul with fire. It was the attack on his father's house in 1781 by a Captain Beard and his band of Tories, briefly alluded to in *Wheeler's History of North Carolina*. In this attack his father, a brother and two neighbors, contended hand to hand with Captain Beard and his company of over fifty tories until they were overcome and cut down, their bodies covered with wounds. Major Drake lived in his native county, Nash (formed from Edgecombe in 1777), for more than seventy-five years... He served in the North Carolina Legislature in the House of Commons from 1792 to 1796, and in the Senate in 1800 and 1805. He was for more than thirty years Clerk of the Superior Court of Nash County... Major Drake was a Master Mason. He was initiated into the Order in the town of Halifax, North Carolina near seventy years ago... sixty years ago he made a profession of religion and was baptized in Swift Creek, near Marne's Chapel, Nash County, North Carolina... After his death on Sunday his body reposed in the house of his son-in-law Maj. J.F. White, where he died, until the Tuesday following. On Tuesday morning an appropriate funeral discourse was pronounced by the Rev. M.B. Hardin, Pastor of the Baptist Church at Auburn. His remains were then taken in charge by the Masonic fraternity and borne to the depot where the last sad honors, peculiar to the Order, were performed. It was then placed on the cars and attended by a number of his children and friends, it was safely conveyed to the house of his son, Dr. John G.F. Drake, Nash County, North Carolina, arriving there on Thursday evening...

Married on the evening of 5th of January by the Rev. C.S. Burks, Mr. John Waller and Mrs. Mary E. Freeman.

By the same on Thursday evening the 16th inst., Mr. William Pugh and Miss Elizabeth A. Johnson, all of Tallapoosa.

3-1-1860

Married on the 1st February by Rev. E.Y. VanHoose, Mr. John M. Curry to Miss Emma L. Garland, all of Glenville, Alabama.

Married on the 20th February by Rev. T.J. Rutledge, Mr. George W. Huguly of Chambers County, Alabama to Miss Rebecca L. Gaines of Mount Sterling, Choctaw County, Alabama.

Mrs. M.C. Tichenor, late wife of Rev. ?.T. Tichenor of Montgomery, Alabama, and daughter of F.S. and Ann B. Cook, was born in Columbus, Georgia November 11th, 1828. Bereft of her parents at the early age of thirteen she was placed in the family of her uncle, Rev. John E. Dawson. ...Having finished her education she removed to Montgomery and resided with her brother-in-law, Mr. E.L. Ellsworth... In the summer of 1858 it was too evident

## Marriage and Death Notices From The South Western Baptist Newspaper

that the Destroyer had marked her for his own and steadily did she advance to his cold embrace. Having removed to the family of Mr. B.F. Noble, her brother-in-law, some five months since, she received the unremitting attentions of husband, and sisters and brothers, and friends... On the evening of the 13th inst. it was all over and our beloved sister now dwells in the presence of her Savior...

Died at his late residence in Foster's Settlement, Tuscaloosa County, Alabama on Thursday, January 26th, 1860, of pneumonia, William Lambert Bealle. He was born in Columbia County, Georgia, September 28th, 1815. His father died while he was an infant. When about eleven years old, in December 1826, he with his two older brothers were placed under the kind guardianship of his uncle and aunt, Mr. and Mrs. John S. Bealle, in this settlement. One of them, however, enjoyed the pleasant home only long enough to endear himself strongly in the affections of all and then Augustus sickened and died. The oldest of the three still lives. He was sent to the best schools the country afforded and when far enough advanced to the University of Alabama... After leaving the University he for a short time served as clerk in a store in Tuscaloosa and then retired to his farm. On November 14th, 1849 he was united in wedlock to Miss Martha C. Townsend. By this union they were blessed with four children. One dear little son preceded the father to the grave. Two sons and an infant daughter still live...

Died near Palo Alto, Mississippi on the 21st ult., Albert Y. Watkins, in the twentieth year of his age. The subject of this notice was a resident of Greene County, Alabama, and grandson of Mrs. M. Fleming...

Departed this life on Wednesday, February 1st, 1860, on board the steamer *Paul Jones* on the Washita River from an accidental discharge of a colt's repeater in his possession, Oliver A. Perry, son of Mathias A. and Susan Perry of Perry County, Alabama, age twenty years. The subject of this notice left his uncle's home in Alabama just eight days before in company with his cousin L.S. Perry on a tour of the West, full of hope and anticipation... The steamer was then landed and his remains deposited on the bank of the Washita River at the Washita City in Union Parish, Louisiana, away from father and home...

3-8-1860
Married in the city of Montgomery on Wednesday the 29th February by the Rev. Platt Stout, Gen. W.B. McClellan of Talladega to Miss Mary Ann, daughter of the officiating clergyman.

By the Rev. J.E. Bell on 7th of February, Mr. R.W. Holaman to Miss Mattie A. Allen, all of Greenville.

By the same on the 15th of February, Dr. D.H. Cropp to Miss Eugenie E. Pou, all of Greenville.

By the same on the 23rd of February Mr. Thaddeus G. Watts to Miss Mary F. Carter, all of Butler County.

## Marriage and Death Notices From The South Western Baptist Newspaper

Died in Marion, Alabama on the 14th ult., in the thirty-third year of her age Mrs. Sarah Muldred Fielding, wife of James H. Fielding, and daughter of Coleman J. and Eunice Brown.
Tribute of Respect from the church at Big Creek on the death of Reuben Dodson.
Tribute of respect on the death of Miss Mary A.A. Roberts.
Died on the 15th ult., Ira Pitt Jordan, youngest son of Ira T. and Mary T. Jordan, age seven months, three weeks.
Tribute of respect upon the death of Mrs. M.C. Tichenor.

3-15-1860
Married on the 1st of March 1860 at the residence of the bride's father by Elder J.D. Kendrick, Mr. F. Curzelius and Miss Catharine McLean, both of Wilcox County, Alabama.
Married at the residence of the bride's father on the evening of the 7th inst. by the Rev. Mr. Mitchell, Col. John W. A. Sanford to Miss Sallie, second daughter of Col. Wm. Henry Taylor, all of Montgomery.
Married on the 19th February by Elder G.L. Lee, Mr. P.B. Glover to Mrs. A. Peavy, both of Conecuh County, Alabama.
Married on the 22nd February by Rev. G.L. Lee, Mr. John G. Betts to Miss Eliza A. Satter, all of Conecuh County, Alabama.
Died near Pleasant Hill, Dallas County on the 24th of February, Addie Catts, the youngest child of Samuel W. and Adeline Catts, age about four years...
Tribute of respect from Benton (Baptist) Church on the death of Rev. Isaac Lyon.

3-22-1860
Married at the residence of the bride's father on the evening of the 16th inst. by the Rev. James P. ?, Mr. D.S. Welch to Miss Catharine ?, all of Smith County.
Died in Patsa? Valley, Pike County, Alabama on the 21st of February 1860, Miss Marietta H. Webb, aged ? years, ten months, twenty-one days...
John T. Sawyer, son of John Sawyer of Talladega County, died on the 26th day of February 1860, in his thirteenth year...

3-29-1860
Died in Scottsboro near Milledgeville on the 8th inst., Miss Catharine McDonald, sister to Hon. Charles J. McDonald.

4-5-1860
Married on the 21st of March 1860 at the residence of the bride by Elder J.D. Kendrick, Rev. John Wilmer and Mrs. E.R. Cook, all of Wilcox County, Alabama.

## Marriage and Death Notices From The South Western Baptist Newspaper

On Wednesday morning, 28th ult., at the residence of C.J. Woodruff in Wetumpka, Alabama by Rev. Platt Stout, Mr. James L. Coker of Society Hill, South Carolina to Miss Sue Stout, daughter of the officiating clergymen.

Died at her son's (V.D. Gresham) residence in Greene County, Georgia on the 29th February, Mrs. Mary Daniel, being, we presume, about sixty years of age...

Brother P.D. Stafford departed this life the 17th of January 1860, in the forty-second year of his age... He left a lovely companion and several children...

Col. Y.B. Jenkins died at his residence Monday night, March 19th, 1860, age fifty years. Born and raised in Greene County, Georgia. Joined the Baptist Church at Old Shiloh, near Mercer University, about the year 1826. Lived some years in Tallapoosa County... moved to Talladega County, was a useful member of Antioch Church... Left a devoted wife and seven children...

4-12-1860

Tribute of respect from Ridge Grove Lodge #128 of Free and Accepted Masons, held at their Hall (Ridge Grove, Macon County, Alabama) on the death of M. Bedell.

Married at Salem on the 29th ult. by Rev. W.B. Jones, Mr. C.T. Floyd to Miss Julia L. Dorsey, daughter of Isham Dorsey, all of Salem.

4-19-1860

Died at the residence of her son, Reuben Cooper, in Russell County, Alabama on the 4th of April, Mrs. Martha Cooper relict of the late Cammel Cooper, in the seventy-fifth year of her age. This venerable lady was baptized at Hardy's meeting house, Edgefield District, South Carolina, in the year 1809...

Micajah Bedell was born in Green County, Georgia on the 4th day of February 1795, where he lived until he moved to Macon County, Alabama in the Fall of 1838. He joined the Baptist Church about thirty-five years ago at Bethesda in Green County, Georgia. [date of death not given]

4-26-1860

Married at the residence of Col. Warren Akin in Cassville, Georgia, John S. Prather, Jr. of the *Chambers Tribune* to Miss Sue H. Verdery. Ceremony performed by Col. Akin.

Married at the residence of the bride's father on the 8th inst. by Robert F. Potilo, Mr. John H. Styron to Miss Sarah A. Ray, all of Upson County, Georgia.

Died at his father's residence Union Springs, Alabama on the 16th of March last Wm. Albert, eldest son of F.H. and J. Rosa Moss, age nine years, three days.

## MARRIAGE AND DEATH NOTICES FROM THE SOUTH WESTERN BAPTIST NEWSPAPER

Departed this life at her residence near Ash Creek, Lowndes County, Alabama, in the twenty-fifth year of her age, Mrs. Mary Ann Gordon, consort of David A. Gordon, and daughter of Calaway and Elizabeth Carpenter of Murray County, Tennessee... She left a little infant...

5-3-1860
Died in Butler County, Alabama, April the 10th of measles, infant son of Bennett and Julia A. Bowden, age six months, ten days...
Died on Monday, 16th inst., Mrs. Sarah Cody, wife of Elder Edmund Cody. A disconsolate husband and twelve children by this providence are bereft...
Married on Thursday morning, April 26th, at the residence of the bride's father in Macon County by Rev. C.A. Stanton, Mr. J.J. Whitaker of Heard County, Georgia and Miss Mary M. Cox.

5-10-1860
Married at 6 o'clock on the evening of the 18th ult. by Elder Geo. L. Lee, Mr. Alexander T. Henderson of Monroe County, Alabama to Miss Amanda Floyd of Conecuh County, Alabama.
Married on the 26th ult. at the residence of the bride's father in Tallapoosa County by Rev. S.E. Swope, Mr. Merit Street to Miss Martha J. Dunn.
Died of typhoid fever on the 23rd of March 1860, in the thirty-seventh year of her age, Mrs. Rebecca Cantey, wife of G.B. Cantey, and daughter of Andrew and M.M. Allen. Sister Cantey was born in Autauga County, Alabama and moved with her parents to Montgomery County in 1833. She was baptized in 1845 and united with the Baptist Church at Liberty. In November 1846 she was married to G.B. Cantey. She leaves a mother, two sisters, a husband and seven children...
DEATH OF REUBEN BLAKEY, Sr. and WILLIAM WATSON BLAKEY: On Saturday morning last Mr. Reuben Blakey, Sr. accompanied by two of his nephews, sons of Dr. B.A. Blakey, had gone to Calebee Cheek fishing. While there, the two little boys went into the water to bathe; the current being strong the youngest of the two (William W.) was carried into a deep hole and the aged uncle seeing him in the ? of drowning sprang in to rescue him from the waves, but his age and infirmity rendered him unequal to the task and they both sunk to a watery grave. Their bodies were recovered in the afternoon and the next day, followed by a large number of deeply afflicted friends and neighbors, were borne to the last resting place... Reuben Blakey, Sr. was in the seventy-second year of his age. He was a native of Georgia but emigrated to Alabama in the early settlement of the country... united with the Cubehatchie Baptist Church... Little "Willie" was in the twelfth year of his age...

## MARRIAGE AND DEATH NOTICES FROM THE SOUTH WESTERN BAPTIST NEWSPAPER

Died in Marion, Alabama on the 21st of April, Mrs. Martha Ann Lide, wife of J.H. Lide, and daughter of the late Jas. Lane of Darlington District, South Carolina. Mrs. Lide was born August 14th, 1814... A husband and eight children mourn...

5-17-1860
Married on the evening of the 1st inst. at the residence of the bride's mother in Lowndes County by the Rev. P.H. Lundy, Mr. Horace D. Rast to Miss Anna J. Pierce.
Married on the 12th of April by Elder Charles Bain, Mr. William C. Logan to Miss Francis Isabella Brown, all of Green County.
Married on the 3rd of May by the Rev. Charles Bain, Mr. James H. Wilkerson to Miss Louisa A. Thornton, all of Green County, Alabama.
Married on Sunday morning the 6th inst. at the residence of the bride's mother by the Rev. C.S. Burks, Mr. Terrell Fielder of Tallapoosa to Miss Fendassa Lanair of Macon County.
Married on the 8th inst. at the residence of the bride's father by Elder A. VanHoose, Mr. John D. Cunningham of Macon County, Alabama and Miss Cornelia Dobbins of Spalding County, Georgia.
Mrs. Sarah A. Cody, wife of Elder Edmund Cody, and daughter of the late Rev. Wm. Henderson, was born August 2nd, 1823 in Monroe County, Georgia, baptized... at the early age of twelve years, into the fellowship and communion of the Baptist Church at Clinton, Jones County, Georgia, was married to Elder Cody in 1840, and departed this life... at the residence of her husband in Henry County, Alabama on the 16th day of April 1860.
James K. Redd, Jr., the subject of this notice, was born in La Grange, Troup County, Georgia, April 19th, 1845, and died at 3 o'clock a.m., Wednesday, 2nd of May, at the residence of his father, J.K. Redd, Sr. of Columbus, Georgia, in his fifteenth year.
Tribute of respect from Antioch Church on the death of Col. Y.B. Jenkins.

5-24-1860
The subject of these lines, Miss Henrietta Campbell, was a daughter of Mr. Jno. D. Campbell and Mrs. Charlotte Campbell of Montgomery, Alabama. She was born in Chambers County, January 23rd, 1838. Most of her life was spent in Tuskegee. A few weeks since Miss Campbell visited her uncle Mr. A.D. Campbell of Kemper County, Mississippi...
Departed this life on the morning of the 6th inst., Mrs. Nancy Lockhart, wife of John H. Lockhart. The deceased was born in Newberry District, South Carolina. She lived several years in Lawrence District, until the winter of 1851; her husband emigrated to Russell County, Alabama where she remained to her death. She united herself with the Baptist Church at New Prospect, Lawrence District, South Carolina.

## MARRIAGE AND DEATH NOTICES FROM THE SOUTH WESTERN BAPTIST NEWSPAPER

Died, December 3, 1859 in Russell County, Alabama, Mrs. Sophronia S. Conway, a daughter of Paten and Eliza Waid, and wife and consort of Charles Conway, age sixteen years, nine months, nineteen days.

5-31-1860

Married on Sabbath morning the 20th inst. at the residence of the bride's father by Rev. C.A. Stanton, Mr. Garland W. Bostick and Miss Sarah Jane Hackney, all of Macon County.

Married on the 16th May at the residence of the bride's father by the Rev. P.H. Lundy, Mr. Mirabeau D. Lamar to Miss A.M. Doster.

Married at the residence of the bride's father on the 15th inst. by Rev. E. Greathouse, Mr. J.R. Melton to Miss A.E. Rowe, daughter of Col. John Rowe, all of Tallapoosa County.

Married at the residence of Col. Dendy in Hamilton, Harris County, Georgia on the 3rd of May by Elder E.Y. VanHoose, Mr. William Monroe Parker of Glenville, Alabama to Miss Emma A. Dendy of the former place.

Married on the 22nd inst. at the Baptist Church by Rev. I.T. Tichenor, Dr. B.F. Blount and Miss Sallie E. Molton, both of Montgomery.

Married at the residence of the bride's father (Mr. J.L. Howard) on the 23rd inst. by S.B. Johnston, Mr. A.J. Bissell of the Marianna (Florida) Enterprise and Miss S.J. Howard of this place.

Died October 4, 1859, Fatama Corbin Speakman, wife of A.H. Speakman, and daughter of William and Sarah Pope of Morgan County, Alabama after a brief illness. Sister Speakman was born 5th of October 1826 in Morgan County, Alabama...

Died at Selma, Alabama on Monday the 7th inst., Mary E. Dawson, wife of N.H.R. Dawson, in the twenty-sixth year of her age.

Died in Marion, Alabama on the 22nd of April, Mrs. Penelope Fagan, wife of Enoch Fagan. Mrs. F. was born in Washington County, North Carolina, March 30, 1814 and was married September 15, 1831. She removed to Alabama in 1834 and was baptized into the fellowship of the Baptist Church at Wetumpka, by Rev. A.W. Chambliss in 1842...

6-7-1860

Married May 16, 1860 at the residence of the bride's father by the Rev. Dr. Duvall, Dr. ? Williams of Allenton, Wilcox County, Alabama to Miss Mollie C. Eldridge of Independence, Washington County, Texas.

Married on the 31st ult. at the residence of the bride's father by Rev. John Robertson, Mr. Wm. Martin to Miss Malissa J. Furlow, all of ? County, Alabama.

Died at his late residence near Crawford, Russell County, Alabama on Tuesday, May the ?, 1860, of pneumonia, Jeremiah S. ?ams. He was born in Gwinnett County, Georgia the 15th of May 1823.

## MARRIAGE AND DEATH NOTICES FROM THE SOUTH WESTERN BAPTIST NEWSPAPER

Died at the residence of her parents near Ridge Grove, Macon County, Alabama on the 27th of May of scarlet fever, Frillia Endalia Herring, youngest child of Isaac and Louisa A. Herring, age three years, three months, fourteen days.
Died on the 8th inst. at his residence in Auburn, Joseph B. Williams, age about thirty-five years.
Died at Fort Browder, Barbour County, on the 6th day of January 1860, Mrs. Elizabeth Marshall, consort of Thos. Marshall. Sister Marshall was born in Sumpter District, South Carolina on the 6th day of May 1799. She attached herself to the Methodist Church in 1827 and (until her removal to Alabama in 1849) lived a consistent and blameless member...

6-14-1860
Departed this life in Griffin, Georgia, May 27th, 1860, Mary Pauline VanHoose, infant daughter of Rev. A. VanHoose and wife, age just thirteen months.

6-21-1860
Married on the 6th June 1860 at the residence of the bride's mother in Russell County, Alabama by Elder E.Y. VanHoose, Mr. Benj. R. Henry of Glenville and Miss Maggie A. Vann.
Married on the evening of the 6th inst. at Rocky Mount, the residence of the bride's father, by Elder J.A. Fonville, Dr. Jno. S. Pitts and Miss Mary S. Allen.
Departed this life in Macon County, Alabama, May 29, 1860, Allen Richardson, eldest son of Jonathan S. and Martha Jane David, age four years, four months, twenty-seven days.
Died at his residence in Autauga County, Alabama on Saturday April 21, 1860, Jasper J. Apperson, with typhoid fever after a painful illness of thirty days. He was the son of John and Mary Apperson. Deceased was born in 1827. He leaves a wife and three small children...
Died, April 8, 1860 at his residence in Butler County, Alabama, James Capps. Brother Capps leaves a wife and four little ones to mourn... [see below]
Died, April 12, 1860, Brother John Capps, brother to James. Brother John, though younger than his brother that went before him only four days, became a member of the church about three years ago... [see above]

6-28-1860
Married at the residence of the bride's father in Lowndes County, June 12th by the Rev. P.H. Lundy, Mr. H.P. Caffey to Miss M.E. Rast.
Married in this county on the 13th inst. at the residence of Mr. John Shackelford by Rev. A.T.M. Handey, Mr. Daniel McGill of Texas to Miss Telitha J. Shackelford of Macon County, Alabama.
Died in Philadelphia, Pennsylvania on the 12th inst., Mary Lizzie Shuck, daughter of Edwin H. and Mary S. Banney, age three years, five days.

## Marriage and Death Notices From The South Western Baptist Newspaper

Departed this life June 13, 1860 at home near Perryville, Perry County, Alabama, in the fifty-fourth year of her age, Mrs. Elizabeth P. Miree, wife of Wm. S. Miree, and daughter of Louis and Cynthy McLendon of Georgia. Sister Miree was born in Wilkes County, Georgia, November 13, 1805. Moved to this state with her husband in the year 1822. Was baptized into the fellowship of the Baptist Church at Shilo in 1826. Became a member of the Pisgah Church in the year 1834...

Maj. Dozier Thornton, the subject of this obituary, was born in Elbert County, Georgia, 21 October 1801 and died at his residence in Cherokee County, Alabama, 10 June 1860. He was for thirty years a member of the Baptist Church and for fifteen a Deacon...

Tribute of respect from Masonic Hall, Penick Lodge #161, June 2, 1860 on the death of Augustus W. Deloach.

Died at her residence near Marion, Alabama on the night of the 7th inst., Mrs. Lucinda Oliver, in the seventieth year of her age. She was a native of Greenville District, South Carolina, removed to Alabama with her husband and settled in Perry County in 1810... She was the last survivor but one of those who constituted the Siloam Baptist Church at Marion.

Died at the residence of her husband, Perry County, Alabama, February 28, 1860, Mrs. Mary V. Hannah, in the thirty-sixth year of her age. The deceased was born in the town of Marion, Alabama, March 24, 1824... In December 1845 she was united in marriage with William S. Hannah, her present afflicted survivor. In 1850... became a member of the Baptist Church (Hepsibah) on Oakmulgee Creek in Perry County, Alabama...

Died on the 20th inst. Alonzo Small, son of John B. and Georgiana Ann Campbell.

7-5-1860

Died on the 27th of April at the residence of her husband, McCreles Corley, Mrs. Mahala Corley. The deceased was born in Edgefield District, South Carolina, September 30, 1806. She was a daughter of John and Sarah Bledsoe... She was baptized by Dr. Manly into the fellowship of Mountain Creek Church, Edgefield District, South Carolina about the year 1823.

Died of congestion at her home in Auburn, Macon County, Alabama on Friday the 25th day of May 1860, Mrs. Volecia V.A. Drake, wife of John W.W. Drake, and daughter of the late Augustus G.C. and Elizabeth W. Mitchell. In childhood she was bereft of her father by death. Soon after the decease of her husband the widowed mother and her little family of five daughters (the subject of this obituary being the youngest but one) removed to Harris County and afterwards to Auburn, Alabama where she died on 16 December 1852... Mrs. Drake was married on 22 February 1848... She leaves three clear-minded, bright-eyed boys to perpetuate her memory. Their ages are eleven, seven, and four years...

## Marriage and Death Notices From The South Western Baptist Newspaper

7-19-1860

Married in this county on the 3rd inst. at the residence of the bride's father by Rev. A.T.M. Handey, Mr. Byron L. Taylor of Texas and Mrs. Charlotte K. Adams.

Married in Centreville, Bibb County, Alabama on the evening of the 5th inst. by the Rev. H.A. Smith, Dr. E.H. Moren and Miss Fannie, daughter of Col. S.W. Davidson, all of Centreville.

Died on Wednesday 20th inst. at his residence in Columbia County, Arkansas after a brief illness of bilious fever, Mr. Thomas J. Watts, in the fifty-first year of his age. The deceased had emigrated to this state from Alabama several years since... He leaves a wife and four young children...

Died in Notasulga, Alabama, the 26th of June, Theodore Ledbetter, youngest son of J.W.C. and P.J. Denson, age ten months, four days.

Departed this life in Tuskegee, Alabama on the 11th inst. Thomas Worrell, youngest son of Dr. S.S. and Mrs. M.S. Oslin, age three years, nine months, eleven days.

Died at Society Hill, Macon County, Alabama on the 3rd of June 1860, in the forty-first year of his age... William Ligon.

Departed this life on the 4th of May 1860 in Chambers County, Alabama Sister Patsey Slaughter, wife of Lawson Slaughter. Sister Slaughter died of dropsy of the chest... was about sixty-two years old when she died... She has left a husband and several children...

7-26-1860

Died at the family residence in Conecuh County, Alabama on the 9th of April 1860, Mrs. Mary Ann Ashley, in the sixtieth year of her age. The deceased was a native of South Carolina, Barnwell District, daughter of Adam McCreary, and consort of Captain Wilson Ashley to whom she married in 1819. They came to Alabama in the year 1821...

Departed this life on the evening of 10 July 1860 after an illness of about two months of typhoid fever at the residence of her father, China Grove, Alabama, Tabitha E. Bass, youngest daughter of Elder Jas. C. Bass and wife Jenette, age one year, six months, eight days...

Died at the residence of her father, Samuel Wooddy, in Chambers County, Alabama on the 8th day of June 1860, Miss Polly S. Wooddy, age twelve years, one month. The deceased was born and raised at the place where she died...

8-2-1860

Died at her residence near Perote, Pike County, Alabama on the 15th July 1860 after six months severe suffering with chronic cough, Mrs. Sarah Rodgers, wife of Thomas E. Rodgers, age about sixty-eight years. She was a native of Elbert County, Georgia. She leaves a husband, six children...

## Marriage and Death Notices From The South Western Baptist Newspaper

Died in Columbus, Georgia, on Saturday the 14th of July of cholera infantum, Mary Birt, infant daughter of T.B. and M.B. Scott, age fifteen months, three days.
Died in the evening of the 2nd day of July ult. Mrs. Laura E., wife of H.W. Watson of this city. She was attacked on Sunday the 17th of June last with what was supposed to be typhoid fever... She died young, her race was a short one, having been born in Camden, South Carolina on the 28th day of November 1828...

8-9-1860
Married on Sunday evening the 29th ult. at the residence of the bride's father by Rev. Sam. Henderson, Mr. Richard A. Buck to Miss Harriet, daughter of Maj. E.S. Grover, all of this place.
Died on the 27th of July 1860 at the residence of Emsley Bearden in Perry County, Alabama, John A. Williams. The deceased was born in Dallas County, Alabama, February 14, 1833. He moved to Perry County five or six years ago and became a member of Friendship Church... Mr. Williams in company with three others went on a fishing excursion to a pond on Oakmulga Creek. While in the pond he received his death wound from a moccasin snake. He survived about twenty-four hours. The deceased leaves a wife and child to lament his loss.
Died in Loachapoka, Alabama, June 14, 1860 Julian W., son and only child of Mickleberry P. and Mary Jane Ferrell of Troup County, Georgia, age three years, ten months, twenty-five days.
Dr. Moses Y. Granberry was born March 26, 1830 in Dooly County, Georgia, moved with his father to Harris County when young. He studied medicine with Dr. Spaulding and attended his first course of lectures in the winter of 1853 at the Augusta Medical College. He was baptized by Brother Thornton and united with the Baptist Church at Liberty in July 1855. He died July 2, 1860 after a short but severe illness of typhoid fever.

8-16-1860
Married on the 7nd [?] day of August at the residence of the bride's mother of Auburn, Alabama by Rev. M.B. Hardin, Mr. P.H. Swanson and Miss Mianda P. Jordan, all of the former place.
Married in Talladega County at the residence of the bride's father on Tuesday evening the 24th by the Rev. O. Welch, Dr. S.M. McAlpin to Mrs. H.G. Wallis, daughter of Col. Wm. Mallory, all of this county.
Died in Talladega on Sunday morning the 29th July, Jackson Thomas, son of J.L.M. and Ann A. Curry, age nine months.
Died on the 22nd ult. near Notasulga, Alabama of a short but painful illness, Mary Jane, eldest daughter of Sam'l and Jane L. Reid, in the sixteenth year of her age... West Point, Georgia, 11 August 1860; Galveston, Texas papers please copy.

**MARRIAGE AND DEATH NOTICES FROM THE SOUTH WESTERN BAPTIST NEWSPAPER**

8-23-1860
Married at the residence of the bride's father in this county on Wednesday morning 8th inst. by Rev. A.T.M. Landey, Mr. J.B. Murrell to Miss Martha A. Lightfoot.
Died in Autauga County, Alabama, May the 25th, Mrs. Isabella <u>Hadaway</u>, relict of Deacon Levi <u>Handaway</u>, in the sixty-second year of her age. The subject of this brief notice was a citizen of Georgia, being on a visit to friends and relatives at the time of her death... For more than thirty years she was a faithful and devoted member of the Baptist Church, and at the time of her death was in full fellowship with the Sandy Creek Church, Morgan County, Georgia. She leaves five children...
Mrs. Ann Haseltine Lasiter, wife of John Lasiter, died in Scott County, Mississippi the 1st of July 1860, in the twenty-fifth year of her age. She was the daughter of Daniel and Emeline Odom. Sister Lasiter was born in Muscogee, County, Georgia and was baptized by the Rev. James Whitten into the fellowship of the Philadelphia Church, Russell County, Alabama... She left three children, a kind husband... She was the granddaughter of Dozier Thornton...

8-30-1860
Tribute of respect from Ezel Lodge #175 upon the death of fellow Brother Wm. T. McLendon, who died April 4, 1860.

9-5-1860
Coosa County, Alabama August 29, 1860. Mrs. Louisa A. Swindal, wife of Manly M. Swindal, died in Montgomery County, Alabama on the 21st of August 1860, in the twenty-seventh year of her age. She was the daughter of James and Jane Adams. She was born in Troup County, Georgia whence her parents removed to Coosa County, Alabama... in December 1859 she was married to Manly M. Swindal by the Rev. Moses Gunn and removed to Montgomery, where she died. She left an affectionate husband and kind parents, and brothers and sisters...

9-13-1860
Tribute of respect from La Place, Alabama, Chilton Lodge #129 upon the death of James G. Clark. Brother Clark was born in Surry County, Virginia the 9th March and departed this life at his residence in this county after a long and painful affliction on Saturday the 25th inst...
Died of congestion at the residence of her son, R.R. Harrell, Daleville, Alabama on the 18th inst., age sixty-three years, Mrs. Margaret Harrell, born January 1797, Gates County, North Carolina where she was married to Miles Harrell in 1816. She emigrated to Jones County, Georgia where she remained for some time; thence to Houston County, Georgia where she was baptized into the fellowship of Hayneville Baptist Church in 1841... From

## MARRIAGE AND DEATH NOTICES FROM THE SOUTH WESTERN BAPTIST NEWSPAPER

Houston County she moved to Pulaski County where she was bereft of her husband in 1846, since which time she remained a widow, living with her children...
Departed this life at the residence of his father in Chambers County, Alabama of typhoid fever, July 27, 1860, John E. Davis, second son of Wm. and Eliza Davis, age twenty-five years, nine months, sixteen days.

9-20-1860
Died at her father's residence in the county of Chambers, Alabama of typhoid fever on the 28th July 1860, Martha Elizabeth Finney, daughter of Wm. H. and Theresa Finney, age twenty years, four months.
Died July 31 at Rock Alum Springs, Virginia, Harden B. Littlepage, a resident of Montgomery, Alabama. Brother Littlepage was born in Virginia, October 21, 1827. Some three or four years ago he removed to this place...
Died at her residence at Clauselville, Monroe County, July 22, 1860 of measles, Martha Jane, wife of L.R. Wiggins, age twenty-five years, eleven months, twenty-two days. She has left a bereaved husband and four little children...

9-27-1860
Died August 23 at his residence in Kemper County, Mississippi, Judson F. Hand, in the thirty-seventh year of his age. The deceased was a native of Georgia where he spent most of his life... About four years ago he moved to Mississippi in hope of regaining his health. Since then he has been quietly living on his plantation until about twelve days previous to his death when he was attacked with fever which terminated in congestion of the brain... A disconsolate wife is bereft of a devoted husband, aged parents of their first born, sisters and brother...
Died at his residence in Randolph County, Alabama on the 24th day of August 1860, in the thirty-first year of his age, Brother J.P. Barnett. The subject of this notice was born in Union District, South Carolina. In early life he removed with his parents to Georgia... joined the Baptist Church of Christ at Macedonia, Coweta County, Georgia. He subsequently came to Randolph County, Alabama where he married Margaret Riddle...
Died in Clayton, Alabama on Sunday the 2nd inst. Henrietta, infant daughter of M.D. and Ann Oliver, age one year, seven months, ten days.
Died near Tuskegee, Alabama on the 3rd inst., in the twenty-third year of her age, Martha Tidwell, wife of John Tidwell...

10-4-1860
Died in Scott County, Mississippi on the 10th of September 1860 after a severe illness of fourteen days, Mrs. Nancy P. Haralson, in the fifty-second year of her age. She was the wife of Mr. ?.E. Haralson and daughter of the Rev. William and Elizabeth May. The subject of this notice was born

## MARRIAGE AND DEATH NOTICES FROM THE SOUTH WESTERN BAPTIST NEWSPAPER

April 4, 1809 in Green County, Georgia whence her parents removed to Lowndes County, Alabama 1823. She married December 15, 1826, united herself with the Baptist Church in Troup County, Georgia in 1829... she leaves a kind husband and four affectionate children...
Tribute of respect from the Tuskegee Light Infantry upon the death of private Lucius M. Bryan.

10-18-1860
Died in Cross Keys, Macon County, Alabama on the 2nd day of July 1860, in her thirty-seventh year, Mr(s) Theodosea H. McGinty, her disease was that fell destroyer of human life, the consumption, with which she was afflicted near two years...

10-25-1860
Died in Macon County, Alabama on the 10th of September 1860, Mrs. Eliza Benton, wife of Mr. George Benton, and daughter of Col. Wm. Davis of Georgia, in the twenty-fourth year of her age. She was born in 1836... was married in the fall of 1859.

11-1-1860
Married at West Point, 21st inst. by J.M. Woodruff, M.G., M.L. Mock to Miss Sarah A. Dayle, both of Macon County, Alabama.
Married in Benton at her father's residence, October 4th by the Rev. D. Lee, Mr. J.M. Baker of Mobile to Miss A.M. Kelly of the former place.
Married on Thursday, 11th inst., in Macon County by Rev. Mr. Handey, Mr. Thos. S. Zuber and Miss Mary N. Nuckolls.
Died, September 18, 1860 at St. Paul, Minnesota, Osborne Parker, a member of the Baptist Church in Tuscaloosa, Alabama. He was born at Burnt-corn, Alabama, December 11, 1833... In 1855 after having graduated at the University of Alabama, with the highest honors, he became a citizen of Tuscaloosa... He had gone to the North in hopes of benefitting his health.
Died at his residence in Russell County, Alabama on the 24th inst., William Lynn, age seventy-six years. He joined the United Baptist Church at Teman, Georgia thirty years since...

11-8-1860
Died in Cusseta, Chambers County, Alabama on the 28th October 1860, Mary Bell, only daughter of E.W. and M.A. Williams, age two years, one month, twenty-one days.

11-15-1860
Died on the 5th September 1860, Thos. F. Morrison, son of Brother Thos. J. and sister Lauretta E. Morrison, age three years, nine months, of that fatal disease called croup... Oakfuska, Randolph County, Alabama.

## MARRIAGE AND DEATH NOTICES FROM THE SOUTH WESTERN BAPTIST NEWSPAPER

Died at her residence in this county the morning of the 2nd of October after an illness of several months continuance, Mrs. Eliza Margaret Hale, wife of Mr. Samuel Q. Hale, and daughter of the late Mr. Joseph B. White of Sumpter District, South Carolina. Mrs. Hale was born in Sumpter District and received her education in Dr. Mark's Seminary at Columbia... In 1836 she was joined in marriage to Mr. Hale and removed with him to Montgomery, Alabama the place of his residence at that time... A disconsolate husband and three sons mourn their irreparable loss.

Thomas B. Pace died at his residence near Coffeyville, Alabama, October 27, age sixty years... The deceased was walking from his house to the gate, when he fell speechless, and never spoke any more; he survived a few hours...

Departed this life on the 28th September 1860 at her residence in Black's Bend, Wilcox County, Mrs. Hannah Elizabeth, consort of Isham Moore; age forty-seven years, five months, twenty-eight days... Sister Moore was born in Darlington District, South Carolina on the 1st of April 1813, came to Conecuh County, Alabama in 1821. She was married to Isham Moore on the 29th of September 1830. She was preceded to the grave by her little son, Jesse Alexander, who died on the 21st of September 1860 (only seven days before her), age six years, seven months, fifteen days.

Departed this life in hope of a blessed immortality, Mrs. Didama Bennet, the widow of the Rev. Mitchell Bennett, late of Russell County, Alabama. She was born December 15, 1786 in Pendleton District, South Carolina and died at her residence in Russell County, Alabama October 11, 1860.

Married in Tallapoosa County at the residence of the bride's father on the 16th October by Rev. E.W. Henderson, Dr. M. Lucius Fielder to Miss Louisa F. Burks, all of Tallapoosa County, Alabama.

At the residence of the bride's father on the evening of 25 October by Rev. Geo. L. Lee, Mr. Euclidus S. Longshore to Miss Mattie F. Hix, all of Butler County, Alabama.

In Conecuh County, Alabama on the 1st November at the residence of the bride's father by Elder Geo L. Lee, Mr. Bryant L. Pritchett of Monroe County, Alabama to Miss Mary A. Thornton, daughter of N. Thornton.

11-22-1860

Married in Russell County, Alabama on the evening of the 13th inst. by Rev. Dr. Lovick Pierce, Mr. John H. Martin, Editor of the *Columbus Enquirer*, and Miss Isabella J. McGehee, daughter of Isaac McGehee of Russell County.

Married on the 1st inst. by Rev. W.E. Lloyd, Mr. J.T. Maxwell to Miss S.A. Robert.

On the 7th inst. by the same, Mr. J.J. Right to Miss L.D. Cloud, all of Macon County.

Married by Rev. Wm. Menefee at the residence of the bride's father on the 6th inst., Mr. R.T. Davis to Miss Mary Forte, all of Macon County.

## MARRIAGE AND DEATH NOTICES FROM THE SOUTH WESTERN BAPTIST NEWSPAPER

Married on the 8th November at the residence of the bride's father by Prof. J.M. Armstrong, R.C. Griffin to Miss Mary J. Abercrombie, all of Perry County.
Married on Wednesday evening, 7 November, in Conecuh County, Alabama by Elder Geo. L. Lee, Mr. William R. Watson of Monroe County, to Miss Susan Page.
Died of consumption at his residence, Union Springs, Alabama on the 20th day of October 1860, Mr. A.J. Bagby. The deceased was about forty-five years old... He has left a wife and several children...

11-29-1860
Married on the 15th inst. at the residence of the bride's father by Elder J.D. Kendrick, Elder J.T. Caine and Miss Drury Hames of Perry County, Alabama.
Married at the residence of the bride's mother on the 21st inst. by Elder Geo. L. Lee, Mr. Thos G. McQueen to Miss Mary A. Page, all of Conecuh County, Alabama.
Tribute of respect upon the death of D.J. Parsons.
Died at his residence in Shelby County, Alabama on the 5th of November 1860, Rev Levi A. Honeycutt. He was born in Bibb County, Alabama on the 29th of December 1827. About the year 1848 he was married to Miss Harriet B. Collier of Lauderdale County, Mississippi. Shortly after this they both united with the Baptist Church and subsequently moved to Shelby County, Alabama... besides a faithful companion he leaves six little children.
Died at her residence in Russell County, Alabama on Wednesday the 31st of October 1860, in her eighty-sixth year, Sarah Aldridge. She was born in Cumberland County, Virginia on the 5th of February 1775 of respectable parents. Her father, Mr. Mathias Liverman, emigrated to Georgia while she was a youth. She was married to Reuben Aldridge on the 17th September 1795 and united with the Baptist Church at Green Brier Church, Columbia County, Georgia in April 1804...
Died at his residence near Hickory Grove on the 6th day of November, Addison Stewart Armstrong, in the forty-second year of his age... He was afflicted fifteen years with a complication of diseases.

12-6-1860
Tribute of respect from West Point Lodge #43 on the death of Brother Samuel T. Whitaker. Samuel T. Whitaker, son of Oroon D. and Martha R. Whitaker, was born in Putnam County, Georgia, November 4, 1825 and died in Chambers County, Alabama, November 16, 1860, age thirty-five years, twelve days. In 1833 his parents moved into this community and here he was reared, educated, lived and has died.
Tribute of respect from Brooklyn Church: We are called upon to record one of the most painful and melancholy events in our church history. On the 26th day of October 1858 our beloved Sister Mrs. Nancie Johnston, wife of Brother Caleb Johnston, departed this life. And on the 28th day of June 1860 our

MARRIAGE AND DEATH NOTICES FROM THE SOUTH WESTERN BAPTIST NEWSPAPER

beloved Brother Caleb Johnston followed his wife in death. They were born in the state of Georgia, the husband January 16, 1790, the wife August 13, 1794. They emigrated to Alabama in the earliest settlement in the year 1819...

12-13-1860
DIED: last week Mr. Junius K. Battle...(*Eufaula Spirit of the South*)
Tribute of respect from the Baptist Church at Tuskegee on the death of Rev. John E. Dawson, D.D.
Departed this life on the 22nd November 1860 at this residence near Skipperville, Dale County, Alabama, Martin M. McLendon, age fifty years, eight months, three days, after a season of protracted afflictions which he bore for near three months... Brother McLendon was born on 19 March 1810 and he was baptized into the fellowship of Bethlehem Church, Barbour County, by Peter Eldredge in 1842... He left a pious and good family consisting of an affectionate wife and ten children...
Mr. Martin H. Day died at his residence in Pike County, Alabama on the 16th ult. after a painful illness of thirty-four days, in the fifty-seventh year of his age. The subject of this notice was born in Green County, Georgia and from thence he emigrated to South Carolina... thence to Alabama of which state he remained a citizen until his death... was baptized into the fellowship of the Cool Spring Church of Russell County in the year 1847... He left a companion and seven children...

12-20-1860
Married at the bride's residence in Marengo County, Alabama on Sabbath morning the 18th November by Elder J.C. Foster, Wm. L. Tucker of Georgia to Mrs. Martha W. Tucker of Marengo County, Alabama.
Married at the residence of Dr. Sprott in Dallas County, December 6 at 10 o'clock a.m. by the Rev. P.H. Lundy, Mr. W.H. Blackman and Miss Lucy Addison.
Married at 8 o'clock p.m., December 6 by the Rev. P.H. Lundy at the residence of Col. Wm. Tarrance, Mr. Charles T. Hrabowski to Miss Elizabeth M. Tarrance.
Married on the 6th inst. by the Rev. D.P. Bestor, Mr. John T. Bostor of Mobile to Miss Tide Barnett of Jasper County, Mississippi.
Died on the 3rd inst. at the residence of Mr. H.H. Bacon in Montgomery, Mrs. Georgia D. Fannin, consort of the late Col. William F. Fannin, and eldest daughter of the late Rev. John E. Dawson...
Died at Collirene, Lowndes County, Alabama, November 9, 1860, Mary Kunklin Tha??, age seven years, two months, fourteen days.
Died near Orion, Pike County, Alabama, Mrs. Mary, consort of M.T. Hall, and daughter of Maj. J.B. Hooten, in her twenty-fifth year. Her disease was typhoid fever... leaves three children.

## Marriage and Death Notices From The South Western Baptist Newspaper

Died in Auburn on the 5th inst., Mary A. Sale, daughter of Major J.C. Sale, age eighteen years...
Died at her residence on the 17th day of October last, after nine days painful illness, Margaret L. Averett, wife of William A. Averett, and daughter of Moses and Susan M. Hamilton of Lowndes County, Alabama. Mrs. Averett was born in Lowndes County, Alabama and received her education, and was married in that county to Wm. Averett on the 20th day of April 1854, with whom she moved her residence to Talladega County... She has left three sweet little girls... Her mortality rests in the grave yard at Fort Williams Church, within a few feet of her sweet infant and much loved three sisters-in-law...

1-3-1861
Tribute of respect upon the death of Professor R.A. Montague from the students of Howard College.
Died in Harris County, Georgia, November 25, 1860, in the forty-sixth year of her age, Mrs. Frances Roberts, daughter of Uriah and Mary Blanchard. She was born in Columbia County, Georgia, April 17, 1814, was married to Mr. K.H. Roberts in 1835 and removed to Harris County, where she continued until her death. She has left to mourn her loss, a husband and five children.

1-10-1861
Married in Marion, Alabama on the 18th December by Rev. F.C. Lowrey, Rev. Wm. H. McIntosh to Mrs. Ann Kirksey.
On the 25th day of December at the residence of the bride's father on Chunnenuggee Ridge by the Rev. Sam'l Henderson, Dr. Moses Worthington of Barbour County to Miss Mary L. Callaway, daughter of Rev. P.M. Callaway.
On the 20th ult. by the Rev. Mr. Matthews, Mr. Esselman Varner to Miss Sallie Wilson, daughter of Wm. A. Wilson, esq. of Weogufka, Coosa County, Alabama.
At 11 o'clock a.m. on 13 December by Rev. Platt Stout, Mr. Andrew H. Plyant to Miss Mattie Letcher, daughter of John D. Letcher of Central Institute.
Also on the 26th December by the same, Mr. Kenneth King of Texas to Miss Bettie Alabama Letcher, daughter of J.D. Letcher, all of Central Institute, Alabama.
Also on the 19th by the same [Rev. Stout], Mr. John T. Carlton to Miss Mollie Plyant of Wetumpka, Alabama.
The subject of this sketch, Junius Kincaid Battle, youngest son of Dr. Cullen and Jane A. Battle of Tuskegee, was born the 12th day of October 1838 and died on the 29th day of November 1860 in Eufaula, Alabama, in the twenty-second year of his age. He had been a consistent and worthy member of the Baptist Church for some seven years, having joined the church in Tuskegee in his sixteenth year. He leaves behind him a young wife to whom he had been married but one year; one child, and two aged parents... brothers, sisters, and numerous friends...

## Marriage and Death Notices From The South Western Baptist Newspaper

Whereas we are informed of the recent sad dispensation of Providence in the death of our sister in Christ, Rebecca Antonett Davis, who was born in Perry County, Alabama, August 30, 1843, and departed this life 28 December 1860, in the eighteenth year of her age. The deceased was the daughter of Mr. A.W. and Emily Davis, and was baptized by Rev. W. Wilkes into the fellowship of the Plantersville Baptist Church in the year of our lord 1856.

Died at the residence of her son-in-law, Brother Isham Moore, Mrs. Mary Mayson, age eighty-three years. She was born in Darlington District, South Carolina and in her youth was baptized into the fellowship of the Mechanicsville Baptist Church. She was soon after married to Thomas Mayson of the same county and state. They moved to Alabama in 1821, and settled in Conecuh County; she there united with Mercer Creek Church where she remained a member four or five years; she then moved her membership to Barlow Church where she lived for several years, much esteemed by all who knew her. She then moved to Black's Bend, Wilcox County, and was one of the members in the constitution of New Providence Church. She remained a member of that church until her death. She lived an exemplary life, for about sixty-three years and was much esteemed and loved by all who knew her. She has left sons and daughters, together with a great many grandchildren to mourn her loss. The *Christian Index* will please copy. Buena Vista, Alabama.

Died in Montgomery, Alabama on the 28th ult., Loymie, daughter of Dr. and Mrs. M.P. Le Grand, age three years.

1-17-1861
Married on the 18th of December at the residence of the bride's father by Rev. W.E. Lloyd, Mr. Sam'l Winslet and Miss Louisa Bowden.
By the same on the 20th of December at the residence of the bride's father, Mr. Samuel Perry and Miss Lou. Miles.
By the same on the 10th inst. at the residence of Mr. John Hairston, Mr. Wm. A. McPhaul and Miss Lucinda Hairston, all of Macon County.
At the residence of B.B. Amos of this place by Rev. H.E. Talifferro, Mr. A.C. Standerfer of Georgia to Mrs. Fannie Standerfer of Tuskegee.

1-24-1861
Married at the Perry House, Columbus, Georgia on Tuesday morning, 15th inst., by the Rev. J. Wright, Mr. H.W. Gibson and Miss Gussa G. Greenwood of La Place, Alabama.
On the 10th instant at the residence of the bride's father by Elder J.D. Kendrick, Mr. W. M. Ulmer of Pleasant Hill, Alabama and Miss Minnie C. Gullett of Wilcox County, Alabama.
On the 13th inst. at the residence of the bride's father by the Rev. J.W. Williams, Mr. Thos. F. Nolin of Wilkes County, Georgia to Miss Rosa C. Huguly of Chambers County, Alabama.

## Marriage and Death Notices From The South Western Baptist Newspaper

On Thursday evening the 17th inst. by the Rev. C.S. Burks, Mr. Henry S. Reed and Miss Louisa E. Golden.

Died at his residence in Montgomery County, Alabama on the 4th of December 1860, John H. Lee, who was born in Dallas County, Alabama, 3 April 1827. The deceased connected himself with the Baptist Church at Liberty in 1849... leaves an affectionate wife and children... mother and sister, a dutiful, kind, and only son and brother...

1-31-1861
Died at the residence of his grandfather, Floyd Webb, in Morehouse Parish, Louisiana on the 25th ult. after a long and painful illness, Sydney Perkins Foster, youngest son of John A. Foster of Clayton, Alabama, age five years, two months, twenty-one days. Perkins was born in Mississippi and removed to Georgia in 1855 with his parents when but two months old; thence having lost his mother he was separated from his brother, sister and father, by his removal to Louisiana two years ago.

Died in Marion, Alabama on the 29th December 1860, Miss Harriet Fagan, daughter of Enoch Fagan, age nineteen years.

Accordingly, Brother Jack Harris, Sr. of Perry County, Alabama died at his residence January 16, 1861, age eighty-six years, eight months, nine days.

2-7-1861
Married on the 31st ult. by Rev. H.E. Taliferro, Mr. M.W. Smith to Miss Piety Jane Hill, daughter of Rev. A.B. Hill of Tuskegee.

On the morning of the 28th of January in Glenville, Barbour County, Alabama by Elder E.Y. VanHoose, Col. W.W. Battle of Macon County to Mrs. Jane A. Curry of Glenville.

At the Perry House, Columbus, Georgia on Monday morning, 29th ult., by the Rev. I.T. Tichenor of Montgomery, Alabama, Mr. W.T. Griffin to Miss M.F. Thompson, both of La Place, Alabama.

Departed this life near Dover, Alabama on the 5th day of January 1861, Edward Hardin Law, in the twenty-first year of his age. He united with the Baptist Church of Christ at Concord, Russell County, Alabama on the 3rd of September 1860.

Mr. John M. Mitchell died at his residence in Perry County, Louisiana on the 19th January 1861, in the forty-fifth year of his age. The subject of this sketch was born in Edgefield District, South Carolina, April 24, 1816. While quite a youth he emigrated to Alabama, which state has ever since been his place of residence... The deceased was a member of the Friendship Church, Perry County. We come now to contemplate the melancholy scene of his death, which was contrary to the common events of nature in closing man's career here below. Having received a serious wound which fractured his leg, mortification ensued and he only survived seven days... The deceased leaves a wife and several children to mourn his loss.

## Marriage and Death Notices From The South Western Baptist Newspaper

Died at his residence in Perry County, Alabama, Solomon Smith, January 6, 1861, age seventy-five years, three months, fifteen days. He was received into the fellowship of the Duncan's Creek Baptist Church, Laurens District, South Carolina.

2-14-1861
Married at the residence of Dr. Russell in Lowndes County, Alabama on the 31st of January by Elder J.A. Fonville, Thomas H. Booth of Dale County and Miss Mary E. Lassiter.
Died at her residence in Muscogee County, Georgia on the 9th of January 1861, Mrs Bathsheba Champion, wife of Elias F. Champion. Mrs. Champion was in her eighty-third year and had been a member of the Baptist Church forty-seven years and a worthy member of Bethel Church, Muscogee County, Georgia for the last twenty-eight years. She left an aged companion with whom she had lived nearly fifty years...
Death of our much esteemed Brother A.G. McCraw, who was born in Newberry District, South Carolina, June 4, 1803, was baptized into the fellowship of the Baptist Church at Ocmulgee, May 1828, was ordained to the full work of the gospel by the same church, September 1831, died at his residence in Selma, January 14, 1861, and was buried January 16th at Ocmulgee... Done by the order of the church at Ocmulgee. January 27th, 1861.

2-28-1861
Married on the 6th inst. at the residence of the bride's mother by Elder J.D. Kendrick, John Bradley of Conecuh County and Miss Mattie O. Nettles of Monroe County, Alabama.
Mrs. Kate Law was the daughter of Joseph Bradford of Coosa County, Alabama... After her marriage with Dr. F.M. Law and removal to Selma her sphere of usefulness was enlarged... When Dr. Law entered upon his labors as a minister his wife was an efficient co-worker... She spent the winter of 1858/9 on the Bethel Ship, Mobile Bay, her husband being chaplin and physician. In the autumn of 1859 Dr. Law and family removed to Texas. The disease, (consumption), which had for years been making ravages upon her vital energies, soon showed more alarming symptoms... She departed this life December 14, 1860 in the twenty-eighth year of her age. S.S.M.
Died near Bragg's Store, Lowndes County of typhoid fever, Mrs. M.J. Moss, age thirty years. She leaves a husband and some children...
On the night of the 1st inst. after an illness of seven or eight days, Miss Amelia E. McCants, daughter of Wm. and Judith McCants, formerly of Fairfield District, South Carolina, died in Pleasant Hill, Dallas County, Alabama. She was thirty-two years of age... Written by her affectionate cousin, Zodie.

## Marriage and Death Notices From The South Western Baptist Newspaper

Preamble and resolutions of Selma Baptist Church: The Rev. A.G. McCraw died in this city after a lingering illness on the 14th day of January 1861. He was born in Newberry District, South Carolina in 1803, was ordained to the ministry in 1831... Alabama was the field of his labors, Perry and Dallas Counties more particularly... In 1859 when the charge became too great for his increasing and already advanced years he voluntarily resigned the pastorate to serve several country churches, Oakmulgee among them, of which he became and died a member, while others of his family belonged to this church. Jno. Haralson, T.C. Daniel, C./O. Thames, comm. Selma. February 7, 1861.

3-7-1861
Married in Tuskegee on the evening of the 26th inst. at the residence of the bride's father, Dr. W.R. Cunningham, by the Rev. Mark Andrews, Mr. Thomas L. McGowen and Mrs. M. Louisa Cole, all of this county.
On the 26th ultimo at the residence of the bride's father by the Rev. J.W. Williams, Mr. S.J. Combs to Miss Eleanor Towles, all of Chambers County, Alabama.
Died at his plantation on the night of the 12th inst., Wm. George Goldsby of Marion, Perry County, Alabama. Left devoted mother, brothers, sisters, wife and children...
Tribute of respect, Fort Morgan, February 16, 1861, on the death of the Garrison Chaplain, Rev. N.L. DeVotie...

3-14-1861
Departed this life on the 11th day of January 1861, Thomas Marbury Steed, in the sixty-seventh year of his age. He was born in Columbia County, Georgia. In early life removed to Wilkes County where in 1815 he married Miss Mildred Ashmon, who with himself was baptized into the fellowship of the Baptist Church of Christ called Ebenezer (Upson County) in July 1828. In 1838 he removed to Alabama and for the last nine years resided in the city of Wetumpka where he had a name and a place in the first Baptist Church... Husband,father, neighbor, citizen, Mason, Christian... Funeral under direction of the Masonic Lodge of Wetumpka.
This Church has been called to mourn the loss by death of two of her old members, who have long been recognized as fathers in Israel... Deacon George Peak had numbered his seventy-sixth year; had been a member of the Baptist Church forty-two years... It may be said of him, that during the six years he was confined by a painful disease, of which he died, he was a remarkable example of christian patience... and gave him victory over death and the crown of life on the 17th day of October 1860. Brother Lewis B. Turner fell asleep in Jesus on the 19th of October 1860. Brother Turner had nearly accomplished his sixty-third year... At a conference meeting of the

## Marriage and Death Notices From The South Western Baptist Newspaper

Union Baptist Church, Coosa County, Alabama held on the 2nd day of March 1861, the foregoing paper was read... Platt Stout, Mod'r. Wm. M. Lindsey, Ch. Cl'k.

Died of chronic ulceration of the tonsils and larynx on the 9th of October 1860 at the residence of her brother in Troup County, Georgia, Miss Adelia Drummond, daughter of the late Maj. Jas. and Mrs. Eliza Drummond of Jackson County, Florida...

3-28-1861

Married at the residence of the bride's mother in Pike County, Alabama on the 19th inst. by the Rev. J.M. Wood, Mr. W.S. Botsford of Chambers County to Miss L.C. Whaley of the former place.

Married on the 3rd inst. at the residence of the bride's father by Rev. J.B. Parham, Mr. Wm. Thomas and Miss Aylsee Poteet of Union County, Georgia.

Died in Tuskegee, Alabama on the 17th inst., in the thirty-fifth year of her age, after a painful and lingering illness, Mrs. Sarah Elizabeth, wife of Dr. J.M. Vason.

Died at his residence in Macon County, Alabama on 14 February 1861 after a protracted illness of some six or seven months, Hubbard Holloway, in his sixty-sixth year. Affectionate husband and kind father.

Died at her father's residence in Pike County, Alabama on 27 February 1861 Susannah Malinda Chester, of dropsy. She was born in Harris County, Georgia, October 30, 1841; age nineteen years, three months, twenty-seven days; leaving a father, four sisters and three brothers to mourn her loss. She was mentally afflicted from infancy. A.C.

Mrs. Mary Elizabeth Nolen died at the residence of her husband in Talladega, January 14, 1861 after a severe illness of more than twelve months. She was born in Ashville, St. Clair County, October 14, 1832 and while she was quite small her parents removed to Talladega Town where she grew up and remained in the midst of many friends to the day of her death. She was married to Mr. J.M. Nolen, June 3, 1850 for whom she was the mother of four children. Two of them went to heaven before her and she left two--a son and a daughter--with her bereaved husband and mother... Her pious, faithful mother and devoted husband, patiently gave her every attention. Her disease was pulmonary consumption. J.J.D.R.

4-4-1861

Funeral discourse for Rev. N.L. DeVotie. The military companies of Selma, Independence Blues and Governor's Guards, stationed at Fort Morgan, at the time of the drowning of the Rev. N.L. DeVotie, have selected Rev. Basil Manly to deliver a funeral discourse on Sunday next, at the Baptist Church of this city.

## MARRIAGE AND DEATH NOTICES FROM THE SOUTH WESTERN BAPTIST NEWSPAPER

Married on the 26th March 1861 at the residence of the bride's father by the Rev. J.W. Williams, James E. Williams of California to Miss E.J. Bennett of Russell County, Alabama.
Married, 28 March at the residence of the bride's grandfather, Elder J.D. Williams, by Rev. G.E. Brewer, Mr. A.G. Due to Miss Emma G. Watkins, all of Wetumpka, Alabama.

4-11-1861
Died in Sumter County, Alabama, March 25, Frances A., wife of Maj. Wm. Hibbler, and daughter of Mrs. Martha Green, in the thirty-sixth year of her age. Born in Green County, Georgia she removed to Mississippi in early life. In 1848 she was buried with Christ in Baptism... Member of the Providence Baptist Church... Her bereaved husband deemed himself unworthy so saintly a wife... In the management of her children she was singularly happy.

4-18-1861
Died in West Point, Georgia, March 29, 1861, Mrs. Antoinette T. Erwin, wife of Capt. Jas. H. Erwin, daughter of Jas. Simms, of Chambers County, Alabama. She was born in Hancock County, Georgia, March 28, 1834 and was converted in September 1858 and joined the M.E. Church, South... She was a lovely woman, an affectionate sister and daughter, and a devoted wife... bereaved husband and two little children. Wm. A. Simmons.
Married at the residence of Mrs. Smith by Elder J.D. Kendrick, Mr. William M. Longmire to Miss Virginia J. Powe, all of Wilcox County, Alabama.

4-25-1861
Married in Columbus, Georgia by Rev. J.H. DeVotie, Rev. I.T. Tichenor of Montgomery, Alabama to Miss E.C. Boykin of Columbus, Georgia.
Died in Mobile, January 3, 1861, Pattie Bolling, youngest daughter of M. and S. Threefoot, age one year, ten months.

5-2-1861
Married on the 27th of April at the residence of the bride's father, Allen Gibson, by the Rev. M. Smith, W.A. Robertson to Miss Lottie A. Gibson, all of Rusk County, Texas.
Died on the 10th of September last in Lavaca County, Texas, Mr. John M. Peters, son of Matthew Peters of this county, in the thirty-third year of his age. The deceased was a young man of marked social qualities... He had lived for many years in Macon County... The letter containing the sad announcement of his death never reached his respected parents until full six months after his death... The *Tuskegee Republican* and the *Southern Home Journal* will please copy.

## Marriage and Death Notices From The South Western Baptist Newspaper

Died in La Grange, Georgia on the morning of the 22nd of April at half-past one o'clock, Andrew Fuller Teague, son of Rev. E.B. Teague, age twelve years, one month, one day... Was baptized by his father.

5-16-1861
Married on the 7th of May at the residence of Mr. Joseph Jarrett by Elder E.Y. VanHoose, Mr. George W. Mayo of Preston, Georgia to Miss Sophronia L. Jarrett of Glennville, Alabama.
At Cross Keys, Alabama on the 7th May 1861 by Rev. A.T.M. Handey, Mr. John T. Moran to Miss Maria E. Mount, both of Loudoun County, Virginia.
On Thursday evening the 2nd inst. at the residence of the bride's father by the Rev. C.S. Burks, Dr. Wm. C. Branan to Miss Avarilla York, all of Macon County.

5-23-1861
Died at his residence near Nanafalia, Marengo County, Alabama on the 23rd ult. after a painful illness of two weeks, Elder John G. Williams, age seventy-one years, and more than twenty-five years engaged in the Baptist ministry... Tribute of respect from R.D. Marshall, C.C. Union Church...
Departed this life on the 4th of May, A.D. 1861, John T. Bishop, son of Stephen and J.T. Bishop of Butler County, Alabama, age eleven years, two months, twenty-six days. Thus in the morning of life he has been called in melancholy succession his mother and little brother. Whilst it is a source of unbounded grief to his bereaved father and only brother... He has been diseased for ten years of gravel affliction... He was deprived of speech for some time before his death...

5-30-1861
Married on the 23rd inst. in Harris County, Georgia by Rev. Samuel Henderson, John E. Jones of Tuskegee, Alabama to Miss Catharine Whitehead, daughter of the late Thos. Whitehead.
Tribute of respect from the Evergreen Church, Conecuh County, Alabama on the death of Brother Jeptha V. Perryman, who was born in Twiggs County, Georgia in 1798 from whence he moved to Alabama in 1820 in the early settlement of the country. At the time of his death he was exerting himself beyond his strength to complete an enterprise of vast importance to our state and country under present circumstances, and from the great exposure incident to railroad work, he contracted a severe cold which increased with continued exposure, and settling on his lungs resulted in his death on the 20th day of March last... The deceased leaves a family of five members, an affectionate wife and four children...
Miss Mary E. Stewart, daughter of Dr. and Mrs. Wm. C. Stewart, died May 7, 1861... Long years of illness wrecked her feeble frame.

## Marriage and Death Notices From The South Western Baptist Newspaper

6-6-1861
Married on the 23rd of May 1861 at the residence of the bride's father Rev. W.D. Harrington by Rev. J.W. Williams, Andrew J. Ward to Miss Mary J.R. Harrington, all of Chambers County, Alabama.

6-13-1861
Married on Tuesday the 4th inst. at the residence of Benjamin Walton in Tallapoosa County, by Rev. C.A. Stanton, John H. Bryan of Talbot County, Georgia to Miss Frances M. Walton of Lowndes County, Alabama.
On May 16, 1861 by Rev. J.C. Foster at the bride's father's in Marengo County, Alabama, C.J.G. Christian and Miss Demaris Ethridge.
By the same at the bride's residence on the 23rd of May 1861, Edwin Cato and Mrs. M.J. Johnson.

6-20-1861
Married in Tuskegee on Thursday the 13th inst. by Rev. Sam'l Henderson, the Rev. E.B. Teague, pastor of the Baptist Church at La Grange, Georgia to Miss Lou E. Philpot, daughter of W.H. Philpot.
Departed this life May 31st ult. at his residence in Tallapoosa County, Alabama, Deacon Reuben Maxwell, in the sixty-fourth year of his age... In the suddenness of his death... The deceased had gone to the table to take his dinner... Became a member of the Baptist Church in 1834.

6-27-1861
Died in Glenville, Barbour County, Alabama on the evening of 5 June 1861 of typhoid fever, William LaFayette Ivey, age eleven years, nine months, nineteen days.

7-11-1861
Died at his residence in Marion, Alabama on the 28th of May, Dr. Wm. P. Holman, in the twenty-ninth year of his age... Member Marion Baptist Church...
Departed this life near Wetumpka, Alabama on the 15th day of November 1860, William G. Oliver, son of A.G. and Bethany Oliver, in the nineteenth year of his age. The subject of this sketch was born in Pike County, Georgia. While quite a youth he emigrated with his parents to Alabama which state has ever since been his place of residence. Having received a serious wound by being thrown from a horse which fractured his brain, perhaps, he only survived a few hours...

7-25-1861
Died in Tuskegee on the 12th inst. at the residence of Dr. E.W. Jones, Erastus Walcott, son of M.P. and M.G. LeGrand, age two years.

## MARRIAGE AND DEATH NOTICES FROM THE SOUTH WESTERN BAPTIST NEWSPAPER

Departed this life June 21, 1861, Hugh A. Fargason, son of Thomas B. and Laura W. Fargason, age two years, seven months, twenty-six days. It was thought that he had used Cobalt, a poison, severe vomiting ensued sudden enervation insensibility and in a few days death ended the scene.

8-1-1861
Married on Thursday morning the 25th inst. at the residence of the bride's father by Rev. C.A. Stanton, Wiley Bird of Heard County, Georgia to Miss Allie A. Crowder of Macon County, Alabama.
On the 17th inst. at the residence of the bride's mother by Elder J.D. Kendrick, G.B. Dulany and Miss J.A. Raiford, all of Wilcox County, Alabama.
On the morning of the 23rd inst. by Rev. P.M. Callaway, J.B. Whigham to Miss M.E. Glover at the house of her father, H.G. Glover, both of Barbour County, Alabama.
Mrs. Sarah Eliza Blount, wife of Dr. B.F. [or B.E.] Blount, died on 29 June 1861. She was the daughter of late Maj. Thomas Molton and Catherine, his wife, of Montgomery; born July 26, 1838. [mentions the birth of a daughter] Her funeral was attended by multitudes on Sunday June 30, 1861.
Died at Hickory Flat, Chambers County, Alabama on the morning of 8 July 1861 and buried on the 9th with Masonic Honors, Brother L.M. Cook, after a severe illness of fifteen days of diarrhea, in the thirty-first year of his age. The subject of this notice was the son of Brother F.S. Cook and sister Eady Cook. He married Elizabeth, daughter of the Rev. Leland Allen. Leaves a kind, affectionate and pious wife and three little children. Admitted to the bar two or three years. Member of Baptist Church twelve years... He suffered much during the last days of his life...
Died on the 28th of June 1861 at his residence near Glenville, Barbour County, Alabama, Mr. J.W. Hitchcock, in the thirtieth year. The subject of this notice was born in Madison County, Georgia in which state he lived until some ten years since, at which time he removed to Alabama... When he came to Alabama he joined the Church at Glennville...

8-8-1861
Married in Benton at the residence of the bride's father, July 23, by the Rev. P.H. Lundy, Dr. S.E. Winnemore and Miss Mary A. Kelley.
Died on the morning of the 19th inst. at her mother's residence near Allenton, Wilcox County, Alabama, Miss Bettie C. Williams, age sixteen years, eleven days. She was born in Wilcox County, Alabama, July 8, 1845, in which community she lived until death. She had but a short time previous to her death returned home from Camden where she attended school during the session... soon after her return home slow fever developed itself in a severe attack of typhoid which resulted in her death. In a protracted meeting at Friendship Church in September 1859 she made a profession of religion and soon afterwards was baptized into the fellowship of the Allenton Baptist. She

Marriage and Death Notices From The South Western Baptist Newspaper

leaves behind her a bereaved, afflicted mother, four sisters, three brothers (one of them her twin brother).
Died at her residence in Butler County, Alabama on the 9th of July 1861, Sister Sallie Boan, age sixty years, six months, two days. She was born in Lexington District, South Carolina on the 7th of January 1801. In 1822 she united with the M.E. Church and continued an exemplary member twenty-six years. In 1848 she was baptized by Elder A. VanHoose into the fellowship of Siloam Baptist Church...

8-15-1861
Married at Cross Keys on Wednesday morning, August 7, by Rev. A.T.M. Handey, Mr. Jessee Thompson of Macon County to Miss Sophronia F. Mount, formerly of Washington City, D.C.
Departed this life on the 3rd of June at her residence in Phillips County, Arkansas after a painful illness of ten days, Mrs. Mary J. Bryan, wife of A.A. Bryan, and daughter of H.P. and Prudence Slaughter. She was born in Jasper County, Georgia. Her father removed to Russell County, Alabama when she was quite young where she was reared and educated. She was married in 1847 and united herself with the Baptist Church at Union Springs in 1853... She left many kind friends and relatives, a husband and five little children to mourn her loss...
Died after a short illness near Helicon, Lowndes County, Alabama at the residence of her father, Martha Lynn, daughter of Jas. A. and Elizabeth Graham, age eight years, ten months, seven days.

8-29-1861
Departed this life on the 3rd day of August 1861 at her residence in Macon County, Alabama, Mrs. Margaret R. Hand, wife of the Rev. J.R. Hand, and daughter of John and Mary Cowen. She was born on Hilton Head Island, South Carolina and was baptized into the fellowship of the May River Baptist Church (Beaufort District) in her twelfth or fourteenth year by Rev. James Sweat. She moved with her husband in January 1845 to this state...
Died August 11, 1861 at Camp Walker near Manassas, William James Moody, in the nineteenth year of his age. The subject of this memoir was born near Statesburg, South Carolina. He was reared up in his native state. About one year since he came to Tuskegee to reside with his uncle, William Edmonds. He attended the Classical and Scientific Institute in this place until its exercises closed. After the suspension of the school young Moody entered upon the study of medicine under the care of Drs. E.W. and U.R. Jones. He was thus engaged when Captain R.F. Ligon began the formation of his company for twelve months service in defense of our dearest rights. He died from typhoid fever.

## Marriage and Death Notices From The South Western Baptist Newspaper

9-5-1861
On the morning of the 16th August, Miss Mattie S. Williams, age nineteen years, eighteen days, an elder sister of the late deceased Miss Bettie Williams and a resident of Wilcox County, Alabama, while absent from her home at her uncles in Dallas "fell asleep in Jesus." Member of the Allenton Baptist Church...

9-12-1861
Died at his residence near Plantersville on the 12th inst., Jas. Peebles, in the forty-third year of his age.
Died at the residence of his mother (Mrs. Gracy F. Bates) near Cross Keys, Macon County, Alabama, William Henry Bates. William was born on the 12th day of April 1848 and died 17 August 1861, age thirteen years, four months, five days. William Henry was the only child of a widowed mother.
Died at her residence in Talladega County, Alabama, August 27, 1861, Mrs. Mary Chipman, consort of the late Elder Joseph Chipman, and mother of Col. Matthew Turner, in the seventy-seventh year of her age. She was baptized in Mecklenburg, Virginia by the faithful man of God, Elder John Creath. From Virginia she removed with her first husband to Georgia, where she resided many years and he (Mr. Turner) died. Thence she removed to Alabama and was married to Elder J. Chipman in whose pious society she spent several years. He died last May. At the time of his death she was prostrate from a stroke of paralysis and had been for weeks. She was confined to her bed five months and two weeks...

9-19-1861
Died on the 19th inst. at his country residence, Augustus C. Ferrell, in the fortieth year of his age. Two years ago he became a member of this community.

9-26-1861
Died at Culpeper Court House, Virginia on the 21st of July 1861, Samuel Preston, oldest son of Samuel and Mary A. McCreary, age twenty-three years, one month, seven days. The subject of this notice was a member of the Monroe Guards of the 5th Regiment Alabama Volunteers. [see below]
Died at Culpeper Court House, Virginia on the 18th of August 1861, Deacon Samuel McCreary of Monroe County, Alabama. Brother McCreary was born in Barnwell District, South Carolina on the 23rd of July 1811, emigrated to Alabama while a youth; baptized into the fellowship of the Flat Creek Church, in 1842 ordained a Deacon and continued a member until his death. The circumstances connected with his death are of a mournful character. He had been afflicted with asthma all his life, and hearing of the severe illness of his son he went on to see him, arriving a few ----- before his death; his old disease together with fatigue of traveling and anxiety prostrated him under the

## Marriage and Death Notices From The South Western Baptist Newspaper

stroke. To his bereaved widow and fatherless children his loss is felt heavier than any one else. Although away from his family yet "he died in faith" and beside his beloved son, beneath Virginia's green sod he rests...C.W. Hare, Fatama, Alabama. [see above]

Died at the residence of her husband, John R. Bealle, near Warsaw, Alabama, his wife Virginia C. Bealle. She was the daughter of Col. John D. King of Madison County, Alabama. Was born on the 16th day of April 1831, and died on the 10th of August 1861. She was a consistent member of the Providence Baptist Church, Sumter County, Alabama and died triumphant and happy, only regretting to leave her dear friends, and her noble, warm hearted husband and her lovely daughter and son, now of tender years.

Departed this life in Tuskegee on the 26th of June last, Brother Elisha G. Crawford, age eighty-two years, four months, nineteen days. He was born in Hanover County, Virginia and removed to Greene County, Georgia in 1795, was married to Nancy Turner on the 2nd day of October 1808, who preceded him to her final abode about five years. He removed from Greene to Jasper County in 1810 and in 1844 removed to Macon County, Alabama where he lived until the day of his death. He was desirous of visiting his children in Georgia (as he expressed himself) for the last time and while waiting for the cars became impatient, took his carpet bag and started off upon the road. He had proceeded far before he came to a trestle bridge, the night being very dark and he partly blind, fell through the bridge where he was found a few moments after and conveyed to Mr. Brewer's in the above named place. Medical aid was procured and every needful attention bestowed by kind friends but such was the nature of his injuries, all was of no avail and death released him from his suffering in three hours from the time he received the injuries. The subject of this notice attended a protracted meeting at Calebee Church in September 1848...

10-3-1861
Died at Darksville, Virginia on the 2nd August 1861 from the effects of an accidental shot, Powhatan Richard Baptist, son of Rev. Edward Baptist of Marengo County, Alabama, age twenty-four years, four months, twenty-nine days. The deceased had been lately admitted to the Bar... He volunteered for service in Virginia and became a member of the Canebrake Rifle Guards which so lately distinguished itself at Manassas. On the 3rd of July last when Gen. Johnston was marching to meet Gen. Patterson in expectation of battle our army stopped for rest at Darksville, young Baptist lay upon the ground and fell asleep. He was awakened by an accidental shot from the hands of a comrade which pierced his spine inflicting a fatal wound...

A gentleman writing from Manassas to a friend of the death of Dr. S.H. Wimberly, who fell in the battle of Manassas Plains...

Died at the residence of her daughter (Mrs. Martha Barrett) near Burnsville, Dallas County, Mrs. Martha West, in the seventy-sixth year of her age.

## MARRIAGE AND DEATH NOTICES FROM THE SOUTH WESTERN BAPTIST NEWSPAPER

James D. Brassfield, son of Col. M.R. Brassfield, was born near Forkland April 19, 1836, was baptized into the fellowship of Friendship Baptist Church, Forkland, September 1854, and died of measles at Orange Court House, Virginia, August the 6th 1861, age twenty-five years, three months, seventeen days. He was a member of "The Greene County Grays" and left for the seat of war June 9, 1861...

10-10-1861
Departed this life at his residence in Tallapoosa County, Alabama on the 24th day of July 1861, Brother Isaac Smith, after a protracted illness of about seventy-five days. Isaac Smith was born in Sumpter District, South Carolina May 17, 1786. He jointed the Baptist Church in 1811...,He moved from South Carolina in 1818 and settled in what was then Montgomery County but afterwards Lowndes and there he remained until 1836, at that time he moved to Tallapoosa County, Alabama and here remained until his death...

10-17-1861
Died at his residence at Oak Hill, Wilcox County, Alabama on the 20th of August 1861, Mr. T.J. Harrass, age thirty-seven years, five months, five days. He was born in Wilcox County, Alabama, March 15, 1824, in which county he was raised, lived and died. Early in life he became a great sufferer from pulmonary affection from which disease he was never relieved. In March 1856 he was married to Miss E.A. Collins with whom he lived until death separated them. He had been a consistent member of the Methodist E. Church for ten or twelve years... He leaves a bereaved wife, two interesting little sons...
Died at his father's residence in Chambers County, Alabama, Samuel Thomas Adams, son of James D. and Susan Adams, in the nineteenth year of age. The deceased was baptized into the fellowship of Rocky Mount Church in September 1860; he took his letter and united with Beulah Church a short time before his death.

10-24-1861
Died at her late residence in Foster's Settlement, Tuscaloosa County, Alabama on Saturday, October 5, 1861, Mrs. Rachel A. Gates. Sister Gates was born in South Carolina, December 8, 1787; she was married to George Gates July 21, 1802; removed to Camden County, Georgia and settled near St. Mary's. From thence they removed to Madison County, Alabama in 1815 and in 1817 settled in Tuscaloosa County near where she died... She was left for many years a widow... Baptized by John C. Foster into the fellowship of Grant's Creek Church, November 2, 1845.
Died of diphtheria at the residence of the father near Lexington, Holmes County, Mississippi, little James Reuben, infant son of Hardy A. and R. Hassie Foster. He was born January 19, 1860, and died September 25, 1861,

## Marriage and Death Notices From The South Western Baptist Newspaper

age one year, eight months, six days.
Died at the same place and of the same disease September 29, 1861, little Mattie, oldest child of Hardy A. and R. Hassie Foster. She was born in Tuscaloosa County, Alabama, October 17, 1854, and died as above, age seven years, eleven months, twelve days.
Mrs. Mary B. Inzer departed this life at home in Jefferson County, Alabama, 2 August 1861. Mrs. Mary B. Inzer, consort of James D. Inzer, and daughter of Thompson C. Strickland and Elizabeth Strickland, was born 7 January 1819; married 1 March 1836; joined the Baptist Church July 1846 in Talladega County, Alabama. Her lungs seemed slightly diseased a short time before her death. Intermittent fever prevailed a few days of a moderate type. A few hours before her death her husband discovered she was sinking almost without pain... Our sister has left a heart broken companion with eight children, one of them an infant...
Died of pneumonia in camp at Sangster's X Roads in the "Army of the Potomac," our beloved but now lamented friends, H.H. McPhaul on the 12th, and R.L. Hairston on the 20th ult...

10-31-1861
Married on Thursday the 24th October at the residence of Homer T. Crowder of Macon County by the Rev. Sam'l Henderson, Thomas S. Tate of Tuskegee to Mrs. Martha C. or O. [not clear] T. Walker of Dale County, Alabama.
Married on the 25th of September 1861 near Coffeyville, Alabama by Wm. Deese, Mr. Gabriel H. Law to Miss Huberta A. Dunigan, both of Clarke County, Alabama.
Died: Thomas Leverett, son of John G. Leverett, and grandson of Rev. Gideon Leverett. Deceased was born on the 28th of October 1844. He united with the Baptist Church at this place on the 14th day of August 1858... Brother Leverett, though young, was filled with the spirit of patriotism and love of country, volunteered and left his father's comfortable home, joined the company of Capt. Brown, raised at this place, and was taken with the measles while stationed at Auburn and departed this life on the 9th inst. His remains were deposited in the family burying ground at Brother Brisky's by his weeping friends and relatives.
Died near Alpine, Talladega County, Alabama, October 12, 1861, Mrs. Sarah T. Welch, wife of Rev. Oliver Welch, in the fifty-second year of her age. Mrs. Welch was born in the city of Richmond, Virginia, January 11, 1810 but moved in early life to North Alabama where she professed religion when quite young. Was first married to Mr. Alva Finley. Soon after the death of Mr. Finley she moved to Talladega and married the Rev. O. Welch with whom she lived thirteen years within a few days. Upon one of her sisters visiting of her she said Sister Mary "I am not afraid to die."

## Marriage and Death Notices From The South Western Baptist Newspaper

Died at Collerine, Lowndes County, September 25th of congestion of the brain, Mrs. Gerusha May, wife of Dr. H.W. Caffey, and daughter of the late Green Rives, in the twenty-fifth year of her age. The subject of this brief notice was a native of Alabama, lived and died surrounded by those who had known and loved her from her childhood.
Died in Foster's Settlement, Tuscaloosa County, Alabama of fever and inflammation of the bowels, October 12, 1861, John Reason, third son of E. Collier and Velinda J. Foster, age two years, eight months, fourteen days.
Died in Holmes County, Mississippi of diphtheria, October 3, 1861, little Hassie, youngest daughter of Hardy A. and R. Hassie Foster, age two years, ten months, twenty-eight days.
At the same place October 10, 1861 of same disease Virginia, second daughter of Hardy A. and R. Hassie Foster, who was born November 14, 1855 in Foster's Settlement, Alabama.
On Sunday morning the 22nd day of September last, Purnal Philpot died at Culpeper Court House, Virginia of typhoid fever. This amiable young man was a member of the "Macon Confederates," a company raised by Capt. Ligon to defend our beloved country from invasion. His father Wm. H. Philpot of Tuskegee reached the hospital where he was sent from the camp only a short time before his death. His body was brought home and buried on Friday the 29th September...

11-7-1861
Tribute of respect from Chunnenuggee Lodge #121 Free and Accepted Masons, October 24, 1861, on the death of Brother R.L.G. Bozeman, who was cruelly murdered on the morning of the 22nd inst. by his own runaway slaves.
Died at his residence in the county of Bibb on the 2nd day June 1861, Daniel Watson, age about eighty years. The deceased was born in Argyleshire, Scotland and emigrated to the United States about the year 1802 and settled first in Marlboro District, South Carolina but afterwards removed to the county of Richmond in the state of North Carolina where he resided many years. Several years since he removed to the county of Bibb in this state and was baptized into the fellowship of the Baptist Church at Rehoboth in that county by the Rev. Mr. Lloyd. The subject of this notice was afflicted for twenty years with a disease the most painful, which he bore with great patience and fortitude. He was taken suddenly ill on Sabbath morning the 2nd day of June 1861... On Monday evening following his mortal remains were deposited in the grave at Randolph near the church house where he held his membership.
Died in the triumph of faith at his residence in Dale County, Alabama on the 11th instant, Elder Benjamin Stewart, age sixty-eight years. He had been a member of the Baptist Church thirty-eight years. He suffered from dropsy. Haw Ridge, Alabama. S.D.

## Marriage and Death Notices From The South Western Baptist Newspaper

Mary Ella, daughter of Hardy A. and R. Hassie Foster, was born in Tuscaloosa County, Alabama, August 3, 1857, and died in Holmes County, Mississippi, October 15, 1861, being four years, two months, twelve days old. She was the last surviving of five interesting children, all of whom died in the brief period of twenty days.

11-14-1861
Died at Camp Walker near Manassas, Virginia on the 25th of August 1861 of fever, E.H. Strobel, member of the Macon Confederates 12th Alabama Regiment. Deceased was the pride of manhood... the idol of a tender wife and two little children.

Mrs. Emily P. Pinner died in Opelika, Alabama the 1st day of November 1861, in the thirty-fourth year of her age. She was born in Caldwell County, Kentucky and was married in 1845. She was baptized by Elder Joseph Board and at the time of her death had been a member of the Baptist Church seventeen years. She left five daughters and a devoted husband.

Tribute of respect from the citizens of Pleasant Hill, Mt. Lebanon Baptist Church, on the death of Felix G. Butler, who was wounded in the Battle of Manassas on the 21st of July which resulted in his death on the 8th inst. at Brentsville, Virginia... A copy should be sent to his friends in Texas.

Died on the morning of the 1?th of October 1861 at the residence of her husband near Coffeyville, Clarke County, Alabama, Mrs. Margaret Dunagan, age twenty-four years, eleven months, fourteen days. She was born in Clarke County, Alabama, October 31, 1836, in about ten miles of the place she died. Her disease was cold which settled in her throat, something like the quinsy which caused her death on the morning of the third day after she was taken. She leaves a husband, one child, a mother, seven brothers and one sister... Her remains were interred in the family graveyard on the 15th October.

11-21-1861
Marion, son of Deacon Presly H. and his wife Eliza W. Wilkerson, was born in Foster's Settlement, Tuscaloosa County, Alabama, December 30, 1851. During a protracted meeting at Grant's Creek in the fall of 1860 he made known to his mother his desire to join the church... He took sick Monday night, October 14th, and died between three and four o'clock a.m. Tuesday, October 29, 1861. He now sleeps beside his lovely sister whom he never knew in the flesh.

Died of typhoid fever at the residence of John Mountcastle in Richmond, Virginia, Lieut. William T. Nuckolls of the 15th Alabama Reg't. Com. A., and son of Mr. N. Nuckolls of Columbus, Georgia, in the twenty-first year of his age. While in camp near Manassas he was attacked by a disease (measles) which has swept away many of our brave soldiers...

## Marriage and Death Notices From The South Western Baptist Newspaper

Away from home and loved ones has James C. Perry passed a victim to galloping consumption. He was born the 20th of July 1839 and died at Centreville the 6th of October 1861. His health was bad for some time previous to his death; he had chills which resulted in hemorrhage of the lungs and bowels and finally in consumption. At six o'clock on a Sabbath eve his spirit left the frail tenement and though his body sleeps in far Virginia soil may we not hope his spirit passed into fairer and lovelier climes.

Little Philip Peter Burt is no more on earth. The subject of this notice was the son of Richard M. and Elizabeth Burt, who reside in Lowndes County, Alabama. Philip Peter died September 26, 1861, being two years, nine months, twelve days old...

Died at his home in Perry County, Alabama, October 19, 1861, Daniel Kinard, in the thirty-third year of his age. He was born in Perry County, January 6, 1829 where he spent his entire life. He was the son of Jacob and Rosanna Kinard of the same county, formerly of Lexington District, South Carolina. In 1843 it pleased God to bring him from darkness to light and he united with the Providence (Hamburg) Baptist Church. At the organization of the Mt. Eden Church in 1844 he was one of its constituent members. Subsequently having removed to the neighborhood of Pine Flat Church he united with it... An affectionate wife and three lovely little children mourn his early loss...

Died in Marion, Alabama, November 3, 1861, Mrs. Ann McIntosh, wife of Rev. Wm. H. McIntosh, in the thirty-second year of her age...

11-28-1861

Married on the evening of Thursday the 14th inst. by Rev. Geo. L. Lee, Henry Hines to Miss Mary A. Norred, daughter of James Norred of Conecuh County, Alabama.

Married at the bride's home on Thursday evening the 21st inst. by the Rev. Mr. McCoy, Sam. Q. Hale of Macon County to Mrs. Arrie Ann Owen of Tallapoosa County.

Dollie Foster, only daughter of William and Lysina Foster, departed this life at her father's residence in Macon County on the 2nd of October 1861, age twelve years, eight days.

Also at the same place on the 10th of October, Mrs. Martha Long, age seventy-one years, three months, twenty-nine days. She has left three children and a large circle of friends. *Weekly Enquirer* (Columbus, Georgia) please copy.

R. Henry Lee, son of Nelson and Martha J. Plumb, died October 7, 1861 at his father's near Mt. Willing, Lowndes County, Alabama of spasms, age five years, nine months, nine days. Grandpa Lee.

Died on the 26th of June last at the residence of her husband, Mrs. Devicy(?) Bruner, wife of Geo. C. Bruner of Wilcox County, Alabama, after an illness of about two weeks. She was the daughter of Aaron and Catherine Majors, and was born December 7, 1823 in Monroe County, Alabama. In 1842 and 1843

## Marriage and Death Notices From The South Western Baptist Newspaper

she was baptized into the fellowship of the County Line Baptist Church, Dallas County, Alabama by Elder Platt Stout. She was married on the 12th January 1847 and a few years ago moved with her husband to Wilcox County, Alabama and there united with the Enon Baptist Church where she lived until the day of her death. She leaves an aged father and mother, one brother, four sisters, her companion, five little children...

The subject of the following notice Mrs. Margaret J. Kirvin, was born in Darlington District, South Carolina, October 15, 1785. She was married as Margaret J. Evans to William Kirvin, October 10, 1805. She was baptized in October 1809 by Elder Daniel White into the fellowship of the Welch Neck Baptist Church in Darlington District, South Carolina. After her baptism she was ever an active useful member of the church filling well the office of a Deacon's wife until her husband became a Minister of the Gospel after which she was equally efficient as the wife of a minister. She removed with her husband and family to Dallas County, Alabama in January 1836 and was for several years a member of the Centre Ridge Baptist Church... She was the mother of ten children, nine of whom she had the pleasure of seeing baptized, and two of them ordained to the Gospel ministry... She died on the night of the 29th of September 1861 having been for more than fifty years a consistent Christian. Since the death of her husband (July 1845[?]) she and her youngest son have lived together...

12-5-1861
Married by the Rev. Thos. J. Williamson on the 24th November in Chambers County, Alabama, Capt. James H. Erwin of West Point, Georgia to Miss Josephine Simms.
Married near Opelika on the 17th inst. by the Rev. W.B. Jones at the residence of the bride's father, Andrew B. Terrell and Miss Hattie B. Johnson.
Died on the 16th ult. near Cotton Valley, Macon County, Alabama, Mrs. Mary Pennington, age sixty-eight years, seven months, five days. The subject of this notice was formerly a Miss Phillips, born in Hanover County, Georgia, 11 March 1793 and when fully arrived to the years of womanhood was united in the holy bonds of wedlock to Mr.--- Pennington of Georgia with whom she lived in the bonds of peace discharging all the duties of a faithful and affectionate wife for the short space of ten years, when by the monster death he was summoned to his eternal home. She resided several years in Jasper and Monroe Counties. In the former county in September 1826 she embraced religion at the camp ground near Antioch Baptist Church and attached herself to the Methodist Episcopal Church and in 1842 moved to the above place... Her disease was typhoid fever of a lingering character... She called some of her oldest grandchildren to her bed side...
Jefferson Davis, infant son of Thomas and Jane Shelton, died November 26, 1861, age five months, twenty-six days. He died while asleep and is supposed without a struggle.

## Marriage and Death Notices From The South Western Baptist Newspaper

12-12-1861
Eldred Wilkerson died at his residence in Macon County, Alabama, October 16, 1861. He was born in Putnam County, Georgia September 1795 and was married to Elizabeth Philips in 1822 in Jasper County, Georgia. The subject of this notice had for thirty-eight years been a strict member of the Methodist church... He was attacked with typhoid fever some two weeks before his demise... As a husband, he was kind and affectionate; as a father, mild and gentle.
Brother Samuel Adams was born in Virginia, near Richmond, February 1, 1784. He removed with his father to Elbert County, Georgia in 1796 and in his twentieth year was married to Martha Thornton, daughter of Rev. Dozier Thornton. During the same year he professed faith in Christ and was baptized into the fellowship of the Vance Creek Church by the Rev. Dozier Thornton. From thence he removed to Russell County, Alabama where he united with the Rocky Mountain Church... From Russell he removed to Barbour County where he remained until his death. He died at the residence of his son, F.F. Adams, November 6, 1861, age seventy-seven years, nine months, six days...
Burnt Corn, Conecuh County, Alabama, November 27, 1861: Departed this life on the 17th day of June 1861 of apolexy at the residence of her husband Butler County, Alabama, Mrs. Mary L. Hix, consort of Wm. Hix, Sr., Sister Hix was born in the state of Georgia, Oglethorpe County, October 11, 1811, and died in the fifty-first year of her age. She was the daughter of L.B. and Sarah Kinebrew. Came to this state in 1838 and to this county, Butler, in 1857. Was married to Wm. Hix October 18, 1840... Husband, step-children and friends will you meet the loving one in heaven ?... Her last illness was short and severe...
Tribute of respect from Clinton Lodge #287 of Free and Accepted Masons on the death of J.J. Culverhouse, who departed this life on the 2nd day of November inst.

12-19-1861
Little Georgia Augusta, infant daughter of Henry C. and Jane Maharrey, died at Foster's, Alabama, Wednesday, November 29, 1861, age six months, twenty-two days.
Willie J. Kendrick died of remittent fever, September 24, 1861, in the sixteenth year of his age. He was the youngest son of a widowed mother who but a few years ago laid in the cold, silent grave an affectionate husband and the gem of the family a lovely daughter of twelve... He was baptized into the Mt. Zion Church by Rev. F.H. Moss in which Church he lived till he died.
Died at Valley, Pike County, Alabama, November 7, 1857, Mrs. E.L. Alford age twenty-eight years and three days. Sister Alford was born in Elbert County, Georgia and with her father (F. Webb) moved to Harris County, Georgia where she was married to W.H. Alford in 1847. In 1848 she was baptized into the fellowship of Pine Grove Church by Elder T.J. Miles. Shortly

## Marriage and Death Notices From The South Western Baptist Newspaper

after her baptism she removed with her husband to Coosa County, Alabama where they remained four years thence to Pike where she died. She left five little children and a devoted husband...
Also died in Butler County, Alabama, August 28, 1861, Mrs. Narcissis Alford, second wife of W.H. Alford, age twenty-two years and seven days. Sister Alford was born in Muscogee County, Georgia. With her father (Mr. Pudgett) moved to Russell County, Alabama thence to Butler County where in 1859 she was married to W.H. Alford and introduced as step-mother to five little children... She was baptized by W.G. Williams in September 1860 into the fellowship of Spring Hill Baptist Church... John J. Webb. Millville, Butler County, Alabama, 12 November 1861.
Died at her step-father's (G.W. Merritt) near Tallassee, Alabama on the 16th September 1861, Mary Skipper, eldest daughter of William H. and E.H. Skipper. She was born the 10th of July 1847; she was fourteen years, two months, six days old. She was going to meet her father that had gone long before her.
Abel John Pouncly ?, who was in the service of his country on the plains of Virginia has been called to his long home.
Thomas Jefferson Brown, son of John and Martha Brown, was born in Tuscaloosa County, Alabama, September 6, 1834. He graduated at the University of Alabama in July 1857. Soon after he began to teach in Manly Academy, Foster's Settlement. He joined Grant's Creek Baptist Church by letter from Gilgal Church and was for some time clerk of this church...

12-26-1861
Departed this life on the first of December 1861, in the forty-first year of her age, Mrs. Elizabeth Long, the wife of the Rev. J.W. Long, and the daughter of the Rev. Alexander Watson. Also her infant daughter on the 8th of December last, age three years, three months, eight days. Mrs. Long was born in Monroe County, Alabama, married in Talladega County, professed a hope in Christ in 1839 and joined Fort Williams Baptist Church and was baptized by her father. She has left a bereaved husband and seven children, four daughters and three sons...
Died at the residence of her husband, Macon County, Alabama, December 15, 1861, Mrs. Jane Emeline Henderson, wife of Dr. Thos. F. Henderson. Sister Henderson was born in Walton County, Georgia, October 14, 1832, and died in the thirtieth year of her age. She was married to Dr. Thos. F. Henderson, August 10, 1848. Moved to Alabama, November 1859, and settled in Macon County... She leaves a kind husband, five small children.
Tribute of respect from the Baptist Church at Concord, Macon County, Alabama, November 9, 1861, on the death of R.A. Cowle. He was born in Washington County in the state of New York about the year 1805, emigrated South many years since... and breathed his last on earth the night of the 9th October last of congestive chill. Wife and five children.

## Marriage and Death Notices From The South Western Baptist Newspaper

1-9-1862

Married at the residence of the bride's brother, Mr. A.M. McIver, on the 12th November 1861 by the Rev. C.F. Sturgis, Joseph M. Lide to Miss Caroline Wilds McIver, daughter of Gen. Thos. E. McIver, all of Dallas County, Alabama.

Departed this life on the 19th day of October 1861 in Columbus, Georgia at the residence of her uncle Col. John Strother, Miss Martha Munnerlyn. She was a native of Marlborough District, South Carolina.

Died on the 23rd of December at the residence of her grandfather, Mr. N. Nuckolls of Columbus, Georgia, "Little Jennie", daughter of Robt. and Mary Kyle, age four years, four months.

Departed this life at his residence in Chambers County, Alabama on the 31st October 1861, Col. Robert Johns, after a protracted affliction of nineteen months. Brother Johns was born in Mecklenburg County, Virginia, October 5, 1783. At an early age he moved to Columbia County, Georgia. After his marriage with Miss Frances Clark he removed to Edgefield District, South Carolina where he was baptized in the Saluda River by Rev. John Bulger in 1809... He served in the war of 1812. [mentions widow and children]

Brother Reason Hobby, Deacon of the New Bethel Baptist Church, Bragg's Store, Lowndes County, died on the 16th of December after an illness of three days. He died of that fatal disease which has been for some time traveling over our land, diphtheria.

Died of apoplexy at the residence of her husband Tuscaloosa County, Alabama, Mrs. Epsey C. Hickman, wife of P. A.? Hickman, and daughter of Daniel and Mary Burgen, on the 20th of November 1861, in the forty-seventh year of her age, being born December 8, 1815. She united with the Roop's Valley Baptist Church by experience and baptism, October 10, 1833, and was married October 8, 1835. Leaving a husband and ten living children. Mrs. H. was taken ill at the dinner table and lived but a few hours afterwards, her summons being so sudden, that she was deprived of the satisfaction of bidding farewell to her husband and children, all of whom were present except one who was in the army. A.C. Thomason.

1-16-1862

The subject of this notice John Talbot, son of John R. and Lucy W. Talbot, was born October 7, 1837, united with the Baptist Church at Sardis in Wilkes County, Georgia in September 1855 and was baptized by Elder Enoch Calloway ...with his parents he drew his letter and removed to Chambers County, Alabama and united with the Church at County Line... Flux terminated his life in camp near Columbus, Kentucky on the 20th of September 1861.

Departed this life December 26, 1861 near Mulberry P.O., Autauga County, Alabama, Nancy Virginia, daughter of W.C. and E.M. Adair, age six years, one month, seven days. The subject of this notice died very suddenly.

## MARRIAGE AND DEATH NOTICES FROM THE SOUTH WESTERN BAPTIST NEWSPAPER

Died on the 25th of October last near Pine Level, Montgomery County, Alabama, Mrs. Matilda Frazer, wife of Allen Frazer. The subject of this notice, daughter of Nathan Wright, Sr., was born on the 5th of February 1805 in Lincoln County, Georgia, and was at the time of her death fifty-six years, eight months, twenty days old. She was married to Mr. Frazer on the 14th of October 1830. From Georgia she moved with her husband to Pike County, Alabama. Some years since they settled near Pine Level where she lived until her death. She was baptized into the fellowship of Surepta Church, near Pine Level in September 1851 by Elder G.G. McLendel. She has left a husband, one daughter and three sons to mourn their loss.

Brother Robert Bryan died at Camp Moore near Mobile, Alabama on the 16th inst., of congestion of the brain. He was eighteen years, eleven months, sixteen days old... was baptized into Rose Hill Baptist Church in the summer of 1860... He was a member of the "Covington Hunters" Capt. J.T. Brady, Col. Bullock's regiment... Being the younger of two sons, the elder having married and moved off. His remains were sent to his father at Leon, Covington County, Alabama and there interred on the 18th inst. John J. Webb, Leon, Alabama, December 21, 1861.

Died at her residence at Hamburg, Perry County, Alabama, Mrs. M.E. White, in the fifty-second year of her age of pulmonary disease. Mrs. White was a native of Sumpter District, South Carolina... [Sick for about five years; mentions children].

1-23-1862

Lumpkin, Georgia, January 9, 1862: Died in Richmond, Virginia on the 10th of November 1861, in the twenty-fifth year of his age, Andrew J.B. Hilliard of Stewart County, Georgia. He was a member and clerk of the Baptist Church of Christ at Summerhill. He had left a wife and child and other friends behind and joined, as recruit, Ball's Company... Also since his death and on the last day of November 1861, his only surviving child, William D., a son, died of congestion of the lungs, age fourteen months. Let not his father, Senator James Hilliard, and brothers and sister weep for Andrew and William...

Died at the White Sulphur Springs, Virginia, John C. Malone, about nineteen years of age. Joining the "Irwin Invincibles" of Henry County, Alabama he was soon with "Wise's Legion" and in actual service... He took the measles which from exposure brought on typhoid pneumonia. Under this after a brief illness he sunk on the 19th of November 1861. His remains were brought home by his brother Y.J. Malone, who was in the service with him...

Died in Camp Law, near Manassas, Virginia, on the 24th day of December 1861 of typhoid pneumonia, William H. Owsley, in the twenty-eighth year of his age. The deceased was a member of the Fourth Alabama Regiment of Volunteers. He escaped the dangers of the battlefield, but fell victim to a disease, from which the care of a brother, friends and medical skill could not save him. Surviving brothers.

## Marriage and Death Notices From The South Western Baptist Newspaper

Died in Richmond, Dallas County, Alabama on the 2nd January inst. after a painful illness of measles of twelve days, Mrs. Avarilla J. Stewart, consort of Alex. Stewart, deceased. She was a daughter of Samuel and Martha Dennis, and was born in Wilcox County, Alabama on the 6th of April 1820 and united herself to the Baptists in September 1837, was married to the above named in December 1838. She leaves behind her a husband, an aged mother, brothers and sisters, ten children, one an infant of seven weeks old.

1-30-1862
Tribute of respect from Perry Lodge #34 Marion, Alabama, January 14, 1862, on the death of Gen. E.D. King...
Died in Marion, Alabama on the 19th December, Mrs. Anabet Huckabee, wife of John G. Huckabee, and daughter of Dr. Clement Billingslea, in the twenty-seventh year of her age.
Fell asleep in Jesus in Auburn, Alabama, on the 6th of September 1861, Joseph C. Sale, in the forty-third year of his age. He was born and raised in Georgia but removed to Alabama where he ended his life... Lingering consumption was his disease... [mentions a widow and children]
Died on Thursday morning the 26th of December last, at the residence of her husband in Centre, Alabama, Mrs. Ruth Allen, age fifty-three years, ten months, twenty-nine days. She was born in Union District, South Carolina and emigrated with her father to Alabama many years ago. John B. Appleton, Van Buren, Alabama, January 20, 1862. *Mississippi Baptist* please copy.

2-6-1862
Preston Bowden, son of Wm. B. and Naney Bowden, departed this life after a protracted illness of typhoid fever in the hospital at Charlottesville, Virginia, on the 15th of September last. He left his parental roof for the seat of war in Virginia on the 26th of June... He joined the Ebenezer Baptist Church in September 1857...
Died on the 14th of January, Nannie, daughter of Fannie H. and G.E. Seaman, age three years, ten months, sixteen days.

2-13-1862
Married on Thursday evening the 23rd of January at the residence of the bride's mother near Orion, Alabama by Elder J.T.S. Park, W.H. Pennington and Miss Lizzie only daughter of Mrs. Eliza McCullough.
Married on the 5th of February 1862 at the residence of the bride's grandmother (Mrs. E. Strozier) by Rev. J.W. Williams, Mr. Jas. Varner to Miss Aurine E. Little, all of Chambers County, Alabama.

## Marriage and Death Notices From The South Western Baptist Newspaper

Died at his residence near Pine Level, Alabama, Luke Nobles, on the 9th of October 1861 after a severe attack of the typhoid fever of near four weeks which he bore with Christian fortitude. Brother Nobles was born in Edgefield District, South Carolina on the 27th of March 1796, where he was raised and lived while he had a family, for several years; from thence he removed to Upson County, Georgia where he lived several years; from thence he moved to Chambers County, Alabama where he lived for many years and principally raised his family... United with the Rocky Mount Church sometime in the year 1843 where he remained a member until the year 1854 when he took his letter and moved to Pike County... [mentions wife and children].

Travis McKinny is no more. He died at his residence in Macon County, Alabama, January 30, 1862. He was stricken with paralysis... At the time of his death he had almost reached his seventy-fifth year... He was baptized into the fellowship of the Greenwood Church, Lincoln County, Georgia. About twenty years ago he left Georgia and settled in this county near Farmville Church of which he was a member at the time of his death. He has left a second wife and four children and many grandchildren.

2-20-1862
Died in this city on the 31st of October '61, Emma Louisa Walsh, granddaughter of Mrs. Witter, age thirteen years, twenty-three days. Only near relative to mourn her loss is an aged grandmother.

Nathan M. Aldridge, son of Clark and Mary Aldridge, departed this life at the home of Thomas H. Speaks near Evansport, Prince William County, Virginia on the 19th day of January 1862. He escaped the dangers of the battlefield but took the mumps which from exposure brought of typhoid pneumonia...His remains were brought home by his father and interred at County Line Church in Russell County, Alabama. February 7, 1862, Leland Allen.

4-3-1862
Died in Dallas County, Alabama on the 18th day of February 1862, Mrs. Margaret Johnston, the wife of Rev. Samuel Johnston, minister of the Methodist Protestant Church. She embraced religion about fourteen years ago in the city of Montgomery. On the 17th day of January she was violently attacked with an inflammation of the stomach which continued for several weeks. Samuel Johnston.

The *Mississippian* says: Captain McGowan of the Quitman Invincibles, belonging to the 14th Mississippi Regiment, was shot dead. Lieutenant McGowan, of the same company was shot down, wounded, and taken from the field of battle. Lieutenant Alexander Trotter, of the same company, shot down five of the enemy...

## Marriage and Death Notices From The South Western Baptist Newspaper

Died near Buckland, Virginia on the 23rd of September 1861 of camp fever, William Thomas, eldest son of R.D. Marshall of Marengo County, in the eighteenth year of his age. The deceased was a private in the "Marengo Rifles" 11th Alabama Regiment. He died at the residence of Mr. Edwin Basye in Fauquier County, Virginia...

4-17-1862
Died March 24, 1862 Erastus Chilton infant son of Dr. U.R. and Mrs. Mary C. Jones of Tuskegee, age fifteen months.
Departed this life after a short but severe illness in the Baptist Hospital, Richmond, Virginia, in the twentieth year of his age, John Thomas Harrington, eldest son of Rev. W.D. Harrington.

4-24-1862
Died of typhoid pneumonia at Williamsburg, Virginia on the 19th March last, in the twenty-second year of his age, Serg't Thos. W. Bayzer of the Greenville Guards Co. F. 8th Alabama Reg't. Edward.
Mrs. Sidney W. Moss departed this life on the 4th inst. at 7 o'clock a.m. Sister Moss was born October 26, 1806 in Green County, Georgia. Her parents removed to Autauga County, Alabama in 1810. She was married to Mr. S.G. Moss, March 30, 1826. In August 1833 she was baptized into the fellowship of the Church of Christ at Sister Springs, Dallas County. For many years previous to her death she was a member of Ash Creek Church, Lowndes County, Alabama. She has left a husband, three daughters and one son...

5-1-1862
Married on the 16th instant in Marion, Alabama by Rev. Wm. H. McIntosh, Mr. Wm. M. Jordan of the Confederate States Army to Miss Mary J. Fiquet, daughter of J.B. Fiquet of Marion.
Died in Russell County, Alabama, April 2, 1862, Wiley Jefferson, elder son of William J. and Henrietta A. Patterson, age five years, six months, six days. The papers of Troy, Pike County, will please copy.

5-15-1862
Married on Tuesday evening, 15 April 1862, by Rev. G.L. Lee, Dr. R.A. Lee to Miss Missouri Henderson, Monroe County, Alabama. The doctor left a few hours after he was married for the war.
Married on Wednesday evening the 16th inst. at the residence of the bride's father by Rev. G.L. Lee, Mr. E. Chadwick, Florida to Miss Martha Green of Conecuh County, Alabama.
Married in Coweta County, Georgia on the 1st of May at the residence of W.C. Barnes by Elder J.H. Hall, William H.M. Gay of Fayette and Miss Kitty Barnes.

## Marriage and Death Notices From The South Western Baptist Newspaper

J.J. Jenkins died in the twenty-first year of his age at the residence of his father, Rev. S.G. Jenkins, Talladega County, on the 14th inst. of chronic diarrhea contracted in the army in Virginia.

Died at her residence at Beulah, Chambers County, on the 6th of May Elizabeth Howell, wife of Ilsa?? Howell, in the forty-sixth year of her age. She leaves a husband and six children... Isaac Howell.

Died on the 7th of January 1862 in the hospital at Camp Me??inger, near Mobile, Eldred B. Lyon, son of John and Nancy Lyon, of typhoid pneumonia, in the twenty-first year of his age. He left a father and mother, one sister and six brothers, three of which are now in the Confederate service.

Died in Chimborazo Hospital in Richmond, Virginia, April 20, 1862, Spencer G. Stark, age twenty-five years; a member of the Macon Confederates, Capt. Ligon, 12th Alabama Reg't.

Simon G. Macon died at Corinth, Mississippi on the 26th of March, in the twenty-sixth year of his age; leaving a wife, two little children...S.G. and George C. Macon emigrated from North Carolina to Alabama several years ago. Simon, after finishing his education married the daughter of Wm. R. Stone, a Deacon in the Baptist Church at Talladega, Alabama. George was a student of Theology in Howard College. When this savage war for our subjugation commenced against us, Simon left his wife and little ones, George his studies, shouldered their muskets, and marched off side by side to grapple with death, for the sake of freedom, they waited long, dreary months, for a conflict with the enemy at Pensacola; thence they were ordered to Corinth to await the great battle of the 6th & 7th of April. While they were encamped at this place, Simon was seized by a malignant disease that soon claimed him as its victim. His brother, George, although quite ill at the time with typhoid fever, brought his remains to his beloved family and sister at Talladega, where he also took his bed and lingered until the 21st of April, then he too fell asleep in the arms of Jesus... George C. Macon was about twenty-four years old.

5-22-1862

The late Mickelberry Ferrel, Esq. of Troup County, Georgia: Some tribute is due to the memory of this excellent citizen who breathed his last at the residence of his son-in-law, Mr. Presley in Louisiana whither he had gone to settle a planting interest, October 30, 1861... E.B. Teague.

Departed this life at her home in Chambers County, Alabama on the 8th of May 1862, Mrs. Susan J. Penn, wife of Brother Wm. Penn, in the twenty-sixth year of her age. Sister Penn, whose maiden name was Buckelew, was early in life a subject of divine grace... During the last eight months of her life she was deeply afflicted... Sister Penn left an aged, widowed mother, a kind husband and two small children, one but a few weeks old...

## MARRIAGE AND DEATH NOTICES FROM THE SOUTH WESTERN BAPTIST NEWSPAPER

Departed this life April 4, 1862 at the residence of her husband, Mr. James T. Gardner, near Reform, Pickens County, Alabama, Mrs. Rebecca C. Gardner, in the thirty-eighth year of her age. She was born in Camden, South Carolina, May 18, 1824; removed with her parents Everard and Mrs. Rebecca Cuerton to Pickens County, Alabama in 1833 and married James T. Gardner, September 24, 1840. She joined the Baptist Church in 1848... She left a tender babe and several children and a devoted husband...

Died at the residence of Noah Robinson in Butler County, Alabama, March 19, 1862, J.F. Parsons, in the twenty-third year of his age. His sudden and untimely death was from inflammation of the kidneys and bowels causing most excruciating pain... He was fully sensible of his approaching death for several days and often spoke of his departure as of going home where he expected to meet his dear father (who had preceded him only a few months)... He leaves a wife, infant, widowed mother, sisters and brothers... He was born in Harris County, Georgia, May 22, 1839; from Harris his father moved to Russell County, Alabama where he was baptized by Rev. C.A. Stanton in the Fall of 1859. From Russell he moved to Butler, and united first with the Church Sardis and subsequently with the Georgianan Church, with whom was his membership at the time of his death.

5-29-1862
Died at his mother's residence in Monroe County, Alabama of pneumonia on the 13th of April 1862, Henry M. Adkinson, in the twenty-sixth year of his age. Brother Adkinson was born in Edgefield District, South Carolina and emigrated to this state in early life with his father, Rev. T. Adkinson, now deceased. He was baptized by Elder A.J. Lambert into the fellowship of the Salem Baptist Church in 1859... a bereaved mother, brother and sisters mourn the loss... Geo. L. Lee, Burntcorn, May 12th, 1862.

Died at Loudon, Tennessee, May 2, 1862 of typhoid fever, Henry Burt a native of Conecuh County, Alabama; son of Joseph H. and Lucy Burt, in the twentieth year of his age.

Died at the residence of her husband in Russell County, Alabama on the 26th day of April, 1862, in the sixty-sixth year of her age, Elizabeth Thornton. The deceased was twice married. Her first husband was James Elberhart of Chambers County, Alabama, formerly of Madison County, Georgia. She lived only a few years with her second husband, Rev. Reuben Thornton. Sister Thornton was for the last thirty-five years of her life, a pious and devoted member of the Baptist denomination. She has left an aged husband, six children...

6-5-1862
Sergeant Newton Blackburn died of typhoid pneumonia at Tuscumbia, Alabama on the 24th of March 1862. He was born the 21st of April 1845 in Chambers County, Alabama...

## Marriage and Death Notices From The South Western Baptist Newspaper

A young lady, the daughter of James Yarborough, was burned to death at Jonesboro on the 7th inst...

6-12-1862
Tribute of respect from the teachers and pupils of the Sabbath School at Warrior Stand on the death of Sam'l Breedlove.
Tribute of respect from the Clinton Lodge #287 of F. & A.M., Skipperville, May 10, 1862 on the death of James A. Brewer, who died in the service of his country at Nashville, Tennessee, February the 6, 1862. He was a faithful and consistent member of the Baptist Church of Christ at Summerhill, Dale County, Alabama...
Died at Union Springs, Alabama, May 10, 1862, W.E.H. Connell, eldest son of M.M. and Emily Connell, after a very short but severe illness, age eleven years, two months, six days. At the time the bereaved parents were called upon to bid a last adieu to their boy, the afflicted father was lying upon a bed of languishing and pain. He survived his son but a few days, when he too was called upon to go up higher. Died of consumption, Mitchael [sic] M. Connell, at the above place, May 23, 1862, age thirty-nine years, four months, seven days... [mentions wife]
Died at Camp Chilton near Corinth, Mississippi, April 21st, my son, Joseph C. Burks, age seventeen years. He was a member of Col. Clanton's Regiment, 1st Alabama Cavalry. He was in the Friday's fight, taken sick that night and lingered until the 21st. June 1st, 1862, C.S. Burks.
Died at Loachapoka May 23, 1862, Mrs. Kisiah King, formerly Mrs. Shurley. She was married to G.C. King, 22 August 1826. Baptized, 16 November 1835 by Rev. C.A. Tharpe at Antioch Church, Jones County, Georgia... She was fifty-eight years, four months, twenty days old when she was strucken with the palsy. She left seven children.

6-19-1862
Tribute of respect from Antioch Church, June 1, 1862 upon the death of J.C. Jenkins, son of our pastor S.G. Jenkins.
Mrs. Catharine Jones, wife of Lieutenant John E. Jones, died in Tuskegee on the 6th day of June 1862, in the twenty-second year of her age. She had been married a little over a year, her husband had just left a few days before for the seat of war as a member of the 45th Regiment of Alabama Volunteers, her attack was sudden and virulent and she left an infant of only four months old... being a member of the Methodist E. Church.
Died of typhoid fever on the 19th of May last, at Camp Winder Hospital, Richmond, Virginia, William Asbury Starr, youngest son of Rev. R. and Mrs. Phoebe Starr, age twenty-two years. Berry was born on the 27th of November 1839 in Chambers County, Alabama. He lost his father at an early age... Berry you were my friend.

## MARRIAGE AND DEATH NOTICES FROM THE SOUTH WESTERN BAPTIST NEWSPAPER

Fell in the battle of Chickahominy, May 31st, Capt. Thos. J. Bacon, La Grange, Georgia. He leaves a wife and five most interesting children.

6-26-1862
Died on the 9th June 1862 of inflammatory rheumatism, age twelve years, two months, twenty days, William Chappell, elder son of A.L. Haralson of Autauga. [mentions parents and little brother] His Father.
A good man and his son have fallen: Elder James R. Thames and his son, Nataan J. Thames, are no more: They are numbered with the pale nations of the dead. Elder J.R. Thames departed this life on the 7th of June 1862. He was the son of Rev. Cornelius Thames. He was born in the state of Alabama, Macon County, very near the place where he died, March 20, 1819. He was baptized into the fellowship of Salem Church by his father in November 1839. Brother Thames contracted the disease measles which proved fatal while away from home waiting on his beloved soldier boy in or near Mobile. Thus father and son fell by the same disease... Nathan J. Thames, son of Elder J.R. Thames, was born May 27, 1843. Died, May 20, 1862. He was baptized into the fellowship of the Philadelphia Church by Rev. Jno. McWilliams near four years ago; some time after, he by letter, united with the Salem Church... The remains of our Brothers were then borne to the family burial ground and laid by the side of his son while a mother and other relatives sleep near by.
Died in Tuskegee, June 15, 1862, Mrs. J.M. Dancy, wife of A.D. Dancy, in the thirty-seven year of her age. Mrs. D. had been an orderly and consistent member of the Baptist Church for several years, having joined the church in 1853. She leaves a husband and two little children...
Talladega Church, June 7, 1862. Whereas, with mingled feelings of grief, we have learned that our Brother, Jasper D. Wilson, member of this church.. fell in the battle of Williamsburg, Virginia.
Departed this life at the residence of J.N.C. Brown, one miles east of Centerville, Bibb County, Alabama on the 6th day of May 1862, Henley D. Lightsey, age twenty-six years, seven months. Brother Lightsey had a younger brother in the Confederate Army at Richmond and had four dear sisters, two little brothers at home... his father and mother both being dead.

7-3-1862
Died at camp Memminger near Mobile, Alabama on the 20th January 1862, Joab Franklin Goodson, age eighteen years, nine months, eight days. He joined the Baptist Church at Mount Moriah, Bibb County, Alabama, September 14th and was baptized September 26, 1861. He died after a short illness... He bade us all farewell and requested us to send his remains home to be buried in his grandpa's burying ground. In accordance with his dying request his brother brought his remains home, and on the 27th January 1862 we consigned the noble "soldier boy" to the narrow tomb. He leaves a father and mother, brothers and sisters...

## Marriage and Death Notices From The South Western Baptist Newspaper

Mr. J.C. Goodson--Dear sir: It becomes my painful duty to announce to you and your family the sad intelligence of the death of your son, Joab F. Goodson. He has been sick for several days in the hospital, and suddenly died...Joab was a good boy, a true soldier. J.G.

Departed this life on the 13th inst., near Verona, Mississippi, John J. York, a member of company (E) 34th Regiment Alabama Volunteers. As a husband, kind and sincere, and as a father affectionate and devoted...

Death of Mrs. Paulin: Only a few days since the husband and child rejoiced in the angelic love of a wife and mother. Sarah Eveline, wife of Rev. J.S. Paulin, and daughter of A.H. and Mary L. Borders ?, was born in Troup County, Georgia on the first of August 1837, and died in Clayton, Alabama on the 16th of June 1862.

7-10-1862

Married on the 15th of May by Rev. Basil Manly, D.D., Lieut. Albert J. Thornton to Miss Alcesta, only daughter of Judge H.W. Watson, all of Montgomery.

Mrs. Jamie Gray Nichols died in Columbia, South Carolina at the house of H.E. Nichols, Thursday morning, June 19th. She was a native of Chambers County, Alabama. Educated, mainly, under Milton E. Bacon at La Grange, Georgia. On December 1, 1858 she was married to James H. Nichols (of Charleston, South Carolina) in the 1st Baptist Church, Montgomery by the Rev. John E. Dawson. She was ill for two years and since February last, had lost her voice. Her residence was in Lowndes County, Alabama for the last few years...

Thomas L. Whitehurst died in Auburn, Alabama on the 15th day of June 1862, in the twenty-sixth year of his age. He was a soldier in the 37th Regiment of Alabama Volunteers, a citizen of Pike County, Alabama and a member of Capt. Amorine's company.

Died in the city of Tuscaloosa, April 3, 1862, Mrs. Eliza J. Shelton. She was born in Spotsylvania County, Virginia, January 30, 1817.

Died in the 1st Alabama Hospital, Richmond, Virginia, June 6, 1862, in the twenty-seventh year of his age, Lewis G. Aldridge, eldest son of Clark and Mary Aldridge of Russell County, Alabama... United with the County Line Baptist Church in Russell County, Alabama at about twelve years of age. He never gave father, mother or wife a short answer or a cross word.

7-24-1862

Robert L. Mayes, late Captain of the Tuskegee Light Infantry, fell in the battle of "Seven Pines" on the 1st June 1862... Devoted husband, fond father..."

Died in camp at Saltillo, Mississippi, June 2, 1862 of pneumonia, Jasper N. Hurlay, age twenty-three years, fifteen days. Baptised by Elder J.A. Fonville at Orion, 10th day of September, 1857. J.P. Nall.

## Marriage and Death Notices From The South Western Baptist Newspaper

Mary Thomas Owen, the only daughter of Mariah and Thomas E. Owen, departed this life at the residence of her grandfather in Butler County, Alabama on the 4th day of July 1862. Mary T. was born in Chambers County, Alabama, June 24, 1854. Little Mary's father died a few weeks before her birth. Geo. L. Lee, Burnt Corn, July 8, 1862.

Died of typhoid fever on the 19th of June at Dr. Witherspoon's, near Crawford, Mississippi, Lieut. John R. Payne, son of John and Francis Payne of Butler County, Alabama. John was born April 4, 1842; age twenty years, two months, fifteen days. He had been a member of the Baptist Church in Greenville, Alabama for more than two years... He fought as Alabamians know how to fight.

Died in La Grange, Georgia, on the 24th of June, Andrews Batile, son of Col. D.W. and M.J. Morgan; age eight years, three months.

John C. Moore died in residence of his father, Dr. J.S. Moore, near Warrior Stand on the 10th day of July, 1862, in the twenty-third year of his age. He was seized with typhoid fever. His father succeeded with bringing him home some ten days before his death. Member of the Tuskegee Light Infantry.

Tribute of respect from Mt. Lebanon Baptist Church on the deaths of Leslie Waldron and Tho's Fail, while in Virginia upon the tented field, in defence of their country. T.E. Williams, Ch. Cl'k., Pleasant Hill, Alabama.

Tribute of respect from Howard College, Marion, Alabama, June 26, 1862, upon the death of Gen. Edwin D. King, who on the 11th day of January 1862 closed his earthly career.

Died of camp fever in Scott County, Mississippi, June 10, 1862, William Washington, son of Jesse M. and Elmira Pearson, age seventeen years, six months, twelve days.

Tribute of respect upon the death of Wm. F. Beard.

7-31-1862

Married at the residence of the bride's mother on the 12th March 1862 by Rev. E.E. Kirvin, Lieut. J.K. Hawthorn, C.S.A., and Miss Janie H. Williams, all of Wilcox County, Alabama.

Died of typhoid pneumonia at Mound City, Illinois on the 8th of April 1862, in the twenty-second year of his age, Dozier A. Odom, a member of the Forest Guards, Capt. Graham, Company F, 20th Mississippi Regiment, son of D.H. and Emily E. Odom. The subject of this notice lived in Scott County, Mississippi and was a worthy member of the Baptist Church at Hays Creek. His remains were interred on the banks of the Ohio River.

Departed this life on Thursday, June 12, 1862, Mollie Brooks, infant daughter of Captain Henry P. and Ann R. Reid of Lowndes County, Alabama, age four years, four months, four days.

## Marriage and Death Notices From The South Western Baptist Newspaper

Perry Smith died May 6, 1862 on his way home from Corinth, whither he had gone as a member of Capt. F.A. Pinckard's Company of Cavalry... We also chronicle the death of Brother Palmore Mathis, who died at Corinth, ? day of June 1862, a member of Capt. Pinckard's Company. As a husband he was loving and tender. He was baptized 23 June 1860.

We also chronicle the death of Brother Hosea Hood, who died at his father's residence in Randolph County, May ? 1862, after a long and painful illness. He contracted his disease while in the army of the Confederate States, and returned home to recruit his health...

Died at his residence in Tallapoosa County, on the 6th inst. of snake bite, Thomas Jefferson Cooper. The deceased leaves a wife, three little girls, one brother...

Daniel M. Sayre died on the 30th June ult. at Richmond. He was the editor of the *Tuskegee Republican*... He was one of the first to give up his business and the endearments of home and rush to the field of conflict...

Departed this life at Ridge Grove, Macon County, Alabama on the 19th of June 1862, Alburn L. Bedell, age twenty-three years, one month, twenty-three days. He leaves behind two loving sisters and three brothers... Deprived of parents by death when quite a small boy. Taken by measles... Baptized at Farnville Baptist Church, August 1860.

William Preston Kinnebrew, son of M.D. Kinnebrew of Tallapoosa County, Alabama, died on the 2nd day of July 1862 of wounds he received in the battle of "Seven Pines" on 31st of May. He was a member of the Lonchapoka Rifles, 6th Regt. Alabama Volunteers, and in the twentieth year of his age.

Died in the city of Petersburg, Virginia on the 16th of June 1862 at the residence of Mrs. S.C. Morgan, Mr. Francis Debardalaban. The dear strange lady before mentioned found our Brother, a stranger and took him in sick... Francis Debardalaban was born in the year 1825, consequently was in his twenty-seventh year when he died. United with Tuslegee at age sixteen. [mentions mother, brother]

Died on June 3, 1862 at the residence of his father, Perry Kirkland in Autauga County, near Burnsville, in the thirty-second year of his age, Donelson Kirkland. He has left a bereaved companion and parents... Member Shady Grove Church. July, 1862, W.W.

8-7-1862
Tribute of respect for two faithful ministers of the New Testament from Pleasant Grove Church in Talladega County, Alabama for Joseph Chipman, who died at Matthew Turner's the 6th day of May 1861, in the eighty-ninth year of his age; and Brother George C. Macon, who died at the house of Wm. R. Stone, April 21, 1862, in the twenty-second year of his age... Eldest brother, Simeon G. Macon, died at Corinth a few days before.

## Marriage and Death Notices From The South Western Baptist Newspaper

Ira Ellis Payne, son of John and Francis Payne of Butler County, Alabama, was born January 18, 1844, and died of typhoid fever at the hospital in Enterprise, Mississippi, June 20, 1862, age eighteen years, one month, two days. Fought with his brother at battle of Shiloh. Thus has gone John and Ellis Payne - two brothers. They are now slumbered side by side in their graves.

Died in the Yandall Hospital, Columbus, Mississippi, J.M. Cogburn of the 17th Alabama Regiment, Co. I. He was born in Georgia in 1838. He leaves a wife and three children... Professed religion in his seventeenth year... P.P. Neely, Pastor of the Methodist Church, Columbus, Mississippi.

Died at his residence in Monroe County, Alabama, April 22, 1862, Deacon James E. Lett, in the forty-second year of his age. The deceased was born in the state of Virginia, Mecklenburg County, April 4, 1821. On the 13th of February 1845 he was married to Miss Elizabeth Boyken Hunter, with whom he lived happily to the close of his life... The decease of Brother Lett was very sudden and unexpected. He leaves a dear companion and seven fatherless children. Baptized by Elder J.H. Schroble in 1840 when he became a member of Limestone Church.

Died of pneumonia at the hospital in Richmond, Virginia on the 7th of June 1862, Alvin A. Lancaster of Chambers County, Alabama. Alvin was a member of the Cusseta Gray's Co. A., 14th Regt. Alabama Volunteers. He leaves a mother, sister, brother...

Thomas M. Branch of Mobile died of typhoid fever on the 22nd of July, in the twenty-third year of his age. He was wounded in the battle of Chickahominy, returned home, and died a few days after his arrival.

Joseph J. Knight, son of John and Brunetta Knight, died of typhoid fever in the hospital in Richmond, Virginia, June 11, 1862, age nineteen years, six months, six days. He was born in Jasper County, Georgia, December 5, 1842, and in early life removed with his parents to Chambers County, Alabama which home he left in August last as a recruit for the Loachapoka Rifles, Sixth Alabama Regiment... Uncle Joe joined the Baptist Church at the age of sixteen. A Niece.

Mrs. Francis Thomas, the wife of Michael Thomas, died after a few days illness at his residence near Hamilton, Harris County, Georgia, July 6, 1862; in the fifty-fourth year of her age. She was born in Kershaw District, South Carolina and moved to Lowndes County, Alabama about 1835, where she was baptized in the Smyrna Baptist Church by Elder Jesse Lee... Left bereaved husband and five mourning children. In the last two years of her life she witnessed the connecting of two of her children to the church.

Killed on the battlefield near Richmond on Monday the 30th of June 1862, Sergeant John B. Tramill, son of Elias Tramill, age a little over twenty-four. The subject of this notice was born and raised in Perry County, Alabama. In 1854 she made a profession of religion and joined the Baptist Church at

## Marriage and Death Notices From The South Western Baptist Newspaper

Fellowship Brush Creek. Fought at battle of "Seven Pines." [mentions deceased mother and grandmother who died several years ago] The subject of this notice, Judson Bickerstaff, the son of A.R. and S.C. Bickerstaff, was born in Chambers County, Alabama in 1842... He was taken seriously ill and ended this life on the 7th of July 1862 at the Clifton House in Richmond, being nineteen years of age.

Died, Hinds H., son of Octavia L. and William Bailey, deceased, of Tuskegee, Alabama. He was just eighteen years of age. In the battle before Richmond on Thursday, July the 1st, he fell with his leg shattered by a ounce ball... He eagerly watched the battle in front of him until he was struck down by a minnie ball passing through his head. [mentions widowed mother, sisters and only brother]

8-14-1862
Died of typhoid pneumonia at his residence, Fredonia, Chambers County, Alabama, Edwin T. Satterwhite, age thirty-six years, one month. Brother Satterwhite was born December 30, 1825, was baptized by Rev. D.H. McCoy, August 1859, and died January 30, 1862... He was returning home from Evansport, Virginia on a mission. On Sunday, January 26th, he was taken very violently and a physician was called and he was advised to lay over until he got better, but he insisted that they should send him on home, for he thought that he would die and he wanted to get home before he did. So he arrived on Monday 27th, and Thursday night, 30th, he breathed his last in his own house. He left a wife and four daughters, aged respectively fifteen, seven, five and two years... About two weeks after the death of Brother Satterwhite his eldest daughter, Mary Elizabeth, was attacked with the same disease. She was born April 13, 1847, was baptized August 20, 1858 by Rev. D.H. McCoy, and died July 10, 1862. She was confined to her bed five long months, lacking three days. She hated to leave her mother and four little girl children, her mother had brought forth another about three months after the death of her father.

Theodore W. Vernon was one of the number of brave Southern sons who fell a sacrifice in their country's cause in the last days battle before Richmond. He was a member of the 5th Alabama Regiment Company A. He was born in Wilcox County, Alabama, February 9, 1830. He had lived several years at Choctaw Corner, in Clark County... He has left an aged and devoted mother, a lovely young wife and child...

Mrs. Lide, relict of James Lide, gently expired on Thursday, July 3, 1862, at Carlowville, Dallas County, Alabama. She was born November 21, 1778, married to James Lide, August 22, 1793. Baptized by the Rev. James Coleman in the Great Pee Dee River on the second Sunday in July 1803. In December 1835 with her husband she removed to Alabama. She had eight sons and four daughters. Three of her sons died young, all the residue of her children became members of the Baptist Church. In the present war, twelve

## Marriage and Death Notices From The South Western Baptist Newspaper

of her grandsons and great grandsons are in the army. Thus she was born in one revolution and died in another.

On the memorable 31st of May 1862 while fighting with his companions in arms for the independence of our Confederacy, Robert L. Mayes passed from the ranks of our heroes into the smaller and selector roll of those who are honored as martyrs to their country's cause...

Mrs. Mary Larkins, born in New Hanover County, North Carolina, near Wilmington, in the year 1769 and departed this life on the 19th July 1862, age ninety-three years, at her daughters Mrs. C. Larkins in the city of Montgomery, Alabama... Member of Baptist Church for thirty years having been received by old father McLemore, Pastor of Elim Church. For past sixteen years suffered great bodily affliction and for about three years previous to her death was confined mainly to her room.

Dennis J. Perry was born in Perry County, Alabama, April 15, 1824. He was baptized into the fellowship of the Baptist Church at Ocmulgee... of which church he remained a member up to the day of his death which took place at Oakalona, Mississippi, July 10, 1862, while performing his duty waiting the sick. He was a member of Capt. C.H. Harris' Co. 28th Regt. Alabama Volunteers. He was in the battle of Farmington Roads where he displayed great valor and bravery.

Died at her residence in Summerfield, Dallas County, Alabama on the night of the 27th July, Mrs. Sarah W. Goldsby, wife of Col. T.B. Goldsby, deceased. Sister Goldsby had been a member of the Baptist Church at Ocmulgee for a number of years... Pastor. Plantersville, July 29, 1862.

Baptist Church. Greenville, in conference, July 12, 1862. It has pleased God in his providence to remove from our fellowship two of our young and very much loved Brothers, viz: Lieut. John R. Payne and Dr. J.L. Lide. Brother Payne died at Dr. Witherspoon's near Crawfordville, Mississippi, June 19, 1862 of typhoid fever... Brother Lide had left his parents and home in Marion, Alabama and settled in our midst to practice physic but a short time before he volunteered to serve his country... Brother L. was killed on the 27th of June, 1862 by a grape shot through the hips in the last great battle near Richmond, Virginia.

Died in Richmond, Virginia, July 16, 1862, in the twenty-first year of his age, Jesse Mashburn of Fannin County, Georgia. The subject of this notice was a member of the 11th Regiment, Georgia Volunteers. The deceased has left an affectionate father and mother and two brothers, one of whom is a member of the same company that he was, and three loving sisters...

Tribute of respect on the death of J.V. Perryman, Jr., born in the county of Conecuh and state of Alabama on the 24th of May 1837. He united with the Evergreen Baptist Church on the 25th of August 1856. But alas! that common enemy to whom all must submit asked him to surrender, which was done without a murmur, at Knoxville, Tennessee on the 11th of May 1862.

## MARRIAGE AND DEATH NOTICES FROM THE SOUTH WESTERN BAPTIST NEWSPAPER

8-21-1862
Since the commencement of this war, Alabama has mourned the loss of many of her bravest and truest sons. Buloch, Lomax, Martin, Baine, Hale, the Joneses, besides many others of lesser note, sleep in soldiers graves. To the catalogue of her distinguished dead we have to add the name of John J. Woodward. He was born in Fairfield District, South Carolina, and belonged to a family which has contributed much to Church and State. In 1828 he graduated at the University of his native state... He removed to Talladega County, Alabama in 1837 or 8, and commenced planting, which owing to some financial embarrassment, he abandoned to resume his profession. For a brief period he edited the *Democratic Watchtower*... Col. W. leaves a devoted wife and several small children... In 1847 he was elected a representative to the legislature. He was a politician of the Calhoun school, editor, lawyer, solicitor, judge, captain, major, colonel.

Orrin D. Cox, son of O.D. and Emily Cox, died of measles in the hospital in Richmond, Virginia, July 24th, 1862, age eighteen years, one month, five days. He was born in Macon County, Alabama, June 19, 1848 where he lived until August last.

Died at the residence of his father in Conecuh County, Alabama, Jesse Wright Burt, son of Jas. H. and Lucy A. Burt, of typhoid fever and measles on the 28th day of June 1862. He was born on the 20th day of February 1832... He leaves an affectionate and Christian wife and two little children.

Departed this life July 23, 1862 at the residence of his mother near Midway, Alabama, William Early Thornton, in the twenty-seventh year of his age. Weeks of suffering with camp fever. The deceased became a member of the Church of Christ at the tender age of fourteen years, being baptized by Rev. James Perryman into the fellowship of Union Baptist Church, Talbot, County, Georgia... [mentions widowed mother, relative Col. R. Thornton]

Died at her residence in Montgomery after nineteen days illness, Mrs. S.E. Cook, in the fifty-second year of her age. For years the sure and steady ravages of consumption had been wearing away her life. Leaves father, brothers and sisters... two sons in the army... and an only daughter. But death still lingers, to bear away in five weeks the pride of that bereaved household, the youngest, Ellsworth Cook, in the twenty-six year of his age of typhoid fever after sixteen days illness, at Night's Mills, near Tupelo... Leaves brother and sister.

Sarah Quarles Joiner died at Guntown, Mississippi on the 11th of July, having ripened to the honored age of three score and eleven years. Deceased was born in Campbell County, Virginia, her maiden name being Cobb. In early life with her parents, she emigrated to Abbeville District, South Carolina where she was married to S.S. Joiner. Removing to St. Clair County, Alabama she made a profession of faith... [mentions her son, Jas. H. Joiner, the editor of the *Talladega Watchtower*]

## MARRIAGE AND DEATH NOTICES FROM THE SOUTH WESTERN BAPTIST NEWSPAPER

Died, Herbert McDonald. He leaves behind a widowed mother, three sisters and one brother...

Died at the residence of Calvin Stephens, her son-in-law, on the 25th of July 1862, the beloved disciple Eleanor Nobles, daughter of William and Margaret Holloway, in the sixty-fifth year of her age. Sister Nobles was born in Edgefield District, South Carolina on the 25th day of April 1798. She was married to Luke Nobles of the same district on the 19th of December 1816. Was baptized into the fellowship of the Baptist Church, Gilgal, on Turkey Creek, South Carolina by Elder Basil Manly, D.D. about forty years ago. In 1824 with her husband and family, Sister N. emigrated from South Carolina to Upson County, Georgia; thence moved to Chambers County, Alabama in 1831; thence to Pike County, Alabama in 1853; thence to Montgomery County, Alabama in 1858 where she lived till God's appointed time to take her home above. Her sickness was inflammation of the bowels and brain. Her sainted husband had been called of his blessed Lord about ten months before her...

John U. Ingram, a member of the Macon Confederates, 12th Alabama Volunteers, was instantly killed while gallantly charging a battery in the battle of Seven Pines, May 31, 1862. He was twenty years, five months, fourteen days old at the time of his death.

Tribute of respect on the death of F.E. DeBardalaban, our late clerk, who died June 16, 1862 in Petersburg, Virginia, whither he had gone as a soldier in the Confederate Army. La Place Baptist Church. August 2, 1862.

In the battle of Seven Pines on the 31st of May, while gallantly defending his country, fell our noble friend and messmate, John D. Britton, son of Isom and Amanda Britton. John was born the 11th October 1840; age twenty-one years, seven months, twenty days. He was a member of the Loachapoka Rifles in the 6th Alabama Regiment. He left a widowed mother, two sisters and two younger brothers.

8-28-1862
Married on the 14th of this instant at the residence of the bride's father, Magnolia, Alabama, by the Rev. A.J. Coleman, Dr. T.P. Burgamy to Miss Dora Fonville.

Died on the 3rd day of July 1862 from the effects of a wound received on the battlefield near Richmond, Virginia, Benj. Josephus Goss, eldest son of Elder J.D. and Nancy Goss of Autauga County, Alabama, age twenty-four years, one month, sixteen days. He was a member of the Wetumpka Light Guards and attached to the renounced 3rd Alabama Regiment.

Miss Bettie Jones. This amiable and accomplished young lady, the daughter of Amos Jones, late of Tuskegee, died at the residence of her father in Wilcox County, Alabama on the 27th of June last, in the twentieth year of her age, after an illness of only two or three days.

## Marriage and Death Notices From The South Western Baptist Newspaper

Tribute of respect on the death of George W. Giddins. He fell at the battle before Richmond on the 27th of July... He was cut off in his twenty-seventh year. He was baptized into the fellowship of Bethel Church, Muscogee County, Georgia... We sympathize with his wife and two children, parents and sisters.

While noticing the death of George W. Giddins it is our painful duty to announce the death of his brother Frances M. Giddins, who died of typhoid fever at Lauderdale Springs, Mississippi, 15 July 1862, in the eighteenth year of his age.

Died at Lauderdale Springs, Mississippi on the 28th day of June 1862, Euclidus S. Longshore, age thirty-two years, one month. Brother Longshore was baptized, October 6, 1854 by Elder J.G. Branthy and united with the New Prospect Church, Butler County in 1860... He was joined in marriage by the writer of this notice to Miss Mattie F. Hicks, 25 October 1860. At the call of our country for volunteers he left bosom companion and darling little babe. The remains of the deceased were brought home and interned in the family burial ground. Baptized, October 6, 1854 by Elder J. G. Branthy and united with New Prospect Church, Butler County, in 1860 by letter.

Tribute of respect for Mark A. Hill, who was killed in the battle near Richmond, June 25, 1862. He was a member of the West Point Guards (4th Georgia Regiment). The deceased was a son of Waid Hill of LaFayette, Chambers County, Alabama but a Georgian by birth and died in the thirtieth year of his age.

Tribute of respect for Capt. R.H. Keeling, who died at "Seven Pines". He was born in the city of Richmond, Virginia on the 11th day of August 1827 and was, therefore, in his thirty-fifth year...

9-4-1862

Col. Sydenham Moore, of the 11th Alabama Regiment, died yesterday morning of a wound received in his left leg, on the 31st of May at the battle of "Seven Pines." Col. Moore was born in Tennessee but removed when young to Huntsville. He practiced law at Green County. In the Florida and Mexican War...

Lt. B.B. Smith. The melancholy news reached our town in a few days since that this most excellent young man died one day last week at Chattanooga, Tennessee. He was first Lieutenant in one of the companies in the 45th Reg. Alabama Volunteers.

Died at Richmond, Virginia on the 4th July from a wound received in the battle fought near the city on the 27th June, in the twenty-second year of his age, Thornton R. Harvell. Thornton was born in Perry County, Alabama. He joined the Baptist Church of Christ at Shiloh, in his native county, September 6, 1860. He had just finished his literary course and returned to see a widowed mother at the home of his youth... when the news reached him that a ruthless foe was about to invade his country. He was present and was

## Marriage and Death Notices From The South Western Baptist Newspaper

slightly wounded at Manassas on the memorable 21st July 1861. During a charge made by the 4th Alabama in the battle near Richmond on the 27th June, under the leadership of that good and brave man, General Stonewall Jackson, Thornton fell wounded in the leg by a minnie ball. His leg was amputated on the 3rd of July which resulted in his death on the 4th day following.

Died from the effects of measles at the residence of her father in Greenville, Alabama, Eugenia F., eldest child of Jas. G. and Francis Colvin. Eugenia was born October 8, 1852 and died August 24, 1862, age nine years, ten months, sixteen days.

Died near Sweet Water, Alabama on the 4th of August, Mrs. Catharine, wife of Bowen Seabrook; also on the same day, Mrs. Mary, wife of E.W. Keese. They were both members of the Baptist Church.

Died at her residence in Perry County, Alabama, Mrs. Rhody Summers, on the morning of the 26th August 1862. Ocmulgee Church mourns the loss.

On Sunday the 31st of May 1862, Daniel Sturkie was killed in the battle of Seven Pines near Richmond, Virginia... He was slain by a ball through the head... Daniel Sturkie was born and partly raised in South Carolina. His father settled in Russell County, Alabama while he was a youth... The deceased left an affectionate wife, an interesting little boy, a widowed mother, brothers and sisters...

The lifeless form of Thomas Elijah Robbins now lies in the cold narrow home of the dead. He was the son of Rev. James and Elizabeth Robbins, and was born in Conecuh County, Alabama on the 22nd day of November 1841. He died on the 9th of August 1862 of a wound received in the battle at Richmond... His parents died in his early youth. With his brother joined the immortal "Fourth Alabama." His brother fell on the plains of Manassas and his remains now repose beneath the soil of Virginia... [mentions brother and sisters, aunt]

Ash Creek, Lowndes County, July 27, 1862. This day having been set apart for the purpose of having a proper respect to the memory of four of our most prominent and esteemed young men to wit: Frank Haralson, James Gordon, Jr., David Gordon, Jr., and Julius M. Shuford...

9-11-1862

Married on the 28th ult., at the residence of the bride's mother near Eutaw, Alabama, by the Rev. Charles Manly, Lieut. W.A. Child of Tuscaloosa to Miss Mary C. Cockrell.

Tribute of respect on the death of Captain A.S. Flournoy. Killed instantly. [mentions, brother, sisters, a dear niece]

Departed this life the 28th of July 1862, George, the son of J.J. and Moriah Davis. He was born in 1841. His disease was contracted near Richmond, Virginia, and terminated in typhoid, which probably was brought on from a hasty march from Yorktown to Richmond when just out of the hospital...

## Marriage and Death Notices From The South Western Baptist Newspaper

9-18-1862
Died on the 6th day of August 1862 at the hospital in Danville, Virginia of typhoid fever, William Thompson Simmons, in the twenty-second year of his age. He was born in Montgomery County, but at an early age moved to Macon, where he lived until the time of his volunteering... He left a widowed mother, brothers and sister...

Departed this life at Mr. Britton Rodges', near Tupelo, Mississippi, Richard H. Baker, in the seventeenth year of his age. He was born in Macon County, Alabama the 28th day of October 1845... had the misfortune to lose his father when quite young and was raised by an affectionate mother, a kind uncle and aunt... His kind uncle arrived there in time to wait upon him one week before he died.

Adoniram M. Eley was born in Taliaferro County, Georgia the 3rd day of January 1837. His parents moved to Union Springs, Macon County, Alabama January 1838. He died August 27, 1862, in the twenty-sixth year of his age. The eldest son of Rev. M.N. Eley...

On the 23rd of August 1862, Daniel R. Rudulph died of typhoid fever at the residence of his parents in Greenville, Butler County, Alabama; age about twenty-two. He was one of five sons of his parents in the Confederate Army. It was with only extraordinary energies, he was enabled to reach home to die.

9-25-1862
A Good Man Fallen: Richmond, Virginia, September 5, 1862. Some six months ago, Rev. L.B. Robertson, a young Baptist minister, came from his home in Eutaw, Alabama to secure an appointment to labor among the soldiers as colporter. He told us that his churches (four in number)... were willing to give him up for a few months, that he might go on this mission from our Board, Brother Robertson returned to labor among the brave men in his own state. He spent a few weeks at Mobile, preaching and praying and scattering the life-giving pages in the camps and hospitals of that city. Then he went up to the hospitals in Mississippi where he labored with untiring zeal and abundant success. While engaged in this service he contracted the "camp fever" from the effects of which he died on the 12th ult.

10-2-1862
Married on the 21st inst. at the residence of Elder R.B. Brooks, the bride's father, near Midway, by Elder J. Stratton Paullin, William Cato to Miss N. Carrie Brooks, all of Barbour County.

Married at the residence of the bride's father in Montgomery County on the 11th of September 1862 by Rev. W.E. Lloyd, Wm. D. Zuber and Miss Mollie L. Evans.

Died in Tuskegee on Saturday, September 20, 1862, Ione, the only daughter of J.C.H. and Julia Breedlove Reid. Born Monticello, Georgia, March 3, 1842, and was in her twenty-first year... [mentions loving brothers]

## Marriage and Death Notices From The South Western Baptist Newspaper

Ellis, infant of J. G. and Frances Colvin, died at the residence of his father in Greenville, Alabama, September 12th, 1862, age eight months, twenty-six days. The parents lost their eldest, a daughter a few days before... The eldest and youngest of four children.

Died of measles on the 24th day of July 1862 at the residence of her father near Bellville, Conecuh County, Alabama, Miss L.E. Ballard, daughter of Theopleilus and Catherine M. Ballard, in the twenty-fifth year of her age. [mentions little brothers, sister]

Died at the residence of her husband in Sumter County, Alabama, of congestive chill, Catherine Rebecca, consort of Col. James M. Lee, on the 8th day of May 1862. She was the daughter of Nathaniel P. and Elizabeth Deane. The deceased was born in Clark County, Alabama, February 7th, 1830. She was baptized into the fellowship of the Christian Valley Baptist Church in the summer of 1858... left a bereaved husband with four small children... requested husband to keep children together... [mentions mother in law]

On the 9th inst. the infant of Mr. and Mrs. G.T. Flewellen breathed its last at the residence of Col. E.R. Flewellen in the county of Barbour, age eleven months... She was the admiration of her near relatives.

Departed this life at the residence of his father, George Shealy, Chambers County, Alabama, John Noah Shealy, in the twenty-third year of his age. Born in Edgefield District, South Carolina the 6th of May 1831. In early life he with his father and family moved to Alabama... was baptized into the fellowship of the LaFayette Baptist Church... A member of Company F. 47th Reg't Alabama Vols... He was taken sick and suffered severely during his stay in camps and the hospital, from several successive attacks of different forms of fever, which left him in a very low state with chronic diarrhea. Through the intercessions of his sister he obtained a sick furlough and like many others of the noble and brave he returned home to die, in fact he did not quite reach his home, his wife and little ones, he arrived at his father's unable to travel and died the third day afterwards. Brother Shealy leaves an affectionate, devoted wife, (whose parents are both dead) two small sons, father, mother, many sisters, brothers...

10-9-1862

Married Tuesday, September 30, at La Place in this county by Rev. Mr. Handey, Mr. Henry W. Griffin and Miss Aggusta G. Roberts.

Died in Tuskegee on Saturday the 20th of September, Ione, only daughter of Mr. and Mrs. J.C.H. Reid. She was born in Monticello, Georgia, on March 3, 1842, and was in her twenty-first year.

Tribute of respect from Notasulga Lodge #119, Free and Accepted Masons, on the death of E. Winn.

Robert Hardeman Sinclair, son of Albert E. and Elizabeth Sinclair of Tuskegee, Alabama, fell while gallantly charging the foe August 29th, at the

## Marriage and Death Notices From The South Western Baptist Newspaper

late battle of Manassas... being in his twentieth year... After a brief illness Randolph Sinclair, uncle of Robert, but member of the same family, died September 25. He was a discharged soldier recruiting his wasted health... [mentions aged grandmother]
On 22nd of September death came in our midst and took away a pure and lovely girl, Virginia, youngest daughter of J.F. and E.M. Nix; age fifteen years, nine months, thirteen days... For some days that fatal disease diphtheria preyed on her body...
Died in Richmond, Virginia on the 27th of April last, John T.O. Brine, of Tallaferro County, Georgia, after a protracted illness, age twenty-two... [mentions parents, brothers and sisters] [see below]
Died in Richmond, Virginia on the 4th of June last, Bracy O'Brien, father of the above, in the sixtieth year of his age. The deceased was born in North Carolina, 1802, moved thence to Taliafero County, Georgia where he married and remained several years, afterwards he moved to Tallapoosa County, Alabama. He had gone to Richmond to attend a sick son, John T. O'Brine, but when he arrived there his body was reposing beneath the soil of the Old Dominion. [see above]

10-16-1862
Died on the 2nd of October 1862, of brain fever, after a brief illness, in the town of Tuskegee, Eliza P. Hill, daughter of A.B. and Louisa Hill, in the nineteenth year of her age.
Died at Clinton, Tennessee, March 25, 1862, of pneumonia and brain fever, Joel T. Rice, age twenty-eight years, four months, four days. He was a member of Company L., 20th Regt Alabama Vols., which mustered into service September 16, 1861. Though he was not one of the first to rush to arms in defence of our country; a dear mother prostrated upon a bed of affliction (from which she never rose)... His mother died very soon after his return to camps and he survived her just four short months. His brother was with him in his last illness. Oh, cousin Joel. M.J.G.
Died at the residence of his father, Garlan Rice, in Green County, Alabama, July 23, 1862, of congestion of the brain, George W. Rice, age eighteen years and eleven months. In April last this young soldier, accompanied by an older brother, left home and joined the 36th Alabama Regt. ...They had been in camps only three months when both were taken sick, and permitted to return home, where they might receive proper attention... He has left a father, four brothers, a little sister...
Died of typhoid fever at her father's residence in Macon County, Alabama, in the twenty-fourth year of her age, Miss Emeline Smith, daughter of James and Emeline Smith.
Departed this life in Mobile on the 28th of June 1862 of typhus fever, Brother Jesse Knight, in the thirty-fourth year of his age. Brother Knight was born and

## Marriage and Death Notices From The South Western Baptist Newspaper

spent his life in the immediate vicinity of Mount Moriah, Wilcox County, Alabama. Buried Mt. Moriah. [mentions wife and children]

10-23-1862
Died in Eutaw, Alabama, August 12th, 1862, Rev. L.B. Robertson, in the twenty-ninth year of his age. The subject of this notice was born in North Carolina, February 5, 1833, emigrated to Cherokee County, Alabama in 1847, thence to Oxford in 1852, thence to Eutaw in 1860. Graduated Howard College, 30 June 1860.
Died in Richmond, July 12th, 1862, in the thirty-ninth year of his age, Nathan L. May of Benton, Lowndes County, Alabama. The subject of this notice was a member of the 5th Reg't Alabama Vols. and belonged to the Hayneville Guards. He leaves an afflicted widow with whom he had lived but a few months... He was laid in Holly-wood.
Died in Virginia on the 9th June, Brother R.H. Hill, in the twenty-six year of his age. The subject of this notice was born in Macon, Georgia, February 23, 1836. He moved to Alabama in 1857... leaves a devoted wife, two little children, father, mother... He died on the battlefield while gallantly leading his brave men.
J.J. Webb has fallen! He breathed his last on the 22nd of September... His body now lies in the church-yard at Damascus.
Helen May, only child of Mr. and Mrs. Geo. W. Thomas, died in Montgomery, September 24, 1862.
Lucy Finne, only daughter of Mr. and Mrs. Geo. W. Mrquis [Marquis?], died in Tuskegee, October 7th, 1862.

10-30-1862
Died at Big Spring Hospital, East Tennessee, on the 10th of September last, of typhoid fever, James C. Philpot, in his thirtieth year. Mr. Philpot volunteered early last spring and entered the Confederate service in the 46th Regt. of Alabama Volunteers. A younger brother of the deceased died of a similar disease last fall in Virginia. [mentions aged parents, widowed wife, two little children]
Killed by the ruthless invader at the battle of Malvernhill on the 1st of July, John T. Bestor of Co. B. 3rd Regt. Alabama Vol. He was the eldest son of the Rev. D.P. Bestor, and in his twenty-fifth year. In December 1860 he was united in marriage to one of Mississippi's lovely daughters, and soon after, his country called for volunteers... He paid a short visit to his home in Mississippi to arrange his affairs, and bid farewell to wife, father, sisters, and brothers and soon joined his company at Norfolk. Remains among the evergreens of Mississippi.
Died near Glasgow, Kentucky on the 15th September last, Robt. Ivry, third son of Barna and Aley Ivry. He enlisted April last.

## Marriage and Death Notices From The South Western Baptist Newspaper

11-6-1862

Died on the 30th June 1862 at the residence of Mr. Hitchcock in Richmond, Virginia, J.W.D. Jelks, in the forty-fourth year of his age... He raised a company early in the war... [mentions wife and children]

Departed this life in the city of Dalton, Georgia on the 2nd day of October 1862, Casskity, youngest daughter of Merritt and Eliza L. Burns, age twenty-two months.

Died in Auburn, Alabama, October 22nd, of ulcerated sore throat, Lizzie Unice, daughter of (the late) Maj. J.C. and S.S. Sale, age two years, six months.

Died near Tupelo, Mississippi the 8th day of August 1862, in the thirtieth year of his age, Thomas A. Moncrief. He was a volunteer in Captain Stanton's Company of the 1st Alabama Regt. and was on the Island #10 when it surrendered to the Yankees... Baptized at Farmville about three years ago. [mentions wife]

Died at the "Clifton House," Richmond, Virginia on the 7th of July 1862, Mr. J.R. Rickerstaff, in the twentieth year of his age. He left home in Tallapoosa County, Alabama the 9th of May 1861 in Capt. Kenedy's Company 6th Alabama Regiment... lost his right arm in the battle of "Seven Pines" near Richmond. For a few days hopes were entertained of a speedy recovery from the effects of the wound, but being attacked with fever he finally died as stated above.

Also, Andrew R. Bickerstaff, the father of the above noble youth, died at his residence in Tallapoosa County, Alabama, August 6, 1862... Receiving a dispatch from Richmond that his son was badly wounded he went in all haste to see him, and gave him all possible attention till his death. He then returned home and soon prostrated with typhoid fever, suffering for twenty-four days... leaves a wife and children... W.M. Mitchell.

Tribute of respect from St. Frances Baptist Church held in Mobile 3rd of October on the death of Deacon B.W. Miller. [mentions Thos. P. Miller, son of the deceased]

11-13-1862

The subject of this obituary, Benjamin F. Lovelace, age twenty years, nine months, seventeen days, fell on the memorable 17th of September at Sharpsburg, battling in his country's cause; pierced through the head by a minnie ball.

Died at the residence of James Thompson in Butler County, Mary Lula, the only heir of Dora Webb. She departed this life 13th of October 1862; age one year, five months, six days. Dora.

Mrs. Elizabeth Roberson. This Christian woman fell asleep in Jesus in Montgomery County, Alabama on the 16th day of October 1862, after suffering several months from dropsy, in her sixty-seventh year. She was born in Southampton County, Virginia in 1795, was married in her eighteenth year

## Marriage and Death Notices From The South Western Baptist Newspaper

to Wm. Wade of Northampton County, North Carolina, who died in 1827, leaving her with several small children to raise with limited means. She was baptized into the fellowship of Smith's Baptist Church in 1833 and removed to Alabama in 1844. She was twice married after the death of her first husband. Once to Deacon Wm. Baker, and after his death to Rev. John Roberson, who survives her.

H.C. Johnson. This young brother was born May 14, 1840. Volunteed September 10, 1861. [mentions widowed mother, brothers and sisters]. A.J. Russell.

Died on the 17th May last, at Columbus, Mississippi, age twenty-three years, John A. Sledge, son of C.A. and D.C. Sledge. The deceased joined the Baptist Church at Sardis, Macon County about three years since... Another brave soldier. [mentions fond parents, brothers and sisters]

Tribute of respect on the death of John Brinson. Husband and father.

11-20-1862

Married on the 30th of October by the Rev. M.B. Harden, Miss Mary E. Haynes to B.M. Thompson, all of Union Springs, Alabama.

Died at the residence of her grandfather, H.E. Taliaferro, on the 5th of November 1862, Bessie, daughter of William G. and Nancy J. Ham, in the second year of her age. Croup and pneumonia attacked the dear child...

On the morning of the 26th ult., near Greensboro, Alabama, died, Mrs. Nancy H. Burford, in the twenty-eighth year of her age. In the year 1857 she was baptized by Brother Wright into the fellowship of the Newbern Church, Green County, in which she died. Husband and children mourn.

Died at his residence in Pike County, Alabama, September 17, 1862, Deacon Leroy J. Johns, age forty-nine years. The subject of this notice was born in the state of Georgia, Jones County, March 12, 1813, where he grew up to manhood and at the age of twenty-seven was baptized into the fellowship of Bethlehem Church, Harris County. He moved to Pike County, Alabama in 1851 and by letter united with Fairview Church... [see below]

Died at his residence in Pike County, Alabama, October 9th, 1862, Deacon John Emerson, age sixty-five years. The subject of this notice was born in the state of Georgia, Hancock County, April 3, 1797, in which state he lived and at the age of thirty-five was baptized into the fellowship of Sharon Church in Monroe County. He moved to Pike County, Alabama in 1846... Emerson and Johns being set apart to the office of Deacon at the same time in the same church, remained members and Deacons... [see above]

Died: John Barlow, son of Deacon Thomas Barlow of Lowndes County, Alabama. He was born December 3, 1827 and died at Charlottesville, Virginia, July 17, 1862. In 1859 he moved to Texas and at the call of his country he entered the army, 1st Texas Regiment, Hoods Brigade... While performing duties of a soldier he fell victim to disease.

## Marriage and Death Notices From The South Western Baptist Newspaper

11-27-1862
Married in Tuskegee on Tuesday evening the 18th inst. at the residence of the bride's father, John C. Judkins, Jr., C.S.A., and Miss Mollie Thompson.
Departed this life on Wednesday the 5th inst. after a painful illness of eight days, Arcada Tallula, infant daughter of Davis and M.R. Stringer; age three months, eleven days.
Departed this life on Monday 27th of October 1862, Mrs. Bettie M. Hawthorne, consort of J.R. Hawthorne, Jr., in the twenty-third year of her age... was baptized into the fellowship of Rock West Church in Wilcox County... had been united in marriage but seven months... and he was at the time of her decease with his regiment upon the battlefields of Virginia.
At her residence in Tuskaloosa, Alabama. Mrs. Margaret A.E. Furman departed this life, October 22, 1862, in the forty-fourth year of her age. Her maiden name was Cammer. She was born in Charleston, South Carolina. In Alabama, her residence till her marriage with Richard Furman, was chiefly in the family of her maternal uncle Hon. B.F. Porter. She was married in 1841 and baptized in 1842. She was the mother of ten children, three of whom died in infancy, the last she left an infant.
Departed this life on the 10th day of October 1862, at his residence in Montgomery County, Deacon E.S. Leonard, age thirty-eight years, seven months, seventeen days. For several years past the subject of this notice had endured with christian fortitude the untold sufferings which accompany that dreadful disease consumption. He has left a devoted companion, widowed mother, two brothers, two sisters...

12-4-1862
Died on the 11th day of November 1862 of protracted fever at his residence in Monroe County, Alabama, Thomas Wiggins, in the fifty-six year of his age, leaving behind a widow and eight children...
Died in Russell County, Alabama on the 13th October, William H.H. Fuller, with consumption of the lungs. His disease contracted in camps whilst in Virginia, by being exposed to a heavy sleet one night, they being without a single tent. He was taken to the Richmond hospital and remained there nearly five months. After being brought home he only survived six weeks. He was a recruit of Capt. Hardaway's of Columbus. He was young, only in his twenty-first year.
Died at Cross Keys, in this county, on the 21st inst. after a short but painful illness, Robert Marshall, only son of A. S. and Frances R. Mayes, age four years, three months.
Died on the 16th November of typhoid fever in the vicinity of Tuskegee, Mrs. Sarah R. Daniel, in her twenty-fourth year. She was the twin sister of Miss Emeline Smith, who died about one month ago of the same disease. Mrs. D. leaves a husband, an only child, parents and brothers and sisters...

## Marriage and Death Notices From The South Western Baptist Newspaper

Died on the 11th of October 1862, near Cropwell, St. Clair County, Alabama, of ulcerated sore throat, Sarah M. Thompson, daughter of John F. and Caroline M. Thompson, age four years, eight months, twenty days... Brother Thompson having joined the army during summer of '62, Sister Thompson with her two little children, of which this little girl was the oldest, resolved to stay at home and take care of what they had...

Of the many noble martyrs who have fallen in our struggle for life and liberty none more noble nor brave has fallen than Robert G. Andrews, only son of Rev. A. Andrews, who fell at the battle of Sharpsburg, age twenty-seven, a member of Co. A. 4th Alabama Reg.

12-11-1862

Died in Knoxville, Tennessee, November ?5th, 1862, of typhoid, [first name not given] Barganear and his wife Emma F. Barganear. Emma was the daughter of Wm. B. and S.A. Price of Butler County, Alabama. But two months ago Berry bade farewell to father, mother, wife, child and all the endearing scenes of home and flew to the rescue of his country. Soon, fell disease prostrated him on a bed of suffering, and as soon as his faithful, devoted wife heard the sad news she went to endeavor, to alleviate his sufferings and administer to his wants, but she was only permitted to remain with him a few days to comfort and console... and was conveyed to a private house to die... They both died the same day... Berry was twenty-four and his wife seventeen years of age... They left a little girl fourteen months old... Emma was a member of the Bethel Baptist Church at Ft. Deposit.

Died on the 20th July 1862 at Cropwell, St. Clair County, Alabama of flux, Elizabeth Leland Swink, daughter of Leland L. and Nancy J. Swink, age one year, ten months, thirteen days.

During the past week two of our scholars gently fell asleep, as we trust in the arms of their savior. Miss Delle Rambo breathed her last after a long and painful illness at half past one o'clock Sunday morning, October 26th, and little Ada Taylor, of the infant department early on Monday morning following. First Baptist Church. Montgomery Alabama.

12-18-1862

Died in prison at Camp Randall, near Madison, Wisconsin on the 12th of May 1862 of measles, Frank Boykin, in the twenty-third year of his age, a member of Co. G 1st Reg't Alabama Vol., and second son of Frank and Fannie Boykin, Pike County, Alabama.

Died in Richmond of camp fever, N.C. Battle, age eighteen years, son of W.W. Battle, Macon County, Alabama. Volunteed Confederate Army.

Departed this life in the sixty-third year of her age, Mrs. Frances Porter, wife of Henry B. Porter, and daughter of Willis and Kitty Perry. Sister Porter was born in Warren County, Georgia. She was baptized in her twenty-first year by Rev. John Goss into the fellowship of Cabin Creek Baptist Church, Putnam

## Marriage and Death Notices From The South Western Baptist Newspaper

County, Georgia; moved to Alabama 1839 where she spent the remainder of her useful days. On the 29th of October last she fell asleep in Jesus. Union Springs, Alabama. M.N.E.

Mrs. Mary A. Horton, wife of W.S. Horton, died in Perry County, Alabama, November 8, 1862; age thirty-two years. She had been for many years a consistent member of the Baptist Church at Hopewell.

Departed this life some time since at Knoxville, Tennessee, age about twenty years, Alexander, son of our esteemed Brother J. Long of Chestnut Creek. He sleeps far away from home.

Tribute of respect from Auburn Lodge #76, December 2nd, 1862, on the death of Thomas Slaton, Senior Warden of this Lodge, who died at his home in Auburn on the 29th day of November 1862. [mentions widow and orphans]

Tribute of respect from Concord Church, Russell County, Alabama, on the death of Rev. David Elkins. He was severely afflicted with palsy... Could not speak for several days.

12-25-1862

Died on the 25th ult., Francina Cordella, youngest daughter of Britton and Sallie Stamps; age eleven years, two months, twenty-five days. Youngest of the family circle. Parents, brothers and sisters...

Ephraim A. Williams, son of W.B. Williams of Pike County, Alabama, died in Ringgold, Georgia, November 9th, 1862, in the twenty-fifth year of his age. He was born in Chambers County but for several years passed had resided mostly in Pike. Leaving his wife and little ones with his father-in-law, Mr. Dempsey Johnson, near Opelika, he prepared for the contest. Joining Capt. T.F. Flournoy's Company 45th Reg't Alabama Vols... Detailed as a hospital nurse but in a short time took pneumonia from cold contracted while waiting on the sick and died on the 4th day after the attack. He leaves a young widow and one little boy, one having died while he was in the army... In 1856 he joined Baptist Church at Mt. Carmel, Pike County.

Miss Fannie, eldest daughter of Brother Ivy and sister Mary Smith, fell asleep in Jesus on the 9th November 1862, in the twenty-second year of her age. She was buried with Christ in baptism and became a member of the fellowship Baptist Church in Marengo County, Alabama.

Died on the 4th day of November 1862 after a protracted illness of five months at the residence of her husband, Col. Joseph Johnston, in Tallapoosa County, Alabama, Sister Elizabeth W. Johnston, in the forty-seventh year of her age, leaving a kind husband and five children... Sister Johnston was baptized into the fellowship of Pleasant Grove Church many years since by Rev. D.B. Culberson...

MARRIAGE AND DEATH NOTICES FROM THE SOUTH WESTERN BAPTIST NEWSPAPER

## ALABAMA COUNTY COURTHOUSES DESTROYED BY FIRE

| County | Date(s) Burned |
|---|---|
| Butler | 1853 |
| Calhoun | 1861, 1865 |
| Cherokee | 1882, 1895 |
| Chilton | 1870 |
| Choctaw | 1859, 1871 |
| Clay | 1875 |
| Coffee | 1851, 1863 |
| Conecuh | 1868, 1875, 1885, 1895 |
| Covington | 1895 |
| Crenshaw | 1898 |
| Dale | 1869, 1884 |
| Escambia | 1868 |
| Fayette | 1866 |
| Franklin | 1890 |
| Geneva | 1898 |
| Greene | 1868 |
| Jackson | 1864 |
| Jefferson | 1870 |
| Lamar | 1866 |
| Lawrence | 1859 |
| Limestone | 1862 |
| Marengo | 1848, 1965 |
| Marion | 1866 |
| Mobile | 1823, 1840, 1872 |
| Monroe | 1833 |
| Morgan | 1926, 1938 |
| Pickens | 1876 |
| Pike | 1828 |
| Randolph | 1896 |
| Sumter | 1901 |
| Walker | 1865, 1877, 1896, 1932 |
| Winston | 1891 |

**MARRIAGE AND DEATH NOTICES FROM THE SOUTH WESTERN BAPTIST NEWSPAPER**

## NAME INDEX

?ams 144
?ay 50
Abbott 39, 103, 112
Abel 10
Abercrombie 133, 135, 153
Acher 67
Acker 114
Adair 77, 100, 101, 129, 176
Adams 44, 50, 73-76, 92, 99, 104, 111, 114, 117, 125, 147, 149, 168, 174
Addison 154
Adkinson 182
Agee 104
Akin 141
Albert 141
Aldridge 127, 153, 179, 185
Alford 174, 175
All???? 24
Allen 55, 56, 63, 69, 70, 113, 116, 133, 139, 142, 145, 164, 178, 179
Amorine 185
Amos 156
Amoss 133
Anderson 6, 16, 38, 73, 106
Andrews 59, 106, 159, 202
Apperson 76, 145
Appleton 178
Arant 118
Arbery 101
Armstrong 18, 40, 48, 52, 58, 65, 85, 102, 130, 134, 153
Arnold 89, 101
Arnot 30
Arthur 82
Ashcraft 10
Ashking 100
Ashley 116, 147
Ashmon 159
Ashust 31
Askew 28, 135

Atkinson 71, 113
Atteberry 20
Averett 78, 155
Averitt 71
Bacon 29, 35, 154, 184, 185
Bagby 153
Bagget 128
Bailey 15, 29, 111, 112, 189
Bain 134, 143
Baine 191
Baker 25, 66, 134, 135, 151, 195, 200
Baldwin 82, 108
Ball 177
Ballard 196
Bandy 42
Bankston 87
Bannerman 58
Banney 145
Baptist 64, 167
Barganear 202
Barker 60
Barlow 200
Barn?t 68
Barnes 63, 75, 180
Barnet 68, 135
Barnett 150, 154
Barrett 167
Barron 38
Bartlett 72
Barton 50
Bascom 2
Bass 43, 87, 100, 130, 137, 147
Basye 180
Bates 100, 166
Batile 186
Battle 29, 39, 72, 76, 102, 115, 119, 132, 133, 154, 155, 157, 202
Baylor 8
Bayzer 131, 180
Bealle 101, 139, 167
Bean 16, 99

205

MARRIAGE AND DEATH NOTICES FROM THE SOUTH WESTERN BAPTIST NEWSPAPER

Beard  138, 186
Bearden  148
Beck  134
Bedell  141, 187
Bell  94, 115, 139
Belsher  134
Bennet  91
Bennett  117, 122, 126, 152, 161
Benson  4, 48, 82
Bentley  65, 81, 95, 99
Benton  127, 151
Berny  108
Bestor  3, 23, 154, 198
Betts  140
Beverly  64, 66, 117
Bevis  108
Bickerstaff  189, 199
Billingslea  4, 6, 16, 39, 50, 178
Billingsley  72
Billingsly  25
Billups  21
Bird  164
Birdsong  119
Birt  148
Bishop  59, 86, 107, 162
Bissell  144
Black  22, 74
Blackburn  182
Blackman  154
Blackshear  58
Blair  49
Blake  88
Blakey  48, 63, 142
Blan  91
Blanchard  155
Bland  12, 64
Bledsoe  77, 124, 146
Blount  101, 144, 164
Blunt  1, 65, 79
Boan  165
Board  171
Bodell  42
Bolger  125
Bolling  161

Bolton  3
Bond  6, 89
Bonds  55, 112
Boone  133
Booth  98, 158
Borders  12, 103, 185
Boroughs  27
Boroum  80, 108
Borum  98, 104
Boster  3
Bostick  91, 144
Bostor  154
Boswell  100, 136
Botsford  160
Boulware  118
Bowden  116, 142, 156, 178
Bowdon  78
Bowen  85, 88
Bowie  78
Bowlin  16
Boyd  127
Boyken  188
Boykin  161, 202
Bozeman  56, 94, 170
Bradford  11, 73, 158
Bradley  158
Brady  177
Brame  10
Branan  162
Branch  111, 188
Brannon  105, 112, 126
Branthy  193
Brantley  62
Brasfield  119
Brassell  119, 128
Brassfield  25, 168
Brawner  85
Brazelton  39
Breaker  4, 32, 48
Breedlove  94, 183, 195
Brewer  62, 77, 128, 161, 167, 183
Brine  197
Brinson  200

MARRIAGE AND DEATH NOTICES FROM THE SOUTH WESTERN BAPTIST NEWSPAPER

Brisky  169
Britton  192
Broadhurst  118
Brock  10
Broderick  30
Brodnax  116
Brooks  16, 83, 94, 101, 105, 186, 195
Browder  8
Brown  3, 5, 6, 27, 42, 57, 58, 76, 102, 116, 140, 143, 169, 175, 184
Browning  131
Brownlee  34
Brumby  5, 6
Bruner  172
Bryan  9, 76, 91, 115, 127, 151, 163, 165, 177
Buck  21, 148
Buckelew  181
Bulger  176
Bullington  67
Bullock  5, 47, 177
Buloch  191
Burford  200
Burgamy  192
Burgen  96, 176
Burk  34
Burkes  85
Burks  29, 39, 101, 128, 132, 138, 143, 152, 157, 162, 183
Burleson  7, 9, 28
Burnes  5
Burney  84, 112
Burns  94, 101, 199
Burr  43
Burruss  29
Burt  68, 70, 172, 182, 191
Buse  63
Bush  82, 115, 124
Bussey  35
Butler  6, 29, 134, 171
Butts  81
Cadenhead  26
Caffee  107, 114

Caffey  8, 97, 145, 170
Cain  10
Caine  153
Caldwell  17, 46, 62, 82, 98, 103, 111
Calf  4
Calfee  49, 84
Calhoun  130
Callaway  43, 48, 61, 87, 89, 92, 93, 128, 133, 155, 164
Calloway  40, 176
Cameron  28
Cammer  201
Campbell  49, 69, 75, 88, 123, 143, 146
Camron  69
Canady  115
Cannon  3
Cantey  142
Capers  111
Capps  145
Cargile  134
Cariker  77
Carley  63
Carlisle  15
Carlton  155
Carpenter  142
Carraker  34
Carrel  1
Carroll  6, 50
Carson  90
Carter  58, 109, 110, 115, 139
Cater  1
Cato  163, 195
Catts  140
Chaddick  121
Chadwick  180
Chalmon  31
Chambliss  1, 9, 11, 24, 96, 144
Champion  158
Chapman  65, 123
Chappell  184
Chasiene  110
Cherry  60

MARRIAGE AND DEATH NOTICES FROM THE SOUTH WESTERN BAPTIST NEWSPAPER

Chester 160
Child 194
Childs 55
Chiles 87
Chilton 30, 46, 113, 133, 135, 180
Chipman 166, 187
Chisolm 28
Christian 60, 104, 163
Christmas 68
Cilley 7, 73, 121
Clanton 183
Clappe 61
Clark 129, 149, 176
Clarke 135
Clay??? 24
Clement 4
Clements 86
Clingham 36
Clinton 5
Cloud 52, 69, 152
Clower 93
Coats 45, 96
Cobb 56, 80, 101, 131, 137, 191
Cochran 89
Cockerham 16
Cockrell 194
Cody 129, 142, 143
Cogburn 113, 188
Coke 102
Coker 141
Colby 73, 121
Cole 13, 15, 25, 47, 54, 99, 159
Coleman 3, 32, 51, 82, 112, 132, 189, 192
Collier 64, 80, 93, 104, 153, 170
Collins 1, 3, 27, 66, 82, 132, 133, 168
Colquitt 107
Colvard 99
Colvin 194, 196
Combs 159
Cone 5
Conger 30
Conine 43
Conington 121
Connell 183
Connella 21
Conner 92
Conway 122, 144
Cook 44, 70, 71, 138, 140, 164, 191
Cooper 11, 24, 75, 93, 100, 136, 141, 187
Copeland 120
Corbin 20, 53
Corday 88
Corley 146
Cote 3
Cotton 87, 118
Covington 112, 125
Cowart 98
Cowen 165
Cowle 175
Cox 68, 76, 105, 110, 131, 142, 191
Craighead 123
Crane 11
Crawford 6, 60, 128, 167
Creath 20, 166
Creighton 121
Crittenden 136
Croft 114
Crolius 83
Cromwell 44
Cropp 139
Crow 5, 79, 124-126
Crowder 107, 164, 169
Crumly 126
Crumpler 130
Crumpton 130
Cuerton 182
Culberson 29, 203
Culbreth 40, 80
Culpepper 61
Culverhouse 174
Cunningham 8, 21, 24, 59, 78, 110, 133, 135, 143, 159

MARRIAGE AND DEATH NOTICES FROM THE SOUTH WESTERN BAPTIST NEWSPAPER

Curry  19, 33, 34, 48, 55, 56, 110, 113, 114, 136, 138, 148, 157
Curzelius  140
Cushman  85
Dagg  50, 96
Dailey  5, 28
Dalzell  51
Dancy  184
Dandridge  28
Danforth  47
Danghdrill  57
Daniel  3, 95, 141, 159, 201
Darby  112
Davenport  104
David  145
Davidson  147
Davis  1, 10, 48, 79, 96, 99, 110, 121, 150-152, 156, 194
Dawsey  92
Dawson  41, 132, 138, 144, 154, 185
Day  154
Dayle  151
Dean  130
Deane  196
Debardalaban  187, 192
Dees  98
Deese  169
DeGraffenreid  80
DeLoach  65, 146
Dendy  113, 144
Denkins  29
Dennis  100, 126, 178
Denson  6, 24, 147
Derdin  6
Deslar  4
Devore  43, 44, 94
DeVoteo  23
DeVotie  20, 22, 39, 44, 89, 118, 132, 159-161
Dewey  22
Dews  38
Deyampert  44
Dick  67, 68
Dickenson  136
Dickerson  65
Dickey  109
Dickson  97
Dill  123
Dillard  23, 40, 43, 53
Dobbins  143
Dobbs  104
Dockery  15
Dodson  56, 140
Dorroh  23
Dorse  123
Dorsey  141
Dossey  26, 32
Doster  144
Dougherty  135
Douglass  16, 128
Drake  137, 138, 146
Drakeford  63, 89, 135
Draughon  37, 38
Drummond  13, 160
Dryer  96
Du?ham  136
DuBose  62, 75, 87, 92, 129
Due  161
Duke  128
Dulany  164
Dunagan  171
Dunaway  94
Duncan  33
Dunigan  169
Dunklin  125, 134
Dunn  142
Dupree  8, 21, 45
Durham  100
Duskin  121
Duvall  144
Dyer  3
Eady  30, 112
Eaford  91
Eager  6
Early  191
Easley  134
Eberhart  51, 57

MARRIAGE AND DEATH NOTICES FROM THE SOUTH WESTERN BAPTIST NEWSPAPER

Eberheart 122
Echols 26, 48, 58, 59, 68, 105
Edmonds 14, 165
Edmonson 30
Edmunds 11
Edwards 26, 106, 133
Elberhart 182
Eldredge 154
Eldridge 144
Eley 53, 55, 57, 62, 65, 68, 74, 78, 94, 96, 195
Elford 117
Elkins 40, 203
Elliott 8
Ellis 124, 188
Ellison 133
Ellsworth 138
Elmer 33
Elston 35, 49
Emerson 200
English 136
Erving 30
Erwin 161, 173
Estes 11
Ethridge 99, 163
Eubank 53, 76
Eubanks 29
Evans 1, 97, 131, 136, 173, 195
Everett 1, 42, 108, 115
Fagan 144, 157
Fail 186
Fallaw 81
Fannin 154
Fargason 164
Farley 67, 87
Farrar 12, 101
Faulkner 114
Ferrel 181
Ferrell 148, 166
Fielder 121, 143, 152
Fielding 140
Fife 1
Fike 14
Finley 22, 169

Finne 198
Finney 150
Fiquet 180
Fitzpatrick 75, 135
Fleming 22, 139
Flemming 4
Flewellen 196
Flournoy 194, 203
Floyd 132, 141, 142
Flynn 54
Fonville 53, 62, 64, 97, 102, 112, 118, 135, 145, 158, 185, 192
Ford 12, 14, 16, 17, 19, 27, 32, 39, 74, 116
Forte 152
Foscue 128
Foster 7, 15, 28, 29, 46, 71, 97, 103, 104, 113, 115, 127, 128, 130, 154, 157, 163, 168, 170-172
Fountain 27
Fowler 70
Fowlkes 7
Fox 20
Foy 86
Fr(e)drick 67
Fraser 43, 77
Frazer 102, 177
Frazier 19, 97
Frederick 113, 115
Freeman 72, 97, 102, 134, 137, 138
Fuller 13, 65, 114, 162, 201
Fullilove 117
Furguson 99
Furlow 144
Furman 12, 201
Futell 67
Gachet 94
Gafford 130
Gaines 138
Gales 113
Gardner 3, 11, 42, 43, 97, 182
Garland 136, 138
Garrett 36, 67, 80

**MARRIAGE AND DEATH NOTICES FROM THE SOUTH WESTERN BAPTIST NEWSPAPER**

Garrot  64
Garward  65
Gary  37, 85, 129, 135
Gates  168
Gaulden  31
Gay  180
Gayle  67
George  4, 14, 106
Germany  82, 91, 95, 100
Gewin  39
Gibbs  46
Gibson  31, 35, 36, 81, 114, 137, 156, 161
Giddins  193
Gillispie  61
Gilmer  66
Gilmore  16
Gilmore,  42
Gindeat  51
Gladney  42
Glaze  97
Glover  118, 140, 164
Golden  157
Goldsby  159, 190
Gonder  130
Gooch  26, 58
Goodall  78
Goode  28, 115
Goodenough  17
Goodson  184, 185
Goodwin  27, 71
Goolsbie  131
Goolsby  125
Goram  131
Gordon  50, 142, 194
Goree  2, 17, 33
Gorham  111
Goss  53, 192, 202
Graham  64, 89, 165, 186
Granberry  16, 65, 69, 70, 75, 121, 148
Grant  98
Graves  97, 109, 128
Gray  185
Greathouse  144
Green  1, 55, 119, 129, 161, 180
Greene  1, 135
Greenwood  65, 132, 156
Greer  122
Gregory  63
Gresham  141
Griffen  135
Griffin  27, 29, 53, 61, 107, 123, 153, 157, 196
Griffing  117
Griffis  129
Grifling  9
Grigg  28
Grose  31
Grouby  102
Grover  148
Grubbs  117
Guatman  99
Guice  109
Guild  50
Gullett  137, 156
Gun  71
Gunn  39, 40, 57, 84, 85, 93, 149
Gwin  43
Gwinn  40
Hackney  144
Hadaway  149
Hadin  63
Hadley  9
Hagerty  31
Haggard  62
Haggerty  95, 96
Hagin  63
Hairston  156, 169
Hale  80, 134, 152, 172, 191
Hali  66
Hall  66, 72, 154, 180
Ham  200
Hames  153
Hamilton  49, 59, 155
Hammett  136
Hammond  58
Hamrick  115

MARRIAGE AND DEATH NOTICES FROM THE SOUTH WESTERN BAPTIST NEWSPAPER

Hand  47, 62, 96, 150, 165
Handaway  149
Handey  31, 84, 97, 99, 111, 116, 122, 132, 145, 147, 151, 162, 165, 196
Handy  44, 52, 55, 65, 75, 86, 95
Haney  39
Hanks  78
Hannah  146
Haralson  71, 101, 150, 159, 184, 194
Hardaway  201
Hardeman  196
Harden  200
Hardin  138, 148
Hardivick  39
Hardy  12, 36, 50, 65, 102, 104, 118, 122, 125, 130
Hare  32, 167
Harkness  113
Harrass  168
Harrell  48, 108, 134, 149
Harrington  56, 114, 163, 180
Harris  18, 22, 34, 38, 57, 58, 66, 94, 111, 119, 133, 136, 157, 190
Harrison  26, 76, 115
Hart  59, 106
Hartwell  25, 63, 110
Harvell  34, 193
Harvey  85
Harvies  133
Harwell  34, 136
Hatch  8
Hatchett  64, 93
Hatter  134
Haughton  28
Havis  118
Hawthorn  32, 186
Hawthorne  201
Hayley  43
Hayman  32
Haynes  40, 200
Hays  33
Head  105

Heard  17
Hearison  6
Heirston  80
Helms  102
Henderson  26, 38, 43, 47, 57, 58, 62-64, 68, 74, 76, 77, 79, 81, 82, 84, 87, 93, 96, 97, 100, 102, 104, 105, 113-115, 118, 123, 127, 128, 133, 136, 142, 143, 148, 152, 155, 162, 163, 169, 175, 180
Hendon  121
Hendree  72
Hendrick  76
Henley  35
Henry  67, 145
Herbc?t  4
Herrick  52
Herrin  98
Herring  145
Herst  40
Hibbler  44, 161
Hickman  176
Hicks  5, 193
Higgenbotham  102
Hill  31, 64, 65, 67, 69, 74, 75, 87, 118, 129, 157, 193, 197, 198
Hilliard  177
Himes  77
Hines  119, 172
Hinkle  103
Hitchcock  164
Hix  152, 174
Hobbs  91
Hobby  176
Hodge  13, 56
Hodgens  53
Hodges  75, 91, 101, 137
Hodnett  78
Hoffman  136
Hogan  98
Hogue  24, 39
Holaman  139
Holcomb  134
Holden  90

MARRIAGE AND DEATH NOTICES FROM THE SOUTH WESTERN BAPTIST NEWSPAPER

Holland 124
Holliday 28
Holloway 160, 192
Holly 134
Holman 3, 23, 64, 163
Holmes 12, 27, 36, 57, 82, 112, 113, 122
Holt 30
Holtzclaw 23
Honeycutt 153
Hood 133, 187
Hooten 21, 26, 29, 51, 154
Hopkins 47
Hopper 124
Horn 134
Horne 93, 96, 129
Horton 1, 203
House 9
Howard 37, 61, 62, 71, 76, 95, 102, 114, 144
Howe 117
Howell 78, 136, 181
Howlett 24
Hrabowski 154
Huckabee 178
Hudson 17, 20, 34, 73, 89
Huey 117
Hughes 59, 80
Huguly 138, 156
Humphries 55, 110
Hunt 96
Hunter 42, 103, 132, 188
Hurlay 185
Hurst 102
Hutchins 97
Ingram 192
Inzer 169
Irby 86
Irwin 129
Ivey 57, 62, 78, 92, 93, 113, 119, 163
Ivry 198
Ivy 55

Jackson 44, 45, 82, 85, 90, 92, 114, 131, 194
Jacob 54
Jacobs 19
January 96
Jarrell 47
Jarrett 162
Jarvers 137
Jay 66, 101
Jelks 199
Jenkins 16, 28, 51, 141, 143, 181, 183
Jeter 96, 127
Jett 26
Jewell 39
Jewett 2, 8, 15, 110
John 25
Johns 176, 200
Johnson 31, 74, 76, 82, 96, 108, 131, 135, 138, 163, 173, 200, 203
Johnston 31, 57, 81, 91-93, 144, 153, 154, 167, 179, 203
Johston 57
Joiner 191
Jones 20, 28, 31, 32, 41, 44, 54, 63, 66, 89, 92-94, 96, 97, 106, 111, 112, 113, 116, 118, 135, 141, 162, 163, 165, 173, 180, 183, 191, 192
Jordan 1, 40, 42, 69, 84, 86, 87, 112, 140, 148, 180
Judkin 119
Judkins 201
Judson 31, 97, 112
Jurey 30
Kaukle 136
Keel 79
Keeling 193
Keese 194
Keitt 92
Kellam 51, 107
Kelley 17, 164
Kellum 51
Kelly 93, 97, 125, 151

MARRIAGE AND DEATH NOTICES FROM THE SOUTH WESTERN BAPTIST NEWSPAPER

Kelton  43, 88
Kendrick  39, 113, 131, 137, 140, 153, 156, 158, 161, 164, 174
Kenedy  199
Kennedy  5, 86
Kenney  6
Kerlin  32
Kerr  61
Key  62
Kidd  17, 49
Kilkrist  79
Kinard  172
Kincaid  155
Kindrick  131
Kinebrew  174
King  8, 20, 41, 44, 82, 93, 115, 119, 124, 133, 155, 167, 178, 183, 186
Kinnebrew  65, 84, 131, 187
Kirbo  55
Kirkland  108, 187
Kirksey  155
Kirvin  173, 186
Knight  16, 188, 197
Kobb  134
Kotten  68
Kunklin  154
Kurvin  76
Kyle  176
La Plass  99
Lacy  62, 102
Lake  23, 59, 95, 97
Lamar  24, 49, 93, 144
Lamb  80
Lambert  104, 137, 139, 182
Lanair  143
Lancaster  42, 188
Landey  149
Landrum  110, 124
Lane  60, 69, 80, 103, 143
Langford  80
Lanier  40, 92, 104
Larkins  6, 42, 131, 190
Lasiter  149

Lassater  18
Lassiter  158
Latimer  54
Lattimore  21
Law  72, 73, 94, 104, 128, 157, 158, 169
Lawler  95
Lawson  1, 20, 67, 127
Le Grand  156
Ledbetter  147
Lee  18, 22, 36, 54, 72, 94, 101, 102, 118, 132, 135, 140, 142, 151, 152, 153, 157, 172, 180, 182, 186, 188, 196
LeGrand  163
Leonard  201
Letcher  65, 155
Lett  188
Leusueur  107
Leverett  169
Lewis  102, 106, 131, 136
Lide  45, 56, 63, 125, 134, 143, 176, 189, 190
Lightfoot  149
Lightsey  109, 121, 184
Ligon  147, 165, 170, 181
Lilly  96
Lincoln  8
Lindsey  120, 160
Linton  119
Lipscomb  30, 74, 117, 132
Lisenbe  91, 92
Little  178
Littlepage  150
Liverman  153
Lloyd  23, 42, 55, 71, 84, 88, 97, 102, 106, 118, 135, 152, 156, 170, 195
Locke  43, 135
Lockett  17
Lockhard  121
Lockhart  42, 92, 125, 143
Loftin  4
Logan  143

**MARRIAGE AND DEATH NOTICES FROM THE SOUTH WESTERN BAPTIST NEWSPAPER**

Lomax  191
Long  42, 106, 116, 172, 175, 203
Longmire  26, 98, 161
Longshore  152, 193
Love  53
Lovelace  199
Loveless  104
Lovell  59, 97, 98
Lowery  106
Lowrey  155
Lucas  3, 106
Lumpkin  8, 20
Lunds  27
Lundy  49, 110, 130, 143-145, 154, 164
Lynch  40, 63
Lynn  151
Lyon  50, 140, 181
M'Guire  124
Mabson  67, 87
Macon  181, 187
Madison  17, 35
Maginnis  27
Mahan  39
Maharrey  174
Mahe  9
Majors  172
Malichi  100
Mallory  61, 148
Malloy  91
Malone  43, 67, 177
Mangham  98
Manly  22, 94, 101, 106, 146, 160, 185, 192, 194
Manning  38
Marable  31
Marchel  92
Marquis  198
Marsh  41
Marshall  3, 14, 30, 130, 134, 145, 162, 180, 201
Marson  67
Martin  31, 94, 97, 125, 144, 152, 191
Mashburn  190
Mathews  127
Mathis  117, 187
Matthews  118, 128, 155
Matthis  60
Mattison  84, 105
Maxwell  34, 47, 71, 95, 102, 152, 163
May  10, 37, 150, 198
Mayes  127, 185, 190, 201
Mayo  25, 162
Mayson  156
McAdams  126
McAlpin  148
McBryde  30
McCall  28, 132
McCants  158
McCarthy  92
McClellan  139
McCloud  91
McConaughy  83, 126
McConico  41
McConnico  103
McConnio  103
McCormick  129
McCoy  3, 40, 172, 189
McCrary  45
McCraw  9, 16, 37, 38, 43, 59, 60, 94, 126, 158, 159
McCreary  2, 88, 147, 166
McCullough  178
McDaniel  57, 103
McDonald  58, 77, 140, 192
McGar  93
McGee  58, 122, 124, 136
McGehee  152
McGill  145
McGinty  151
McGowan  179
McGowen  159
McGraw  38, 49
McIntosh  39, 50, 72, 73, 121, 130, 155, 172, 180
McIver  176

MARRIAGE AND DEATH NOTICES FROM THE SOUTH WESTERN BAPTIST NEWSPAPER

McKay  62
McKinney  77
McKinny  179
McKinzy  125
McLean  140
McLemore  15, 22, 49, 190
McLendel  177
McLendon  4, 146, 149, 154
McLeod  65
McMath  29, 30, 67, 69
McMilan  87
McNeely  19
McPhaul  156, 169
McPherson  115
McQueen  15, 153
McRae  9
McRie  64
McWhorter  33, 78, 128
McWilliams  184
Meadors  93
Meadows  18
Mealing  31, 75
Means  47
Meek  56
Meekin  76
Megginson  31, 104, 118
Melcher  22
Melton  32, 39, 112, 132, 144
Menefee  103, 121, 152
Mercer  88, 90
Meredith  15
Meriwether  92
Merrill  7
Merritt  175
Mershon  30
Metcalf  79
Middlebrooks  115
Miles  43, 156, 174
Miller  13, 46, 56, 199
Mills  14
Milner  62, 88
Mims  37, 105, 135
Minchen  104
Miree  146

Mitchell  1, 123, 135, 140, 146, 157, 199
Mock  151
Molton  35, 118, 128, 144, 164
Moncrief  51, 52, 109, 112, 118, 199
Monk  118
Montague  155
Montgomery  28, 130
Moody  165
Moon  50, 115
Moore  16-18, 21, 39, 50, 60, 98, 133, 152, 156, 186, 193
Moorefield  59
Moragne  60
Moran  162
Moren  147
Morgan  2, 25, 32, 86, 135, 186, 187
Morris  76, 88, 108, 130
Morrison  3, 151
Morrow  24, 133
Morton  12, 73, 94
Moseley  133
Mosely  66, 69, 126
Mosley  3
Moss  16, 76, 82, 92, 94, 105, 117, 119, 125, 133, 141, 158, 174, 180
Motley  50
Moton  82
Mott  104
Moulton  75
Mount  162, 165
Mountcastle  171
Mrquis  198
Mulder  36
Mullins  14
Mundine  7
Munnerlyn  111, 176
Murph(y?)  60
Murphy  7, 48
Murrah  63
Murray  5, 54

**MARRIAGE AND DEATH NOTICES FROM THE SOUTH WESTERN BAPTIST NEWSPAPER**

Murrell 149
Murry 61
Nall 185
Nance 107, 111
Napper 91
Neal 116
Neely 188
Nelms 38, 118
Nelson 60
Nettles 44, 158
Newberry 101
Newman 137
Newsom 2, 41
Newton 116
Nichols 101, 185
Nicholson 98
Nix 197
Noble 132, 139
Nobles 179, 192
Nolan 121
Noland 43
Nolen 160
Nolin 156
Norred 172
Norris 2
Norton 15, 63
Norwood 89
Notan 121
Nours 31
Nuckolls 47, 57, 71, 117, 123, 126, 151, 171, 176
Nunn 100
O'Brien 197
O'Brine 197
O'Bryan 26
O'Neal 49, 118
Oakes 35
Oden 29, 78
Odom 53, 149, 186
Odum 22
Ogden 14
Old 110, 119
Oldham 67

Oliver 10, 28, 30, 36, 146, 150, 163
Orum 76, 117
Osborn 108
Oslin 147
Ousley 86
Outlaw 26, 32
Owen 134, 172, 186
Owens 69, 76
Owsley 177
Pace 152
Page 153
Palmer 27
Parham 160
Parish 61
Park 17, 38, 46, 95, 99, 111, 113, 137, 178
Parke 18
Parker 52, 97, 144, 151
Parks 2, 98, 103, 113
Parmer 129
Parmly 73
Parsons 60, 153, 182
Paschal 99
Patterson 167, 180
Patton 52
Paulin 185
Paullin 112, 126, 195
Payne 186, 188, 190
Peak 159
Pearce 27
Pearson 73, 92, 186
Peavy 140
Peebles 102, 166
Peeples 114
Peetry 63
Pellum 77
Pendleton 43
Penn 85, 181
Pennington 173, 178
Perkins 5, 19, 125, 157
Perkinson 30

MARRIAGE AND DEATH NOTICES FROM THE SOUTH WESTERN BAPTIST NEWSPAPER

Perry  29, 49, 52, 53, 62, 93, 94, 100, 101, 111, 116, 126, 139, 156, 172, 190, 202
Perryman  21, 48, 94, 162, 190, 191
Persons  60
Peters  161
Pettigrew  134
Pharres  18
Philips  51, 55, 134, 174
Phillips  4, 5, 45, 101, 113, 114, 173
Philpot  163, 170, 198
Pierce  74, 89, 143, 152
Pierson  5, 39
Pihrce  74
Pinckard  47, 58, 131, 187
Pinkard  38
Pinkston  26
Pinner  171
Pitt  140
Pitts  59, 109, 145
Plowman  59
Plumb  172
Plyant  155
Pool  95, 137
Pope  10, 129, 144
Porter  38, 72, 95, 201, 202
Posey  18, 124
Poteet  160
Potilo  141
Pou  132, 139
Pouncly  175
Powe  161
Powell  62, 107, 112
Prather  52, 141
Pratt  28
Presley  181
Preston  166
Prewett  28
Price  106, 202
Prichard  82
Priest  71, 137
Pritchett  152

Pudgett  175
Pugh  138
Purifoy  121
Puriroy  133
Pylant  29
Pyron  133
Quarles  2, 123, 191
Raiford  164
Rambo  202
Ramsey  55, 101
Randal  87
Randolph  4, 16, 62
Rast  49, 122, 143, 145
Ratchford  81
Ratcliff  40
Ray  80, 98, 110, 115, 117, 119, 141
Read  52
Ready  31
Reason  170
Redd  143
Reed  89, 157
Reese  28, 86
Reeves  17, 43, 104
Reid  97, 148, 186, 195, 196
Rembert  87
Reynolds  116
Rice  126, 197
Richardson  41, 46, 81, 145
Rickerstaff  199
Ricks  23
Riddle  150
Right  152
Riley  133, 135, 137
Rimer  13
Ringgold  32
Rives  29-31, 70, 110, 170
Robbins  194
Roberson  199, 200
Robert  152
Roberts  39, 65, 81, 86, 87, 124, 131, 140, 155, 196
Robertson  22, 28, 70, 94, 96, 118, 132, 134, 144, 161, 195, 198

MARRIAGE AND DEATH NOTICES FROM THE SOUTH WESTERN BAPTIST NEWSPAPER

Robinson  13, 98, 182
Robison  88
Roby  100
Rodgers  147
Rodges  195
Roebuck  12
Rogers  39, 41, 55, 134
Rolen  1, 70
Rolfe  126
Rolin  3, 93
Root  60, 63, 76
Ross  14, 76, 115, 131
Rowe  144
Rudulph  37, 54, 195
Rugeley  42
Rupert  126
Rush  94, 97
Rushing  86
Russell  56, 67, 90, 105, 158, 200
Rutherford  133
Rutledge  84, 138
Ryan  76
Saffold  73
Safford  7
Sale  108, 155, 178, 199
Salmon  75
Salmons  69
Salter  84, 99, 102, 106
Samford  117
Sanders  3, 8, 38, 42, 83, 136
Sanderson  8
Sanford  80, 104, 140
Sanger  27
Sansing  58
Satter  140
Satterwhite  189
Saunders  43
Sawyer  140
Say??  88
Sayre  187
Scales  97
Scarbor  34
Scarborough  3
Schroble  188

Scogin  66
Scott  32, 37, 44, 76, 83, 88, 148
Seabrook  194
Seales  59
Seals  9, 115
Seaman  31, 178
Sears  42
Sebastian  66
Sedberry  70
Segrest  73
Seltzer  103
Seriven  18
Sessems  44
Sessions  89
Shackelford  38, 145
Shaffer  36
Shank  75
Sharp  29
Shealy  196
Sheer  17
Shell  59
Shelman  23
Shelton  55, 173, 185
Shepard  33
Shepherd  11
Sherman  64
Sherrer  102
Sherror  50
Sherwood  51
Shet?lesworth  17
Shivers  27
Shores  40
Shorter  33
Shuck  19, 39, 145
Shuford  194
Shurley  183
Shuttlesworth  65-67
Shuttleworth  107
Sibley  82
Simmons  47, 58, 97, 161, 195
Simms  161, 173
Simpson  5, 61, 63
Sims  90, 110
Sinclair  196, 197

## Marriage and Death Notices From The South Western Baptist Newspaper

Skinner  8
Skipper  175
Slack  1
Slade  53, 81
Slater  16
Slaton  203
Slaughter  49, 65, 74, 84, 125, 147, 165
Sledge  31, 200
Small  116, 135, 146
Smart  98
Smilie  17
Smith  3, 26, 33, 37, 48, 49, 57, 58, 67, 74, 75, 77, 83, 84, 87, 96, 120, 127, 132, 136, 147, 157, 158, 161, 168, 187, 193, 197, 201, 203
Smyly  34
Snowden  129, 130, 133
Southworth  28
Spalding  66
Span  41
Spaulding  148
Speakman  144
Speaks  179
Speare  4
Spence  90
Spencer  13, 32
Spires  14
Spivey  21
Spratt  27
Sprott  154
Stafford  141
Stakely  51, 62
Stallings  127
Stallworth  109, 119
Stamps  37, 57, 203
Standerfer  156
Stanford  72
Stanly  99
Stanton  66, 80, 83, 105-107, 113, 115, 118, 129, 134, 142, 144, 163, 164, 182, 199
Star  82
Stark  121, 136, 181
Starke  5, 8, 50, 87
Starke....Georgia  5
Starr  183
Stbinger  94
Steadman  16
Stearns  133
Steed  53, 112, 159
Stein  60
Stephens  62, 192
Stevens  29, 50
Stewart  17, 46, 68, 79, 89, 109, 153, 162, 170, 178
Stigler  10
Stilman  1
Stoker  14
Stone  22, 35, 181, 187
Stout  20, 129, 139, 141, 155, 160, 173
Strange  88
Stratford  50, 62, 64
Straughn  79
Street  142
Strickland  169
Stringer  41, 94, 201
Strobel  171
Strong  72
Strother  176
Stroud  114
Strozier  178
Stuckney  134
Sturgis  176
Sturkie  194
Styron  141
Sugo  134
Summers  135, 194
Suttle  120
Swan  26
Swanson  35, 51, 58, 109, 110, 123, 148
Swear?ngen  65
Swearingen  84
Sweat  165
Swindal  149
Swink  202

**MARRIAGE AND DEATH NOTICES FROM THE SOUTH WESTERN BAPTIST NEWSPAPER**

Swope 142
Sydnor 28
Tabor 7
Taggart 34
Tait 2
Talbert 9, 13, 49, 113, 114, 122
Talbird 18
Talbot 95, 176
Taliaferro 67, 74, 86, 93, 126, 134, 200
Taliferro 85, 157
Talifferro 156
Tallaferro 97
Tarrance 109, 154
Tarrant 23
Tarver 49, 112
Tate 169
Tatum 27, 126
Taylor 20, 35, 59, 118, 137, 140, 147, 202
Teague 37, 44, 79, 101, 103, 133, 135, 162, 163, 181
Teel 130
Terrell 46, 84, 173
Terry 89
Tha 154
Thames 159, 184
Tharin 96
Tharpe 183
Thigpen 91
Thomas 7, 23, 24, 46, 54, 58, 61, 73, 94, 97, 113, 118, 129, 160, 188, 198
Thomason 69, 98, 114, 176
Thompkins 70
Thompson 26, 42, 55, 56, 100, 101, 134, 157, 165, 195, 199-202
Thornton 29, 57, 76, 78, 86, 91, 104, 122, 143, 146, 148, 149, 152, 174, 182, 185, 191, 193, 194
Thorton 76, 78
Threefoot 126, 161
Tichenor 29, 70, 118, 138, 140, 144, 157, 161

Tichnor 64
Tidwell 43, 150
Tillman 40, 108
Tilman 12
Tobey 94, 114
Todd 45
Tolbot 87
Towles 159
Townsend 95, 99, 139
Tramill 188
Trammel 56
Trammer 56
Tranquila 107
Travis 3, 122
Trawick 113
Traylor 16, 31, 76, 120
Treutlen 123
Treutlin 73
Trother 56
Trotter 179
Trotti 39
Truss 130
Tubb 2, 5, 20, 39, 68, 99, 102
Tucker 29, 60, 154
Turner 5, 24, 107, 118, 159, 166, 167, 187
Turnipseed 117
Tuttle 52
Ulmer 156
Underwood 1, 7, 68
Vance 67, 84
VanHoose 18, 40, 42, 51, 62, 76, 94, 98, 112, 116, 131, 134, 136, 138, 143-145, 157, 162, 165
Vann 65, 100, 127, 129, 145
Varner 57, 136, 155, 178
Vason 160
Vaughan 2, 5, 101
Veasy 44, 46
Veazey 25, 31, 73, 85
Venable 23
Venaqle 23
Verdery 141
Vernon 115, 189

**MARRIAGE AND DEATH NOTICES FROM THE SOUTH WESTERN BAPTIST NEWSPAPER**

Vickers 29
Vincent 124
W(i)lson 119
Wade 200
Wadsworth 49
Waid 144
Walcott 163
Walden 19
Waldren 47
Waldron 90, 186
Waldrop 50
Walker 16, 23, 27, 38, 53, 63, 76, 80, 81, 99, 104, 105, 123, 126, 134, 136, 169
Wallace 23, 61, 67
Waller 8, 20, 138
Wallis 80, 148
Walsh 179
Walton 99, 107, 163
Ward 46, 163
Ware 64, 118, 128, 129
Warford 15
Warner 71
Warnock 61
Warren 54, 98
Washington 13, 44, 186
Watkins 139, 161
Watson 19, 37, 56, 64, 106, 133, 142, 148, 153, 170, 175, 185
Watt 53
Watters 108
Watts 47, 51, 130, 139, 147
Weaver 72
Webb 81, 134, 140, 157, 174, 175, 177, 198, 199
Webster 102, 136
Welch 36, 61, 88, 130, 140, 148, 169
West 25, 59, 83, 167
Westmoreland 64
Whaley 160
Whatley 37
Whigham 164
Whitaker 142, 153

White 1, 19, 32, 44, 67, 85, 124, 138, 152, 173, 177
Whitehead 162
Whitehurst 185
Whiteside 81
Whitfied 15
Whitfield 22, 94
Whiting 117
Whitlaker 135
Whitlock 39
Whitman 62, 85, 98, 121
Whitten 7, 149
Wiggins 150, 201
Wilds 176
Wilkerson 4, 53, 143, 171, 174
Wilkes 23, 38, 40, 49, 114, 124, 156
Wilkins 78
Willard 94
Williams 10, 17, 35, 37, 40, 43, 47, 51, 53, 55, 60, 65, 70, 74, 91, 93, 96, 99, 110, 113, 115, 121, 129, 132, 133, 135, 144, 145, 148, 151, 156, 159, 161-164, 166, 175, 178, 186, 203
Williamson 81, 97, 132, 173
Willingham 137
Willis 1, 134
Wills 74, 95
Wilmer 78, 140
Wilson 4, 51, 73, 119, 121, 135, 155, 184
Wimberley 94
Wimberly 62, 97, 167
Windham 3
Winn 85, 196
Winnemore 164
Winslet 156
Winter 29, 51
Wintworth 35
Wisham 53
Witherington 108, 133
Witherspoon 186, 190
Witter 179

Wittisch  103
Womack  40, 88, 99, 100
Wood  12, 45, 61, 69, 70, 82, 83, 120, 130, 160
Wooddy  147
Woodfin  23
Woodruff  141, 151
Woods  13, 84
Woodward  22, 191
Woolshy  3
Wooten  7, 64
Worrell  147
Worthington  60, 155
Wray  29
Wright  1, 30, 32, 81, 115, 124, 156, 177, 191, 200
Wyatt  122
Wyne  94
Wynn  133
Wynne  16
Yarborough  183
York  162, 185
Young  16, 27, 50
Zimmerman  55, 106, 122
Zodie  158
Zuber  151, 195

www.ingramcontent.com/pod-product-compliance
Lightning Source LLC
Chambersburg PA
CBHW071713160426
43195CB00012B/1667